Computer-Based

J. T. SHAH
APRIL '1974

Management Information Systems

Leonard I. Krauss

American Management Association, Inc.

To my mother and father

International standard book number: 0–8144–5223–X
Library of Congress catalog card number: 73–119382

THIRD PRINTING

Preface

UPPER management in many companies has become justifiably apprehensive about what popular business literature glamorously describes as management information systems. Indeed, qualms may represent the beginning of wisdom.

Ever since the computer was recognized as a management tool, the subject of MIS has been receiving increasing attention. Its interpretations have been both broad and narrow, its implications both sophisticated and naïve.

Discussed in the abstract, it avoids the critically relevant management issues. Discussed in detail, it is best understood by computer specialists or mathematical programming experts. Between these often encountered extremes is what management needs to know—about the concept, development, and implementation of MIS.

Central among the tasks of this book, then, is to present a clearer idea of the subject for executives, administrators, systems managers, and others who need to assay MIS from a management perspective while also keeping some of the weighty technical issues in view. Toward this end, the book attempts to dispel some of the fantasy surrounding this fashionable topic by providing practical advice and guidelines for dealing with many of the problems encountered in MIS projects.

The search for relevant information took us from popular business magazines to computer and other trade journals, to erudite publications of professional societies, and to various books covering the subject from a number of vantage points. Hundreds of titles were involved. We also talked with executives, managers, consultants, and people attending information systems seminars, to find out what they were thinking and what they wanted to know.

Out of all this came these key impressions: (1) that popular management literature was too general, (2) that technically oriented literature was too technical, (3) that management seminars were not technical enough to impart a "gut" feel for MIS, and (4) that the two ingredients in MIS—management and the information system—were hardly ever examined from an integrated point of view.

These impressions, as well as our own experience and knowledge of what things companies are doing well and poorly under the general heading of MIS, suggested the path to be followed. Hence, we have attempted to set forth widely applicable general guidelines, to be specific where advantageous, to present some of the important technical considerations for the benefit of the curious management reader, and to focus on MIS in such a way as to place management and the information system in meaningful juxtaposition. Whatever contribution may be made through this book, it is our hope that this work will enable the reader to crystallize his own point of view concerning MIS in a perspective relevant to him.

Whether the book has accomplished its goals can be judged only by you, the reader. The one word of advice we wish to pass on is this: Stay on the lookout for new MIS ideas, because the computer world changes fast.

The management aspect has been emphasized throughout, with technical matter interspersed where appropriate. About midway through the book, several chapters will be found to have a richer technical flavor than is normally the case. However, even in those chapters, the aim is only to survey important areas in an attempt to bridge significant gaps and improve the reader's understanding. No attempt is made to provide comprehensive technical coverage.

The early chapters try to set the stage, summarize what has to be faced squarely, and condense the major issues in order to arrive at crisply stated sets of guidelines. The last chapter attempts to assess the longer-term impact of MIS on the way businesses are organized and managed. The chapters in-between deal with MIS development and implementation considerations. The book has been planned so that readers who have a limited interest in these details can concentrate on the first two and last two chapters.

"MIS" is used throughout this book as singular, plural, and possessive. Syntax and context will ordinarily decide. Also, the editorial "we" is used. We hope that these things will make the book less formal and easier to read.

Our trying to establish a nearly complete summary-level framework for executives and managers concerned with MIS has resulted in our being introduced to the work of numerous writers, some of them MIS experts, who have done a fine job of "telling it like it is." Because we think some of their contributions to the growing body of knowledge about management systems are well worth repeating, we have made room in the book for these authors to speak for themselves. In this way, we have sought to enrich the presentation with facts and opinions that have emerged from a diversity of firsthand experiences that have their own special flavor.

Leonard I. Krauss

Acknowledgments

AUTHORS must always assume full responsibility for the shortcomings in their published work. But they can find some comfort in the fact that a select group of colleagues contributes their insights toward improving the finished material. Such is certainly the case with this book.

I would like to express my deep appreciation to my father, William N. Krauss, who gave unsparingly of his time in suggesting editorial improvements during the book's preparation, and in particular for his extensive assistance on Chapter 6, "Data Communications Concepts and Facilities." To my wife, Sharon, I owe a great deal for her patience and proofreading help. For his taking time out of a busy schedule at Systems Research Institute to review and make constructive comments on the final manuscript, I am indebted to Jim Vacirca of International Business Machines Corporation.

To Roger Clavey of Union Carbide and Jack Wadsworth of the First Boston Corporation, I am grateful for the review and suggestions provided on the final manuscript. Thanks are also due members of the editorial staff of AMA, whose efforts brought about improvements in many areas. Last, but not least, I wish to thank IBM and the various publishers that gave me permission to reproduce their copyrighted material.

Contents

1

Laying the Groundwork

AT the start of a recent business seminar on MIS, the chairman solicited definitions from the 15 systems executives and analysts present. Reading the definitions aloud, the chairman quickly showed that communication on the subject of MIS could hardly be effective with 15 people using a term in 15 different ways. The chairman then offered his definition, which he probably thought would help standardize the meaning, at least for the purposes of the three-day seminar. But, as one guest speaker after another presented MIS concepts that were almost entirely different, the elasticity of the definition was shown repeatedly. During the closing hours of the meeting, the chairman again asked for definitions. This time he received 16 and seemed jolted to find that all were different once again. Someone in the group, he observed, had obviously submitted two definitions. This was indeed the case. The executive who had written the extra definition explained that the seminar was so informative that he now was in a position to think about MIS from two distinct reference points. Having 15 people advance a total of 16 definitions certainly presents an unparalleled opportunity to conclude that people find the subject befuddling. But this need not be so, for reasons to be explained shortly.

In considering what definition we might declare sacred in this book, we faced several possibilities. One was to devote a lengthy monologue to the definition. Another was to advance a shorter, omnibus definition, one sufficiently vague to encompass just about anything. However, we chose a third alternative: We are going to try to get along without a specific or standard definition of our own. Instead, we will borrow definitions from the subject matter at hand and in so doing try to get at the real nature of the beast. Like the 15 systems analysts with the 16 definitions, you too should have one or two of your own. Putting this burden on your back, as we are, is in keeping with the kind of realism demanded if you are to have a successful MIS program. Incidentally, do not be fooled by the new acronyms that come into vogue as rivals to MIS; they have no consistent definition either. One seminar chairman found this out when he changed over to IIS (integrated information systems) and asked for definitions from the participants.

A growing appreciation of what we have been watching take place led us to conclude that the pivotal issue in a successful MIS program is the question of how well a particular company's interpretation of MIS reflects its information needs. Unless this issue is properly addressed, definitions mean little. All efforts must be relevant to local conditions and company information needs.

However, a conceptual framework to aid MIS planners in defining and organizing management's information needs can be valuable in facilitating MIS development work. It should come as no surprise that a conceptual delineation of an MIS framework closely parallels areas of managerial responsibility. Correspondingly, we have settled for four information classes, recognizing, as a practical matter, that all are related:

1. Operations, tactics, logistics, or working information. (Can we fill an order for 2,000 widgets today?)
2. Performance or control information. (How are we doing?)
3. Planning or forecast information. (Where are we headed?)
4. Strategic or policy information. (What should we be doing?)

Because these four areas are both general and universal, the MIS problem quickly gets out of focus when we try to look at just one level of detail beyond them. To improve the focus, we must understand the *usage environment*—that is, the business or organization. However, the focus may not be that much better unless you comprehend the complexities of managing your business. Many questions need to be asked and much information gathered and organized to change abstractions to specifics. For it is specifics that provide direction in the analysis, design, and construction of the end product. And this is not an MIS, but rather *your* MIS.

Defining MIS

The integration of the computer with management decision-making processes has been described variously in the past ten years as IDP (integrated data processing), as TIS (total information systems), and more recently as MIS. You should know and we would like to make clear the following: that hardly any existing IDP is truly integrated; that TIS never existed and never will; and that MIS as represented in much of today's literature is something of a hoax. This seems to leave us with nothing more to say, except that you may be spending (or may be about to spend) a lot of time and money trying to develop your MIS. We hope to explain here how you can get the most out of it.

As has already been indicated, a great deal depends on how we define the subject. Since the definition will depend largely on the context, it is your problem. Putting it bluntly, you must understand the bargain—what you are getting for how much and when. It cannot be done superficially.

Not too long ago, in a conversation between two systems analysts waiting for an elevator in the corridor of a large manufacturing company, one made the comment: "We've spent over a million dollars on this project [MIS] and we still don't know what we're doing." Cases of this sort are a sad commentary on the management spending the money, a sad commentary on the use of human resources, and, all things considered, just plain sad. Now that everyone has shared in the blame, we can turn our attention to seeing what relevance this has to defining MIS.

First, since management is spending the money, it should be specifying what it wants in return. What often happens is that the specifying gets delegated, and one of three situations prevails: the delegate cannot find out what management wants; he has his own ideas about what management wants; he lacks the know-how to carry out his responsibilities. Regardless of the cause, the outcome is always highly predictable. The message is simply this. Management must define, in order of priority, what it wants, and it must also specify the important characteristics of the information system. Key performance requirements must also be spelled out, as must the criteria that will be used to judge the system's effectiveness.

Definition as Related to Company Objectives

A simply stated MIS objective might read: "to collect and make available such information as is needed by management to run the business." Another could be: "to improve overall operations by providing management with decision information that is accurate, up to date, and rapidly accessible." Yet another might go: "to improve profit and customer service by getting the right information to the right people so they can make the right decisions."

American Telephone and Telegraph Company has been putting together its interpretation of MIS, which is called Business Information System. AT&T's broadly stated objective: ". . . to meet the increasing problem of keeping Telephone people supplied with the information they need, when they need it, and in the form most useful for decision making."

Definition Implied by Company Activities

Major business functions of a typical industrial enterprise provide a good clue as to the logical stratification of information systems. They may be described generically as shown in Figure 1-1.

Within each function may be found common areas of management activity, which may be classified as planning, administering, controlling. Management's basic need for business information pertains to these activities. And information systems are usually organized to correspond to business functions as well as activities within those functions. Additionally, types or levels of information within an activity must be taken into account. For

FIGURE 1-1
Business Functions Related to MIS

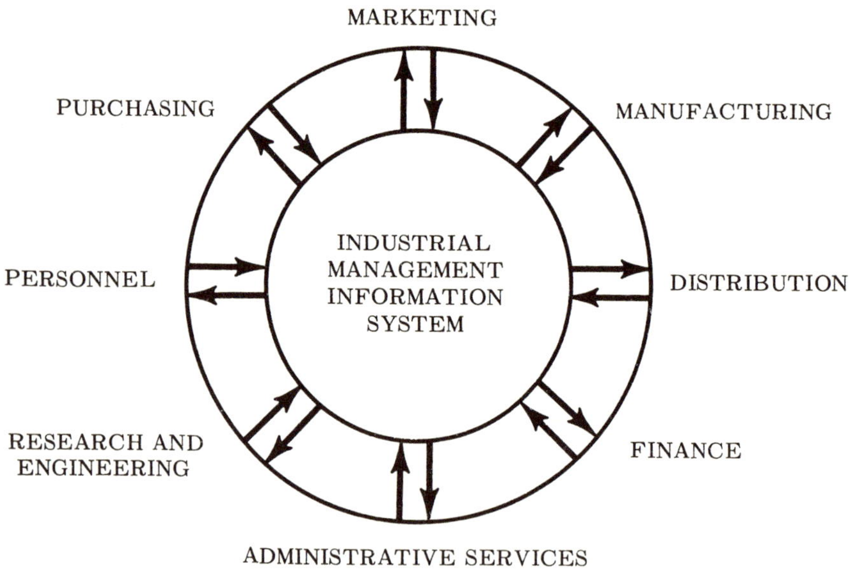

example, consider a marketing planning system. Here, the types of information required relate primarily to customers, sales, advertising, pricing, products, and competition. With each type of information, the job responsibilities of the person using that information and the level of the problem confronting him will determine what pieces of information are actually needed. Information on the distribution function, as an illustration, is of interest to the chief executive trying to decide whether to purchase a fleet of trucks or choose an alternative distribution method. It is also of concern to the supervisor on a shipping–receiving platform, who must plan the daily activities of his crew and the use of distribution facilities.

To summarize the points made thus far, we can list the elements needed to establish a major part of the definition of the information system:

- *Functions* it relates to, such as distribution.
- *Activities* it concerns, such as planning.
- *Areas of management use,* such as transportation.
- *Management levels,* such as department manager.

Factors needed to complete a much more comprehensive working definition consist of (1) *classes of problems* within each management level (for example, comparison of common carriers' service), (2) *information needed* for each problem (for example, common carrier identification).

With a definition formulated along the lines just outlined, it should be possible to answer most of the questions concerning what the system will do and to indicate what can be done with the system. A definition encompassing the six points just outlined will help eliminate the guesswork involved in unscrambling such popular catchall phrases as ". . . provides the information needed by management to make marketing decisions."

Make no mistake about it, a great deal of hard work is required to formulate a working definition that has substance. If you stop to think about the analytical efforts needed, perhaps you can form some preliminary opinion as to the potential magnitude of MIS in your own business or the functions and activities with which you are concerned. Keep in mind that the management information system will be designed to accomplish many of the things that cannot be done effectively without it, so we are talking about much more than just improving what now exists.

Preparing a definition of the kind suggested offers the opportunity to state and delineate known and short-run information needs, but is not complete. The other side of the definition should concern itself with projections about the more distant future, which is the work of people with vision. More often than not, they are found in the top two levels of management.

Beginning with a blueprint of current or known MIS requirements, you have to try to *predict* what else you should do today to be prepared for the much more distant future. Then you can back up and work on the things you know how to do, making provisions as you go for what you believe the future will require.

Dynamic Properties of MIS Definition

While we have touched on the need to consider the long-range aspect in formulating an MIS definition, we also must recognize that neither the company nor its problems are static. Taking our cue from past experience with computer-based business systems, we know that it would be foolhardy to have a definition that is mute on the adaptability of MIS.

Alterations in company emphasis and goals, as well as the emergence of new management information needs, dictate that the system be viewed as a dynamic product. This does not mean that a company has to throw away the old system and build a new one every year or so. On the contrary, it should expect change and be prepared to cope with it. Later chapters will examine some of the methods and modular MIS design approaches that can accommodate or readily adapt to new problem-solving situations.

Promoters, supporters, and developers alike will find it imperative to adopt a posture that permits them to be effective in dealing with the inevitable metamorphosis of MIS. But change can be dangerous if it comes as a surprise. Also, remember that, in a viable MIS, system changes and upgrading activity may wax and wane over a period of time but never truly stop.

Data Processing's Relation to MIS Definition

MIS development can be frustrated by two opposing views. An old-school view is that management information is the byproduct of big data-machining jobs like those that carry out accounting functions. The more current view is that management information is the ultimate aim. Resolving these conflicting notions is not too difficult provided that someone who understands systems is in control of the situation, in which case a balanced point of view should prevail. That is to say, it will be recognized that management information and routine data processing go hand in hand—with neither considered inferior. Adopting this coproduct, rather than byproduct, orientation makes it possible to serve multiple needs conveniently. It further opens up new avenues for creative uses of the system by offering a broader and more accurate picture of the real interrelationships.

Every manager concerned with MIS needs to offer stubborn resistance to "blue sky" implementation projects where the practical consideration of basic data processing questions is disregarded. The failure to consider such questions is the earmark of a shallow systems definition and analysis, the consequences of which are most unpleasant.

Management, Technology, and the Information Explosion

If we were limited to choosing the single most important reason for MIS, we would have to name *time*. Not too many centuries ago, a man could know almost everything there was to know. Once he did, his information needs were filled.

Around the turn of this century, the sum total of knowledge was doubling at a rate of perhaps every 20 years. By the middle of the century, it was doubling at a rate of perhaps every ten years. And within this decade, according to some sources, knowledge may be doubling at a rate of every five years. This geometric progression is the substance of what has been called the information explosion. Managers and many others are caught up in it. We see its effects in the need for more specialized specialists. Although the "renaissance man" is needed now more than ever, in industry he is a bygone phenomenon. Technologically, we seem to be going along fairly well in this environment, though not without pains. But, with respect to management, there are very serious problems that become more serious with every passing year.

At one major electrical equipment and appliance manufacturer, there was a standing joke that shipment could not be made till the paperwork weighed as much as the product. Indeed, paperwork can exceed the product's weight, as has been reported in connection with the design of jet aircraft, where the engineering drawings weigh more than the plane itself. Such developments can also be burdensome to executives, since excessive paperwork can engulf all levels of the organization.

The effective executive of the past knew a great deal about what was going on in his organization. He had to. This continues to be the case, except that today there is much more to be known. Therefore, the executive must either settle for less success or find a different approach. That organization charts of numerous major corporations now have four or five names in the box that used to contain the president's alone is no accident. It reflects the increased complexity brought about largely by the information explosion.

Another problem is that many of the tools management uses to cope with these business complexities are the same relics used when the management affairs were much less complex. Despite efforts to delegate and decentralize, many top executives find that the changing scene makes an ever growing demand on their time and energies. Most are looking for answers that will offer relief greater than that provided by their short-lived predecessors. An increasingly frequent answer is computer-based systems, which offer the greatest opportunity yet for executives to resolve their information needs.

Information Crisis in the Executive Suite

Against the background of the information explosion, it is little wonder that the computer age was ushered in so swiftly. Numerous problems were ushered in with it, many of them quite serious. Significantly, however, most managers would agree that the point of no return was passed some time ago. Only a handful of people are seriously proposing that we do without computers.

Management's motivation to surmount the information crisis has two aspects. One is that managers, inundated with the sheer bulk of information, *want* a way out. The other is that they *need* an answer, because the first companies to find an answer to the information crisis will realize important, if not critical, advantages. Here are some of the key needs that management must fill in order to resolve the crisis. In part, they are what companies hope MIS will bring about.

1. *Render faster decisions.*
    - *a.* Detect and authenticate opportunity.
    - *b.* Identify and isolate problems.
    - *c.* Define and analyze situations.
    - *d.* Evaluate and appraise alternative courses of action.
2. *Accomplish more in the available time.*
    - *a.* Think more deeply about the situations.
    - *b.* Ponder other variables.
    - *c.* Gauge and contemplate ramifications.
    - *d.* Investigate more alternatives.
3. *Make more thorough analysis.*
    - *a.* Review more meaningful information.
    - *b.* Obtain a better collection of relevant viewpoints.
    - *c.* Use advanced management techniques; that is, methods of industrial operations research.
    - *d.* Simulate more conditions.
    - *e.* Ask and examine more questions, particularly the "what if" type.

With the advent of MIS technology, there is good reason to believe that these needs will be satisfied. However, as one observer put it in this connection, "No one is going to get there very fast." Now, at least, some of the tools with which to begin an assault on the information crisis are available.

Real-Time Management Control Concepts

Information increases in value to the degree to which it enables management to decrease the time required to exercise control. Value also increases to the extent that information permits more effective, higher quality decisions. A consideration of the concept and economics of management control systems will make clear how MIS can increase the effectiveness of control decisions.

Figure 1-2 illustrates events that occur in a management control environment. Note that in each of the three graphs shown in the illustration, the passage of time is represented by the horizontal axis. The diagram at the top of the illustration is a control chart. Based on a known standard operating condition of any type, and acceptable limits of variance, measurement of actual performance would permit the detection of an out-of-control condition. Such controls might relate to manufacturing performance, collection of accounts receivable, personnel turnover, customer service, sales, inventory, or almost anything else.

The graph in the middle of Figure 1-2 illustrates the cumulative effects of an out-of-control condition over a period of time. Such effects might include increased operating costs, reduction in value of service activities (maintenance and repair, customer service, and so forth), and opportunity losses of almost any conceivable kind (inability to produce products for an existing market, inability to realize interest income from receivables, inability to take or exercise profitable options).

A key objective of a system of controls is to minimize the time between the point at which a condition goes out of control and the point at which a correction is successfully executed. A number of things take place during this time.

Looking at the lowermost portion of Figure 1-2, we can see that *measurement* against a preestablished range of variability is a continuous function in a system of management controls. After an out-of-control condition occurs, there is a passage of time during which the *detection* of this condition takes place. This is made known to the appropriate parties in the form of a *communication* of some type, which also takes place over some time interval.

When information concerning the out-of-control condition has been disseminated, a *situation analysis* takes place, again over some time interval. Following this, there is typically additional communication with one or more

FIGURE 1-2

Management Control System Economics

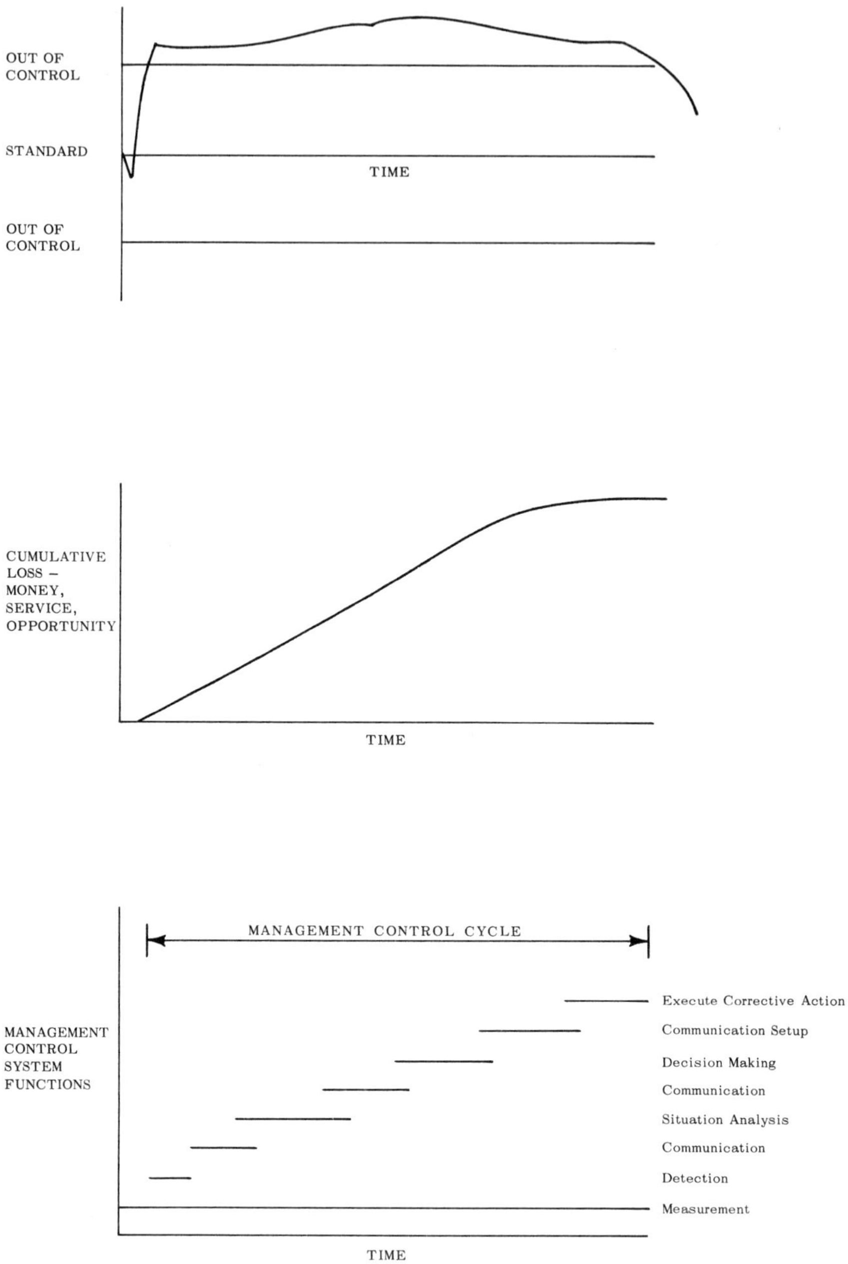

key managers, who render a *decision* as to the best course of action for rectifying the situation.

Further *communication* is required to notify appropriate individuals as to their responsibilities in carrying out the decision. This, plus the "setup" time (if any), takes place over still another time interval. Finally, the wheels are set in motion to *execute corrective action,* which, of course, also takes place over some period of time.

These seven stages illustrated in Figure 1-2, exclusive of measurement, constitute the *management control cycle,* or, to put it another way, the *react and rectify time.*

Real-time management control systems are often associated with react and rectify times measured in seconds and minutes (milliseconds in some process-control applications). And, in general, these are the time frames people have in mind when they refer to real-time MIS. However, it is important to recognize that generically, "real time" relates strictly to the nature of the business situation being addressed. The critical time cycle for management control varies greatly, depending on what is to be accomplished. The frequency of measurement is also affected by the critical time cycle. A management control system measuring sales may be working in weekly time intervals, while a bank teller transaction-control situation is likely to relate to seconds. Data acquisition, measurement, and reporting requirements in each case take up different amounts of time.

Often, shortening the management control cycle permits substantial economic and other benefits to be realized. It is under these conditions that well-conceived real-time MIS can be overwhelmingly effective. In every management control system function (measurement, detection, communications, situation analysis, decision making, and executive corrective action), computer-based real-time systems can permit time-interval compression.

The Changing Role of Computer-Based Systems

Everywhere there is mounting evidence that the role of computer-based systems is changing in the direction of more extensive management uses. But numerous companies are going to miss the opportunity because inappropriate criteria are applied and the wrong people are in control of deciding on the new direction. They will face an impossible task of catching up. And meanwhile, the timetable of progress in systems is being compressed by more and more advanced computer uses.

As The Pillsbury Company's president, Terrance Hanold, pointed out in "A President's View of MIS":

> The test of the new system is not data cost but data value. The proof of data value is no longer found in the reduction of administrative personnel, but in the profitable utilization of highly qualified middle management people. . . . The design and development of this new data system must serve value creation first and cost reduction later.[1]

He went on to say:

> For both the creation of these values and their measurement, the executive management is altogether dependent upon its newly sophisticated middle management. And this middle management is increasingly managed and motivated by the information system itself rather than by the executive group.
>
> The corporate presidency has never been a comfortable spot. Its status under these conditions of employment can only worsen.[2]

John Diebold, a long-time observer on the computer scene, discussing this subject at length, has noted:

> Nowhere is this lack of sophistication [in standards for justifying and evaluating computer applications] more apparent than in the way in which computers are applied in American industry today. Most companies carefully weigh the decision, consider the alternatives, compare the relative costs, and then reach a conclusion—on the basis of the wrong criteria entirely.[3]

With regard to setting goals for computer automation, the Diebold Research Program surveyed 2,500 executives in order to provide answers for the 140 companies sponsoring the program. The results of the survey indicated that "technicians, not management, are setting goals for computers. This is one of the prime reasons why companies often fail to realize the true potential from their data processing investment."[4]

Figure 1-3, which appeared in the article from which the foregoing quotations were drawn, predicts the evolution of management systems and the criteria applied to evaluate them through the year 1985. Absent from the applications shown in Figure 1-3 are scientific and engineering subsystems that should certainly be included as areas of great potential.

[1] *Datamation,* November 1968, p. 61, © F. D. Thompson Publications, Inc.
[2] *Ibid.*
[3] "Bad Decisions on Computer Use," *Harvard Business Review,* January–February 1969, p. 15.
[4] *Ibid.,* p. 16.

FIGURE 1-3
The Changing Role of the Computer

A. Management application

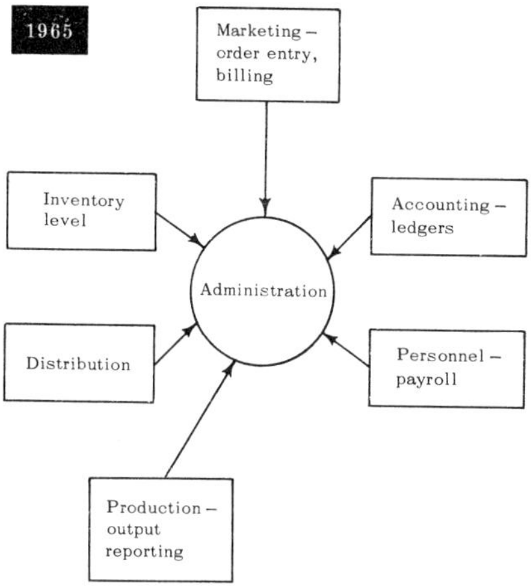

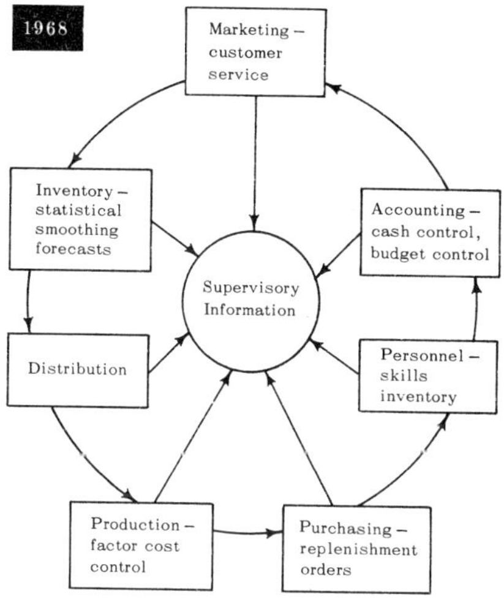

In the two-decade span from 1965 to 1985, computer systems applications will evolve from the unrelated elementary uses which were typical of the 1950's and early 1960's to the highly integrated and interdependent systems projected for 1985. In this first time frame, computers are doing essentially what clerks had done before, only doing it electronically. The value of the computers, when it was measured at all, was calculated by the rather primitive methods of cost displacement of clerical and machine resources.

In this second time frame, roughly the present, the computer is beginning to effect change not only in how a business operates but in what it does. Supervisory management is undergoing transformation in all the basic areas of corporate activity. Measurement by cost displacement has already become obsolescent.

B. Criteria used in evaluation

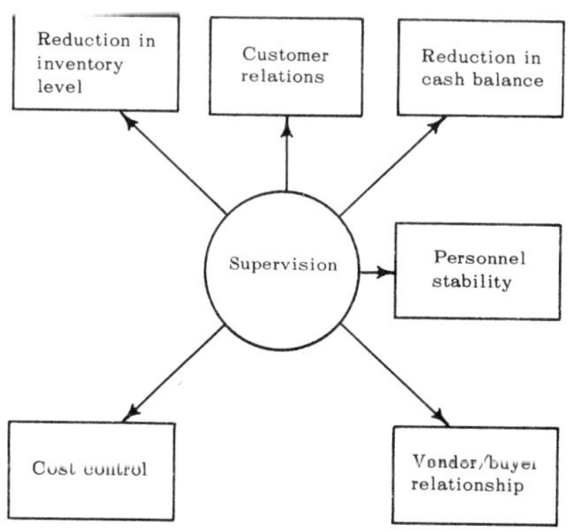

FIGURE 1-3

The Changing Role of the Computer (continued)

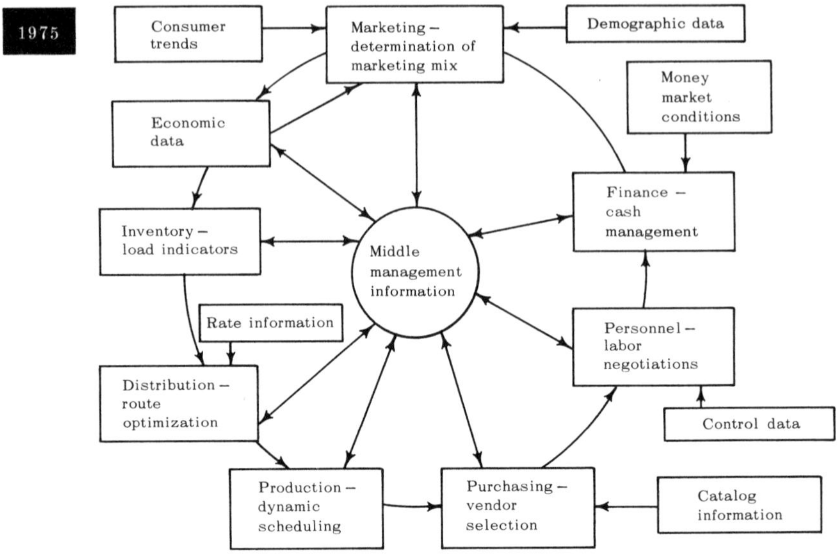

By the mid-1970's, computer systems will no longer be merely a management tool for accomplishing the functions recognized today as the basics of business. Corporate success will be determined by the effectiveness of computer applications at all levels and in all areas of business activity. Substantial progress will have been made in tapping external data for analysis in business decision making. The computer will be used for tactical planning purposes in many key areas.

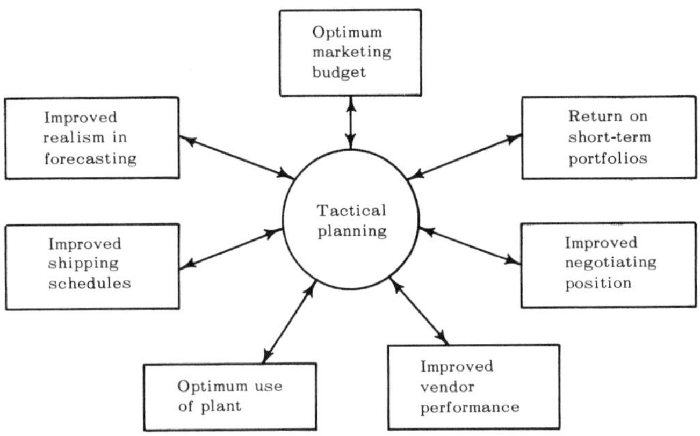

FIGURE 1-3

The Changing Role of the Computer (continued)

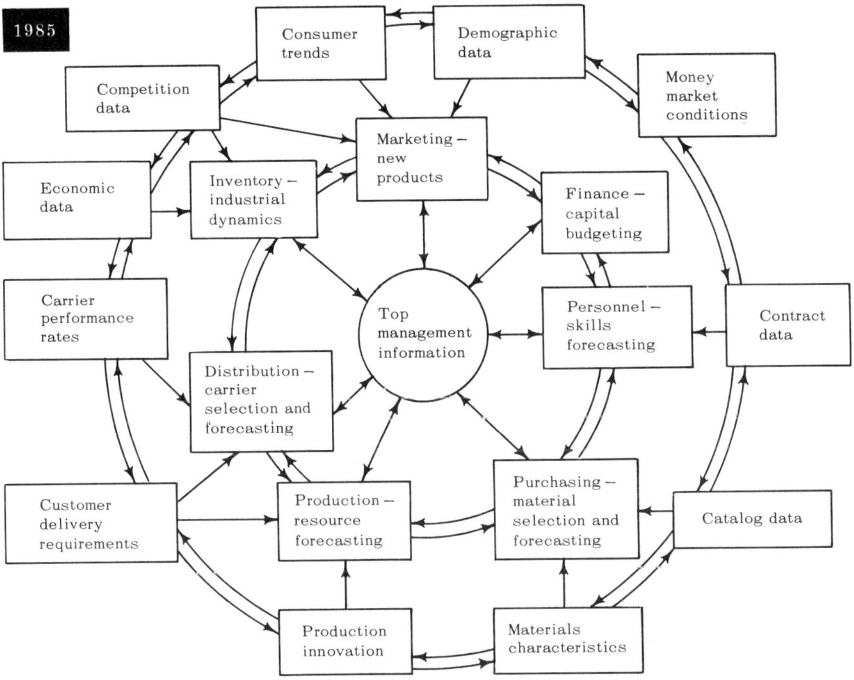

The mid-1980's will see a totally new kind of business structure centered on information processing in which internal and external data interact with each other in countless variations. The information system will then be the heart of the structure. All levels of management will be involved in one or another information processing activity. Companies will be information service centers whose highly automated plants will be making this or that product, performing this or that service – all dependent on a total corporate planning system.

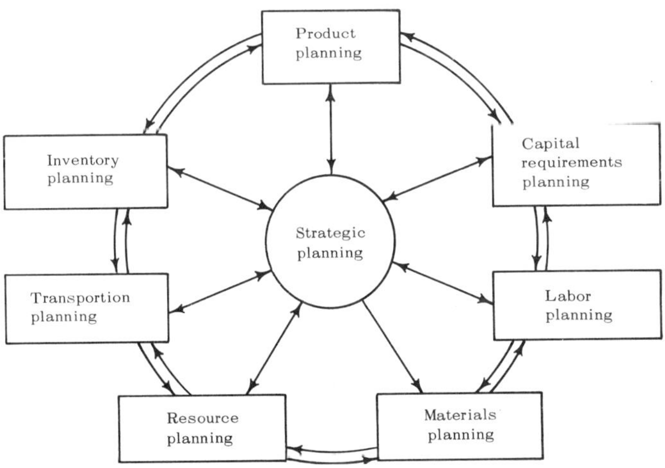

Source: John Diebold, "Bad Decisions on Computer Use," *Harvard Business Review,* January-February 1969.

Technological Basis for MIS

Changes in computing technology and related economics have acted as a catalyst for MIS, triggering advances in half a dozen important areas that have formed its technological basis. They include:

1. Direct-access data storage.
2. Data communications.
3. Advanced central processors.
4. Advanced software.
5. Data-base management and information-retrieval methodology.
6. Management-science techniques.

Because management will be asked to make the purchases relating to these items in the MIS development program, it is appropriate that we consider each, especially with regard to the role they play in MIS.

Direct-Access Data Storage

In contrast to magnetic tape, from which data can be obtained from the middle of the reel only if the computer reads every record preceding the one desired, direct-access data storage devices provide what their name implies—that is, direct access to the desired data record.

The necessity of mass, directly accessible data storage for MIS is fairly obvious in the case of on-line systems that provide fast response to inquiries entered on remote terminals. Where this is not a requirement, this kind of storage may not be needed, although it is often economically justified on the basis of the computer time it saves, since only data of interest are accessed.

Even though direct-access devices have been around for a long time, their limited capacity and high cost have until recently made them unattractive. Today, these undesirable aspects are being minimized, and there are a variety of devices from which to choose.

The principal media for direct-access storage are disks, strips, and, to a lesser degree, drums. All are coated with a magnetically chargeable substance (such as ferrous oxide) that makes reading and writing on them similar to reading and writing on magnetic tape.

Disk storage is the most popular direct-access medium today. A typical system provides for a number of disk packs (removable storage containing 10 or 20 usable surfaces) each of which has a capacity measured in millions or tens of millions of data characters. Nonremovable disk storage also exists. The cost and access speed for disk storage are lower than for drum and higher than for strip storage. Magnetic tape storage is the least costly of all, but does not permit direct access.

Strip storage is growing in popularity as a relatively inexpensive means of storing large masses of data. Capacities for fully loaded strip devices, containing perhaps 2,000 strips, are measured in the hundreds of millions of data characters, with popular models having capacities approaching half a billion characters. Considering that a number of such devices may be attached to a computer system, it is easy to see how all of a company's active records could be stored for quick retrieval and processing.

Drum storage, by comparison, is not a mass data storage medium. Typical capacities per unit are under 10 million characters. Its major advantage is speed of data recording and retrieval. Some are well over 10 times faster than disk and well over 50 times faster than strip. For this you pay handsomely. As a result, drum is used more for program storage, where it becomes an extension of the central processor's main storage, which must store the program when it is being executed. Disk devices of a particular design (having many read–write heads) have drum-storage attributes and offer the additional advantage of being removable—a feature not available with drum.

Research is now under way to determine how lasers might be used for mass storage, and recently reported developments indicate that their use may not be far off. A tape-storage device using lasers has been built. Experiments involving photochromatic media and other techniques, including holography (three-dimensional photography using lasers) are also in process.

Data Communications

Data communications refers to the transmission of information over distance. For our purposes, we will assume that a computer system controls the flow of information.

Telephone and telegraph companies, as well as some new communications companies, have responded to the increased demand for data transmission and to changes in computer technology by providing services necessary to accommodate requirements of the MIS type. These include broad-band services, which permit faster transmission; new and improved tariffs for high volume and wide-area users; central-office equipment that switches calls electronically (under the control of the telephone company's computer); and specially conditioned lines that minimize interference or stray noise, which can play havoc with data. Services also include data sets and foreign-attachment adapters to permit computer and terminal hookups; and consultant aid to customers in data communications network design, selection of carrier services and equipment, and special problems.

Terminal devices, where data originate and are received, are growing rapidly in number and variety. Produced by both computer manufacturers and independent companies specializing in peripheral gear, these terminals may simply transmit and receive prerecorded data involving magnetic tape, punched cards, paper tape, and other media, or they may be of the variety designed for direct human interaction. The last-named are important components of many MIS and include typewriter terminals, teletypes, visual-display terminals (cathode-ray tube and similar devices), audio-response systems, large image-display systems (for group use, as in management briefing rooms), strip-printing terminals (like ticker tape), computer-controlled microfilm viewers, and special-purpose terminals for banking, airlines, hospitals, brokerage firms, and so on.

Advanced Central Processors

The heart of a computing system, a central processor executes the stored program and activates and controls the functioning of all devices attached to the system. Changes in central-processor technology are related in part to electronic components. Large-scale integrated (LSI) circuits and microminiaturization permit faster and cheaper computing than their transistor and vacuum-tube predecessors. Micrologic flexibility in the form of read-only storage, sometimes called firmware or microprogramming, permits the central processor's interpretation of programmed instructions to be changed and new instructions added. Thus it is possible for programs written for one computer to be run on another by changing the micrologic. Expanded use of firmware in the future is expected to have a number of important benefits, including the elimination of much of the compilation (translation from a source language like COBOL—an acronym for common business-oriented language—to a computer-recognized language) now required. Although micrologic flexibility can be used to promote systems compatibility, it can also create incompatibility because of its diversity of uses.

Aside from purely electronic advances, new capabilities and design characteristics of modern processors have made MIS functions possible. Channels permit concurrent operation of many devices, such as terminals, and allow input and output functions to overlap themselves as well as to overlap arithmetic and logical processing of data. Different storage-addressing methods (base displacement) permit much larger memory addressses to be represented in shorter instructions. New and more powerful instructions of all types are available to accommodate various needs. For example, in data communications it is sometimes necessary to change one coding scheme to another; now this is accomplished with a single instruction. Larger, less costly main memory is another important component of MIS-oriented systems. Finally, a number of other highly technical internal features permit the concurrent operation of multiple programs (multiprogramming), time sharing, data communications network control, sharing of mass data storage by multiple computers, and the operation of interconnected central processors (multiprocessing).

Advanced Systems Software

Advanced systems software consists of programs that facilitate the use of computer hardware. Among them are operating systems (executive or monitor systems) that manage system resources, input–output control programs that handle the functioning of data communications and storage devices, compilers for the various programming languages, and programs that perform utility functions, such as copying magnetic tape.

Systems software is needed to control the exotic functions of the hardware described previously. Operating systems even have special hardware instructions that they alone can activate in the course of controlling the execution of a user's job.

A great deal more could be added about systems software, but not without getting into technicalities. For now, suffice it to say that advanced software manages the use of computing equipment in a management information system.

Data-Base Management and Information-Retrieval Methodology

Data base management and information retrieval are mainly concerned with the creation of data files, methods by which the information they contain is updated, ways by which specific records are retrieved in response to a user inquiry or as a regular reporting activity, and means for removing unwanted records from data files.

With the advent of mass direct-access storage devices and MIS information-access requirements, a great deal of work has been done (and much more remains) in order to (1) organize and structure files to minimize access time, (2) index a single file in such a way that inquiries keyed to various criteria can be handled without reading the entire file, and (3) make it easier for management or any other user (noncomputer person) to communicate his information demands to the system.

The relationship of the *single-entry concept* to data-base management is vital to the proper functioning of an MIS. Simply put, a transaction should be entered into computer files once and only once, and from there all other affected records should be updated and the appropriate actions triggered. An integrated MIS approach seeks to do this, thereby overcoming some age-old problems concerned with keeping multiple sets of the same information. Duplication is usually wasteful, but vastly more serious problems arise where the same information is being updated in different ways by different people at different times.

Management-Science Techniques

Management-science techniques provide management with analytical tools for problem solving. For the most part, they comprise a number of mathematical procedures often found under the heading of *operations research*. Some people say it is a branch of mathematics; others call it a branch of industrial engineering. In general, operations research techniques guarantee a mathematically correct (within prescribed limits) problem solution. The solutions that are derived are therefore objective. Of course, like so many other techniques, if you solve the wrong problem or use the wrong data you will get invalid answers.

Problems that can have many possible answers are what management-science techniques are often applied to. Some business problems are so complex that it would take a lifetime to obtain an optimum solution by hand. Enter the computer, which can do the job in a matter of hours or even minutes —and you have a viable MIS component. Since great masses of data often go into solving complex problems, and since such techniques provide management with problem answers (which is a big improvement over information), there is a natural partnership with MIS.

The management-science techniques that pertain most closely to computer-based MIS are as follows.

1. Linear programming and extensions.
2. Simulation and modeling.
3. Queuing and sequencing.
4. Decision theory and gaming.
5. Capital investment, replacement, and maintenance analysis.
6. Data correlation and regression.
7. Inventory analysis.
8. Network methods for project control.

The practical application of most of these techniques depends on the use of a computer to process data concerning history, current conditions, projections, and trends. Management's benefits from the application of operations research can come in the form of new guideposts and also in the form of a new, in-depth appreciation of the problem. Reasons why one plan is better, or why action should be delayed, or why conditions in the current operations need to be rectified, can be evaluated more thoroughly before swinging into action.

Categories of Management-Science Problems

Common categories of management-science problems include these.

Resource allocation, where an optimum solution is sought that, in general, minimizes cost or maximizes profit. For example, in manufacturing, the problem may be to minimize production cost where there are many options. The answer sought is how much of what products to make or buy at what plants, given product demands, plant capacities, costs, and other constraints or requirements. A requirement may be a contract binding the company to buy specified units of raw material or to make a specific number of units of finished product. Manpower levels and labor-agreement provisions may also be reflected.

Inventory management problems, where the fundamental objective is to keep inventories as low as possible consistent with maintaining good customer service. Such problems involve elaborate forecasting techniques that project demands for each time interval. They may involve correlations of demands with external variables such as gross national product, new housing starts, inflationary trends, and so forth. Inventory management is also concerned with economic order sizes and the consideration of volume discounts, with warehousing and other kinds of storage costs also entering the picture. Seasonal demands are analyzed, and peaks and valleys in demand may be "smoothed" in a way that permits level production and lower unit costs.

Queuing problems relate to waiting-line characteristics and economics. Such problems may involve customer services where the customer who has to wait in line too long steps out of line, or the customer who sees a long line does not wait at all. Queuing problems arise in production, transportation, traffic (telephone, city planning, computer inquiries, highway design, and many others), banking, and almost any situation where waiting lines of people or things can form. Variables in such problems include serving-time statistics, waiting-line characteristics and statistics, service-cost rates, effects on business when people refuse to join the line or renege.

Routing, sequencing, and scheduling problems. Routing problems are concerned with situations where there are many possible ways to transport a resource. The objective is to establish a route that means the least distance, travel time, or cost. Such situations come under the heading of transportation problems (which are a special kind of resource-allocation problem). A classic one is the "traveling salesman" problem, where the salesman may have to make calls in as many as 20 cities. He visits each city once during his trip and returns home. There are innumerable ways to lay out a route to accomplish this. Combining the management-science technique (which eliminates having to calculate each possibility, as it contains mathematical shortcuts) and the computer, it is possible to calculate an optimum or near-optimum solution. Thus we have another viable component of MIS.

Scheduling and sequencing problems may also be amenable to solution by transportation methods and may incorporate queuing considerations. Production-line balancing problems, which involve bottlenecks, may be solved by these and other techniques.

Competitive analysis problems are usually marketing-oriented. They may concern pricing, new product introduction, timing of promotional activities, and other variables. One area of growing importance is in competitive bidding "situation analysis" where the history of competitive tactics, new approaches likely to be employed, strategy alternatives, and other considerations enter the scene. In such problems, the computer is used for simulating the outcome where a number of assumptions have been made. Because this can be done rapidly, numerous conditions can be tried. These give strong indications of what factors are sensitive under various sets of assumptions. Methods used to solve such problems come under the heading of decision and game theory.

Financial analysis. The main area of application here arises in capital-investment analysis. Projected rate of return, selection of the best alternative uses of capital, and expected value are some of the answers sought with these methods. Such analysis involves cost and tax data and may have risk introduced as another variable. This kind of use often depends upon the reduction of vast amounts of statistical data and takes advantage of the computer's speed.

Project analysis. One of the important functions of project management is to isolate the series of consecutive jobs that, among all jobs, are critical and that if overextended will cause a project overrun. Another is to understand the degree to which each of the other jobs can be extended or delayed without affecting project-completion time. Knowing these factors, project management can so allocate resources and attention that critical jobs receive a higher priority than noncritical ones. The usual situation involves subprojects or jobs that must be performed according to a planned sequence. Certain jobs can be performed concurrently while others depend on someone's having previously completed one or more jobs. The time required for the completion of each job may be a weighted average. In PERT (program evaluation and review technique), time for job completion is calculated using three figures:

most likely time, optimistic time, and pessimistic time. The last two figures are given one-fourth the weight of the most likely time.

Project analysis is vital not only for project planning but also for implementation. Scheduling and control are maintained by a systematic analysis of project performance against a plan that is updated regularly. Computers and the special project network-solving techniques join together to provide an effective way of planning and administering project activities.

Are You Ready to Tackle MIS: Can You Get There from Here?

Modern developments in computer technology would have us believe that the question of "getting there from here" has already been answered—yes. The problem, however, is not so much concerned with what is said as with what is not said.

For example, we might learn that the XYZ Company, a competitor, has a marvelous new MIS (or is working on one). Our first reaction might be "Why don't we have one?" whereupon commences a frenzied effort to catch up. What you may not know is whether XYZ actually has what it claims, what its operational status is, and what benefits XYZ's management is really getting. Even if the system is fully operational and the company is reaping tremendous benefits, it does not necessarily mean you should get the same thing to stay in business. Moreover—and this is what is critical—the fact that XYZ did it says nothing about your ability to do it. Rather, it says only that it can be done. What you must concern yourself with is whether your available talent, environment, and accomplishments indicate that you can accomplish similar results. In short, the determination as to whether you can get there from here cannot be based completely on someone else's having done so. This is true, first, because their circumstances may be vastly different from yours, and second, because they may have talent and experience that you do not have.

Organization Experience: A Perspective

Perhaps one of the most reliable indications of probability of success at implementing MIS is the company's historical ability to do simpler things well. Simpler things include the basic or routine computerized accounting and reporting systems—but, while they are simpler than MIS, they are not necessarily simple. If serious project overruns, various foul-ups, and systems that operate in fits and starts have become routine, then there is a good chance that the company will not be able to cope with MIS.

Of course, it is reasonable to allow for what a fresh approach under new management would bring to a crisis-ridden operation. But, unless it is absolutely clear that the old problems can be overcome, grave reservations about MIS are in order.

More than a few times we have seen promoters sell MIS to a management unaware of the seriousness of its problems with existing systems. Not being acquainted with these problems, management did not probe for answers as to how the MIS project proposed to overcome them. In the case of a large bank, for example, programmer turnover in the computer department was so bad that people hardly learned about problems they were to solve before they left. At this bank there happened to be two MIS proposals (for two different divisions of the bank) up for consideration, neither of which discussed how staff turnover problems would be overcome. Requiring considerably more continuity of professional personnel than this organization had beeen experiencing, both MIS proposals would have had a slim chance of successful implementation in the absence of measures to meet the turnover problem. Yet, though no such measures were advanced, both proposals were approved and went into development.

Within 15 months, both projects were cancelled. A half-dozen reasons were cited as having brought about the failure of these projects. One of the principal ones was turnover, which caused havoc in the definition phase of these projects. The revelation that this was to be a serious problem need not have been the result of 20–20 hindsight—a cursory look at existing computer-project situations was all that was needed.

Events of the kind just set forth happen every day in all kinds of organizations. Some of the biggest and best have gone through similar experiences four or five times in succession. They learn a little more each time but do not really stand back to take a hard look at the root causes. Between the efforts of professional bottleneckers and a management having dubious qualifications, one manufacturer reportedly went through three MIS fiascoes in different divisions before top management put a stop to such undertakings. Fairly reliable sources quote $1.2 million and $800,000 as the loss figures on two of the three projects. Considering the circumstances surrounding these projects, the company was fortunate that the systems never became operational.

Buying protection against such MIS hazards must involve more than a blank check. Management must get into the potential crisis center and develop plans and ground rules to govern subsequent efforts.

Why MIS Efforts Fail

Describing reasons for failure is not a surefire way to tell someone how to be successful. Nevertheless, there is merit in examining major problem areas so that we can profit from the experience of others. Following are some reasons for poor MIS development:

- Crash installation, rather than an orderly, well-thought-out effort.
- Standards for data definition and identification handled sloppily, rather than being given serious attention early in development.
- Unreliable data in terms of accuracy and completeness.
- Undependable data sources.
- Hypothetical information needs instead of actual information used for design basis.
- Information provided with no distinction between critical and noncritical organization factors.
- Heavy emphasis on data having little or no bearing on business objectives.
- Absence of enthusiastic management support and participation.
- Analysts and programmers not of sufficiently high caliber to handle an MIS.

Management responsible for MIS, in keeping its focus on ultimate performance, should be constantly aware of these "failure factors" and the ones about to be enumerated. Walter M. Carlson, in "A Management Information System Designed by Managers," mentions certain pitfalls that have generally resulted in unsatisfactory systems for managers:

1. Use of analysts having no proven managerial qualifications.
2. No supervision of the project by anyone who will have run some part of the operation with the system that results.
3. Use of outside "consultants" with no stake in the operating benefits to be achieved.
4. Criteria for system design based upon computer-room efficiencies.
5. Lack of data-element standardization, especially in the face of reluctance to agree that existing subsystems have to be changed.
6. Requirements for extensive use of codes at the data sources rather than at data processing centers.
7. Use of codes rather than English titles in output reports.[5]

In "Why Management Information Systems Fail," John R. Gale suggests that the following factors are to blame for MIS difficulties.

Orientation of the system to the computer rather than to the user.

Incorrect definition of the system's prime users and their related priorities.

[5] *Datamation,* May 1967, p. 41, © F. D. Thompson Publications, Inc.

Vesting and responsibility for the system's development and implementation with the incorrect management group.

Inadequate communication to company personnel of the nature and purpose of the system.

Failure to recognize and control effects of company power politics.

Underestimating of the complexity in the designing and implementing stages of the system.[6]

Success Parameters for MIS

According to James H. Greer, controller of CBS, quoted in the article "Television Network's On-Line Management Information System" by James A. Walsh, there are 11 key requirements for a successful on-line management information system:

1. Management must recognize that an information problem exists and want to do something about it.
2. Management information is a line, not a staff, responsibility. Therefore, line management must be given the responsibility for, and must actively become involved in, the development of any management information system from the outset.
3. Initial applications should be in the critical action-oriented areas of the business, and the system should deal with the basic current and future business data as differentiated from historical, financial, and accounting data.
4. Any information problem must be approached first by a definition of the content, format, and timing of the end-need rather than by a nonselective attack on the mass data available. Each end-need must be given a relative priority to prevent the system's development from being delayed or bogged down by minutiae.
5. Once the end-need is defined and a priority given, the place that the information required to satisfy the need is first available within the organization must be identified, and a method of input control set up at that point.
6. Once data is entered into the system, all needs for data within the organization should be serviced from this one record.
7. All data should be entered into the system by the organizational unit having primary responsibility over the function creating the data; that is, sales information by the sales department, etc.
8. All routine reports should be eliminated unless they serve a specific purpose which can be served in no other way.

[6] *Financial Executive,* August 1968, p. 45.

9. For data in the system, no auxiliary records should be tolerated except those required as part of the system's backup or input–output control.

10. All input and output should be in a form and language easily understandable to line people and should conform to terms and practices of the industry to the greatest extent possible; that is, the system must talk in the executive's language, not vice versa.

11. The system should be under line supervision. Personnel manning input–output stations should remain a part of their functional units.[7]

Interdepartmental Politics: A Gray Area

People who write about MIS development projects, and most other computer applications, sometimes talk about a gray area between the defining of business problems and the technical considerations in a computerized system designed to solve them. This gray area is a people problem, and it arises most often from the way in which the MIS project is chartered.

A charter for an MIS project containing gray areas will tend to magnify the project problems that may later arise. One of the more common difficulties is the familar jurisdictional dispute between operating people and computer specialists. If there is no official word in the charter to clarify the relationship, the disputes go on and on, and progress grinds to a halt.

Everyone has to understand that people, and not charters, are the vital force. A charter alone cannot do anything but guide people with good intentions and help each one to understand his role and his common goals.

Top management, in particular, often has little if any awareness of organizational infighting. Because presentations rarely disclose roadblocks and deadlocks of this kind, top managers are deluded if they do not further explore the matter. Of the many questions to be answered concerning whether you can get there from here, the problems involving important jurisdictional relationships are as important as any.

Avoiding Pitfalls After a False Start

Recovering from a bad start can be simply a matter of stopping one project and starting another, although it is almost never a painless transition to shut down one project and recharter another in its place. But when the need for doing so becomes evident, there is usually no purpose to be served in permitting work to drag on to the point of maximum frustration. Unfortu-

[7] *The Office,* May 1968, p. 15.

nately, in some projects, monitoring and controls are so weak that they fail to point up anything short of a disaster condition.

One way to avoid an all-out crisis is to make regular checks of the work in process. This can best be accomplished by conducting periodic meeetings with the systems analysts or programmer–analysts who are defining the business problems and devising systems for their solution. Their comments are generally frank and to the point concerning what areas are presenting the greatest problems. It is common to find these individuals giving unemotional descriptions that management will find of value. Should they be confused, however, it should be determined whether they are confused by the problems they are trying to solve or by the way they and the users have been charged to carry out their assignments.

In some instances, systems people may find that certain business functions are not as well organized as they might have initially expected them to be. At other times, the project staff will describe fundamental problems concerning the way the project is being run, including conflicts between computer people, users, and company management. Sometimes a conflict arises because, as mentioned, the project charter does not make it clear who is supposed to be doing what. People who are on the firing line every day will sometimes point out serious problems by saying things that give the impression that the work is drifting aimlessly. It is not uncommon to uncover confusion—pure and simple. It may be that project-team members have not been in clear communication about project goals and the division of assignments and, as a result, are floundering. On the other hand, the problem could well go deeper than this —perhaps no one has even thought about the proper management conditioning and effective organization of the project.

Conducting a Project Audit

The recovery from a bad start must begin with a thorough review of the problems experienced by people at all levels of the project team, including those individuals participating as advisers and potential users of the system. A reevaluation of this kind is sometimes called a *project audit,* which is best done by someone whose judgment is respected and who has no ax to grind in the situation. When this is not possible, it is usually necessary to have two individuals with offsetting prejudices perform the audit and render independent opinions. If they are asked to offer a jointly prepared evaluation, there is a risk of compromise wherein important elements may be traded into oblivion.

Having lost information of vital importance to the success of a revamped future project, you might be asking for the same trouble all over again in reinitiating the project under incomplete or misshapen guidelines. On more than one occasion, we have seen the unfortunate consequences of acting on compromised or biased evaluations.

Common Findings of Project Audits

Project audits have identified a host of difficulties. Key MIS problem areas that seem to be most common are reported in the following six categories, along with external indicators and end results for each.

1. *Management definition.* Failure to understand and take an orderly approach entailing setting objectives or goals, developing plans, preparing schedules, monitoring and evaluating progress, decision making, action on plans, and the making of continuous or periodic changes to the foregoing to incorporate new and better ideas.

Observations: Activities are disjointed and uncoordinated. Excessive rework is needed, with more time spent on making changes than on making progress. Loss of knowledge continuity caused by turnover.

End result: Project cancellation; salvage value negligible.

2. *"Too many cooks" syndrome.* Group size two to three times what it should have been initially. People getting in each other's way. Work subdivided too finely, introducing responsibility conflicts, boundary and interface disputes, and serious communication problems. Accountability made difficult and the skill and talent of personnel supposed to be doing a systems job grossly underutilized. Many project administration and control problems experienced.

Observations: Interaction is substituted for work. Project never gets off the ground and costs-to-results ratio skyrockets.

End result: Project cancellation; salvage value 10 to 25 percent of cost.

3. *Visibility of contributors.* "Bosses" fail to engage one another and subordinates in deliberations concerning objectives, alternatives under consideration, revisions to plans, top management directives, project administration, serious problems of all kinds, and the vital problems facing the business. Action taken with poor contributor involvement is often ineffectual or falls far short of desired result. Support of completely unilateral determinations is relatively weak. Contributors' direction of their own action is typically based on misinformation and lack of information. Communication by means of rumors and "grapevine" is very active and distorted.

Observations: Activities tend to be redundant, are not directed toward goals, and generally have low productivity and yield.

End result: Excessive turnover, serious project overruns, and possible cancellation with 20 to 40 percent salvage value.

4. *User-systems staff relationship.* A problem comprising one or more

serious breakdowns. These include lack of understanding of what roles each side was to take in MIS development, deficient user conditioning and education on computer automation, deficient systems-staff education on user problems, general failure to set the stage for mutual respect of abilities, incompetent user representation or incompetent systems representation or both. Also, arguments over who was ultimately responsible for the project's outcome—user or systems staff; user's worry about job security, which produces negative attitude toward MIS, especially if thrust on him without consultation; user's failure to react in constructive way to systems staff's questioning and evaluation of detailed problem definitions; systems staff's neglecting to engage users in meaningful review and evaluation of the system design; systems staff's uneasiness about the depth of top management's knowledge of the MIS project and support of it.

Observations: Overt political maneuvering, considerable infighting, emphasis on gamesmanship instead of getting the job done, and much buck-passing and destructive criticism.

End result: Usually project cancellation—sometimes drastic reorganization under new management, with salvage value negligible. Hard feelings make a new try quite difficult, unless there has been a cooling-off period of six months or more.

5. *Accumulation of minor difficulties.* These are termed minor only because they appear less often than the others and because some of them can be more easily rectified. While any one problem can become severe, more often two or more problems in combination are severe, while by themselves they are not. Many of the combination problems occur in groups of three. They include: (a) lower-level management know-how questionable, importance of subordinate's work underrated or belittled, lack of cohesiveness due to human relations breakdown; (b) dishonesty concerning project direction and opportunities, unstable user participation, sense of urgency replaced by sense of futility; (c) gross inequities in pay, deadwood personnel, environment where professional staff members are suspected instead of respected; (d) computer turnaround time very poor, excessive overtime demanded of personnel, stingy attitude about normal working expenses and participation in professional affairs.

Observations: More than half of these problem situations were characterized by an "our work is not appreciated" attitude among MIS staff members. The world's cheapest form of reward was rarely if ever used—a simple "thank you" and a compliment.

End result: If the project does not disintegrate under the impact of one or more of these three-part factors, the efficiency with which it is carried out is bound to be quite low and the quality of the end product quite poor.

6. *Stability and quality of upper management support.* MIS project gradually or rapidly loses the enthusiastic interest and involvement of key

top-level executives. Several predominant causes are : (a) The failure of the project organizers and promoters to impress on top management the level and type of continuing support needed; (b) management's "rubber stamping" the project, without serious review and comprehension of its implications, partly because MIS is fashionable and partly because of not being prepared to probe the claims of benefits attainable; (c) failure of project organizers to demand that top management act in an advisory capacity on a regular basis (no steering committee or advisory board); (d) project results too far out—no chance of seeing some early payoffs before biting off too much—and therefore no results and divided and waning support.

Observations: Status of project acceptance varies greatly, project-team members filled with uncertainty about destiny of project and their own fate, lack of spirit and enthusiasm, and loss of key contributors.

End result: If project not cancelled, progress is minimal; "don't give a damn" attitude undermines effort; careless workmanship in evidence; costs out of control in light of achievement.

Salvaging Remains of the Old Project

In the previous section we mentioned salvage value in connection with project failure. To improve the value of whatever remains, several steps must be taken.

To the extent that it is feasible, a summary of the progress to date should be prepared prior to beginning a phaseout. Members of the project team should be directed to put the finishing touches on whatever they are doing and prepare a status report telling what has beeen completed and what remains. With these documents in hand, it is possible to avoid starting again from scratch, although a lot of the same ground will have to be covered.

The people working on the project should be carefully considered. It is not unusual to find qualified and competent individuals who could be of great help on the next project. There is usually a problem in convincing some of these people that the newly constituted project will be any better than the old, which usually means that they are not anxious to repeat the experience.

Taking a Realistic Position on Time and Cost

The question of the money and time required to get to MIS is sometimes answered as "a lot" and "long." And in many cases this is accurate, relative to the requirements of other systems. Of course, in an absolute sense, it is not at all helpful.

Recently one candidate for the position of project leader for advanced systems, whose résumé listed extensive MIS experience, said he wanted to continue as a specialist in MIS. When asked what he meant by MIS, the candidate responded by describing the interaction between major accounting systems that passed data among themselves. Curiously, management was not mentioned much in his description, and it was not clear whether his idea of MIS reflected the more commonly held views about the goals of MIS.

When asked to give an off-the-top-of-the-head estimate of the time and cost required to develop and implement MIS, he started asking questions about the company. In reply he was told about a hypothetical company with $1.5 billion in sales, $1 billion in assets, diversified manufacturer, 100,000 employees, 10,000 salable products.

The answer given by the MIS expert, after a few minutes of thought, was that it would take 200 to 250 people from five to seven years to develop MIS for the company. He was then asked to put a price tag on the MIS, whereupon he said $4 million to $5 million per year. Judging from these estimates, it appeared that this project-leader candidate had a good feeling for what a full MIS comprised.

An important phenomenon that should not be overlooked is that MIS development costs can be quite similar regardless of company size, assuming that the businesses are the same in most other respects. What this usually means in practice is that the bigger company can often afford to do more in a shorter time, partly because the results of a cost-effectiveness analysis make it more compelling to do so.

Sizing Up the Time Dimension

MIS needs to be contemplated in a time span of five to ten years. As will be seen in the next section, even smaller types of MIS require no fewer than three years' work. Many systems people and some management staffs, not accustomed to such long-term affairs, find this disturbing. However, even in organizations used to making five- to eight-year capital commitments, management gets edgy over computer automation projects lasting so long. The key to success is to have a series of planned implementation phases that have payoffs at shorter time intervals.

How Much MIS Costs

The crux of the MIS cost question, of course, is what the system will be designed to accomplish. But, as pointed out earlier, other factors can cause costs to escalate. Later chapters will treat them and related management considerations. However, in this section it would be helpful to try to remove some of the vagueness concerning the cost issue, largely by surveying the experiences a number of companies have had with management systems. We hope to scan enough cases to provide perspective and insight.

The Southern Pacific Company has developed a $22 million MIS version called TOPS (Total Operations Processing System), one function being to provide fast response on inquiries concerning the company's rolling stock. The system can handle some 93,000 freight cars and 2,300 locomotives and will provide service to offices in 12 states and 25 major cities. TOPS is expected to pay for itself in four and half years or so as a result of the $5 million to $6 million per year return to be realized through operating-cost savings. A company official was quoted as saying there would be little personnel cutback.

In 1963 Lockheed Missiles & Space Co. was reported to have undertaken the development of a $2.25 million production control system. Called the ADA (Automatic Data Acquisition) System, this is just one part of an overall MIS envisioned by the company. ADA was being developed to provide executives with continuously updated information about the location and status of 65,000 active shop orders and related parts throughout the manufacturing process for missiles, space vehicles, and other products. About 5,000 production workers at two producing facilities are linked to the central computers by about 210 remote input stations. ADA experts were forecasting that a net annual savings of $2.8 million would be realized by reductions in personnel—mostly expeditors—and in machine process costs.

Northrop Corporation's Norair Division is saving nearly $1.9 million annually with its Integrated Management System (IMS), according to a 1965 report. IMS is used to help management run Norair's aerospace job shop operations. The system was designed to handle ten general areas concerned with up to 65,000 production orders in process daily. Annual operating costs of IMS are $585,000. Systems development costs as such were not given, although they were probably in the neighborhood of the $2.25 million spent by Lockheed to develop a similar system.

American Airlines' pioneering Sabre system, used for reservation processing, among other things, was implemented over a number of years within the last decade at a cost of some $30 million. Similar systems cost anywhere from $20 million to $50 million.

With an MIS system built at an initial cost of around $225,000, the Metals Division of Olin Corporation was recently reported to be saving $184,000 annually. (Its monthly operating costs are $9,000.) This system has integrated the order-to-shipment cycle and provides management with timely planning and control information. As a result, profits have greatly increased, performance on delivery promises has jumped from 70 to 95 percent, and numerous other benefits have been realized by management.

RCA's MIS effort, initiated in 1966, was budgeted at $30 million a year for development over a five-year period. It called for the implementation of various subsystems during the five years and was being carried out with very close coordination between line management and the MIS systems staff.

In 1968 the Department of Defense was reported to be running its MIS development on an annual budget of $40 million. Where this effort will end is not plainly in view; the department is said to be a "long way from combining the various pieces of its system into an integrated whole."

IBM's management information system will cost $100 million by the time it is completed. IBM's aim is to improve the efficiency of running its business with its MIS, which, according to one article, will consist of "some 3,700 terminals connected to dozens of central computers."

One of the earliest examples of MIS on a much smaller scale was that put together by the Micro Switch Divison of Honeywell, Incorporated in the 1960s at a cost of about $500,000. This was the amount spent for MIS development, which included system definition, design, programming, and conversion. Six main functions were accomplished by the Micro Switch system: (1) design and manufacturing engineering, (2) sales order processing, (3) materials planning and control, (4) production scheduling and dispatching, (5) financial control, and (6) management planning. At the time this system was implemented, Micro Switch employed several thousand people and was handling some 440 orders per day for switches and other products. Among the benefits: Orders delivered on time jumped from 82 to 97 percent; product variance costs, sometimes as much as 36 percent above standards, brought to within 1 percent; clerical costs reduced from 4 to 3 percent of sales; sales to inventory ratio improved by 20 percent.

In the mid-1960s International Paper Company announced a plan to lease $10 million worth of computers to form a comprehensive information and control system. International Paper's long-term program is no doubt along MIS lines, and it is probably safe to say that they are at least equal to the equipment's value of $10 million.

The Weyerhaeuser Company, a forest products business with sales of around $1 billion, embarked on its interpretation of MIS in 1963. Its plan called for $2.5 million worth of hardware.

Westinghouse Electric Corporation has beeen quite active in MIS-type work since the early 1960s and has one of the most comprehensive systems in existence. Undoubtedly, Westinghouse has spent prodigious sums of money. Handling around 90 percent of all industrial orders, the real-time system's inventory management capabilities have permitted an $18 million, or 50 percent, cut in company inventory and the closing of 8 out of 35 warehouses.

Other benefits include a reduction of order-processing costs from $12 to $2 per order.

AT&T reportedly has over 400 people working on its $40 million MIS. And in 1965 Deering Milliken, the giant textile and fabric company, was reported to have organized a team of over 250 people to get started on its total information project.

Other companies working on MIS that have been mentioned in the press include Mead Corporation, U.S. Rubber, General Motors, Pittsburgh Steel, U.S. Steel, First National City Bank, Pillsbury, Ford, Union Bank of Los Angeles, Grumman, Bank of Delaware, Standard Oil of New Jersey, and Chemical Bank.

The Stakes Are Too High to Follow the Leader

These days, riding the tide of what seems to be fashionable portends crisis. Those who have grown accustomed to muddling through will almost surely suffer heavy losses. James W. Taylor and Neal J. Dean sum it up in the closing paragraph of "Managing to Manage the Computer":

> As the computer becomes more embedded in the fabric of business, as management molds these general-purpose machines to the configuration of individual corporate goals and objectives, it becomes increasingly dangerous to look to industry averages for guidance in proportioning computer effort. The alert management group will find useful guidelines in the experience of other organizations. But it will be the company that shapes the computer to its own destinies—influenced perhaps, but not awed, by the practices of others—that will find itself most competitive and best prepared to meet the challenges of the future.[8]

When you consider the number of people (sometimes hundreds) on some of the MIS projects highlighted in the preceding section and add up salaries, fringe benefits, general overhead, and computer time used in development, it may be apparent that we are talking about annual dollar expenditures in seven figures or better for medium-size companies. Besides this, there are computer and systems support costs to be considered once the MIS goes into service. These kinds of numbers are not to be taken lightly. Certainly, no management can risk going into an MIS blindly, using a follow-the-leader justification.

As a guess, a typical MIS will cost a medium-size company something on the order of 1 percent of sales and will take three years or more to develop.

[8] *Harvard Business Review,* September–October 1966, p. 110.

"Typical" means that it will cover the major business functions at a moderate level of sophistication. A more sophisticated MIS will take five years and up (in fact, some managers suggest a ten-year perspective), and the total development cost will probably go beyond 2 percent of sales. These numbers apply to single businesses or divisions of corporations and do not, we feel, reflect integration of conglomerate or multidivisional operations. Integration of this variety is a whole new ball game, one that it is not wise to play unless functions are centralized—at least not yet.

Vexing MIS considerations are certain to be in store for upper management when expenditures like those just outlined are involved. At this point the razzle-dazzle has to yield to a hard look at the MIS blueprints, the objectives, benefits to management, cost-effectiveness expectations, and return on investment. Purely trend-following decisions on MIS can easily bring an organization to the threshold of an MIS disaster. And, in fact, it has helped to bring bankruptcy to two stock brokerage firms. The upshot of this is that management must prepare itself to look beyond the theoretical appeal of the gadgetry of MIS. The company's systems people must promote this through more thorough investment analysis as well as business analysis. Safety valves, in the form of comprehensive reviews, are indispensable if a company is to cut the risk to an acceptable level.

2

Project Analysis and Selection

JUST how a company should approach MIS project analysis and selection is largely a matter of individual taste. That taste, however, should be seasoned liberally with facts about key variables in the business, supersensitive current issues, and general notions regarding company philosophy.

Many professionals duck the question of evaluating alternative approaches. Everyone does this in one form or another, and we can hardly indict anyone for proposing something known to have gotten the desired results. However, it is of the utmost importance to pay particular attention to the local variables, which you are in the best position to understand. Like the physician, you have to zero in on specific cases, not make dogmatic generalizations.

Where you start and what you do at the beginning often has a profound effect on what you wind up with. Clearly, no one who is not intimately acquainted with your company can tell you what is appropriate for your special circumstances. For this reason, guidelines must be adapted in nearly every case.

This chapter examines major management factors in project analysis and selection, including considerations in getting started, initial assumptions, the nature of management information, MIS characteristics and scope, opportunity evaluation, and system functions and data flow.

How to Get Started

Quite often middle managers do the spade work that leads to the commencement of an MIS project. They have typically read about and otherwise familiarized themselves with computer applications. Some will have enough direct exposure to computer applications to be able to visualize how an MIS would work. Beyond this, they can appreciate the immediate benefits to be gained in connection with the problems they face every day.

The other major impetus for MIS is the company's data processing function. Members of this group usually have no difficulty seeing how MIS would work and may be familiar with many of the technical design considerations. But they typically have much less familiarity with operating problems than middle management, and their awareness of the value of such services may be limited. Computer people, however, often see the interrelationships that exist between isolated applications and may see how more of the total problem can be solved more efficiently through systems integration.

Most of the time, for better or worse, top management does not suddenly come along and order an investigation of MIS possibilities for the company. Such action, when it is forthcoming, generally follows quite a bit of prodding from lower-level management, although it has been known to result from an alarming revelation of the organization's problems or a competitive threat.

Depending on whether middle management or the computer people get to top management first, the "pitch" either oversimplifies the technical nature and complexity of the systems effort or fails to consider many of the real management issues. The imbalance created by either approach can be misleading to uninitiated upper-level executives. Preconceived notions that may be formed as a result of a premature assault then become additional obstacles that have to be overcome in the future. Advocates of MIS will almost certainly find the MIS program difficult enough without introducing self-inflicted problems.

Synchronization of Action

Those who champion an MIS concept sometimes exhibit a flash of genius that is forgotten as quickly as it appeared. The importance of expending substantial time and effort in an attempt to pull together the relevant power structure cannot be emphasized enough. Lining up the backing needed to promote something having such a potentially broad impact on the organization is usually not done quickly or easily. Frustration can turn the principal MIS enthusiasts away from the arduous task of garnering support. But those who ultimately succeed will be those who, for the most part, steadfastly reject expedients.

Every management that becomes involved in the MIS effort also needs to do its part in coordinating the factions vital to the project's success. In this connection, consider the following recommendations.

- *For upper-level management.* Before deciding anything, go out of your way to get both sides of the story—from your operating people and computer personnel. If a course of action is decided on, such as an exploratory study, insist that operating management and the computer people carry out every aspect of it together from the very beginning.
- *For middle operating management.* Be sure to call on the computer department for participation starting very early in the discussion and investigatory stages.
- *For computer management.* Do not rush headlong into proposing MIS before ascertaining operating management's interest in the project's possibilities, and never proceed without the user's participation in developing the proposal itself.

Two Sides of the Preconditioning Need

Preconditioning has to do with one's state of mind or general philosophical outlook concerning MIS. Preconditioning is necessary for both user management and the systems staff. On the systems side, we find analysts expecting, if not demanding, clear-cut problem statements and rules such as those to which they became accustomed in developing accounting systems like payroll, in solving engineering and scientific problems, and in programming computers to solve mathematical problems. On the user's side of MIS, we find managers and administrative specialists expecting the systems analyst to design an MIS from a few bright ideas and some vaguely stated business rules. The outcome of these conditions is that both sides repeatedly disparage each other, something that will eventually cause the total collapse of any working relationship.

Preconditioning in advance of definition is designed to explain that an MIS cannot be slapped into the mold of past systems and simply pressed into place. In this educative process, the analyst needs to appreciate that managers find it difficult to specify how they do their jobs. Typically, they have given little thought to their information requirements, and, as likely as not, their perfunctory assessment will reflect old habits. Users, on the other hand, need to understand that MIS cannot be implemented in the absence of rigorous specifications. Sophistication also plays a major part in determining how difficult it will be to arrive at a set of specifications, and it seems to increase as MIS is directed toward higher levels of management.

User Management Conditioning

An orientation program for all managers who will in any way participate in the MIS definition and development is an absolute necessity. It must be so structured as to unify thinking about how systems come into being and where mistakes have been made, and it must instill realistic notions about the true advantages and practical limitations of such systems.

At least six major areas must be explained in order to establish user appreciation of the technical factors that will serve as the foundation for fruitful rapport.

1. *Systems development process.* Step by step, including problem definition, systems analysis, systems design, programming, testing, and implementation.
2. *Programming.* Using any programming language, demonstrate how thinking must eventually be reduced to simple logical, arithmetic, input, and output commands.
3. *Data-base concepts.* Maintaining data files and records of various kinds for retrieval by management and the related indexing considerations.
4. *Operations research.* Optimization, model building and simulation, applied probability and statistics, and other selected topics as deemed appropriate.
5. *Hardware.* Central processing units, direct-access storage, terminals, input and output devices, microfilm and related storage, and systems configuration.
6. *Data communications.* Common-carrier offerings and private line capabilities, network concepts, message switching, and other selected topics.

Osmosis and serendipity are poor means of getting this information across. A training program, a lecture series, informal seminars, or something comparable is required. A minimum beginning program would entail about 40 hours. The most successful applied systems are found in companies that have put up the resources to provide user management with a genuine orientation.

Systems Management Conditioning

A systems manager's role can best be understood if it is looked at through the eyes of a programmer–analyst who, in the final analysis, is confronted with the MIS development problem. Through orientation in the management problems of the organization, he is led to expect in MIS something different from what he may have been exposed to in the past.

The programmer–analyst, besides being otherwise qualified, has to satisfy two prerequisites to be prepared to tackle MIS. First, he has to gain an understanding of the business, the industry group in which it operates, its policies and practices, and its objectives and long-range plans. Often, it is also useful for the programmer–analyst to understand the company's history. Second, he must bring into clear focus the interrelationships that exist between the business function or activity being observed and the rest of the organization. In addition, he must be educated or must educate himself on the finer details of the decision making that goes on in the particular function or activity being studied. Before any analyst can hope to design a successful MIS, he must have a real understanding of the function or activity involved. Superficial or generalized knowledge is not enough.

Beware of Opening Assumptions

Systems people and managers both make dozens of assumptions in order to provide a framework for investigating MIS possibilities. Some of these concern the relationship between information and management. More specifically, the assumptions have implicit MIS requirements built into them and are often made in the very beginning of MIS investigatory work.

Eight Assumptions to Watch For

Promoters of MIS sometimes try to emphasize its value by proceeding according to what seem to be rational conclusions concerning management and its information requirements. The problem, however, is that these are assumptions, not conclusions. Let us briefly analyze eight of the common assumptions made in the early stages of an MIS program.

1. *Decision makers can state what information they need to be effective.* This is perhaps the most unfortunate assumption. While management understands its problems, it does not necessarily follow that it knows what information should be brought to bear on them. MIS developers who have expected

management to set forth its requirements in lucid and unambiguous terms have almost always been disappointed. MIS is a departure, as we have already said, from old data processing systems that merely speeded up manual labor.

2. *Decision making will improve as more information is made available.* Several faults can be seen in this assumption. First, of course, more information of the wrong kind will not help. Second, the presence of more information will not help unless accompanied by more sophisticated methods for locating and retrieving what is of interest. And, finally, the sheer bulk of information makes it more difficult to analyze and set apart what is important from what is less important or irrelevant.

3. *Managers are starving for information.* This is the assumption that is least likely to be valid. Anyone who has seen the piles of information that surround the busy administrator will quickly acknowledge that a simple lack of information is not his problem. What is needed is the appropriate information properly presented. In fact, even too much of the *right* information is a problem, and therefore we may need to look for solutions that go beyond information into, for example, organizational changes.

4. *Information will improve communication, which in turn will improve executive performance.* Two fallacies may be found in this assumption. On the one hand, communication has never depended exclusively on information. Rather, its effectiveness depends on the relevance of information to its receiver, and the clarity of the message as composed by the source. On the other hand, more communication, improved or otherwise, may prove to be a burden on the manager—he may be involved in too much communication as it is. Hence removal, and not improvement, would produce greater benefits. Here again, the problem may have less to do with information systems than with other management problems.

5. *Better and more accurate information means better decisions.* On the surface this assumption may look all right, and perhaps in some cases it is. In many situations, however, quality and accuracy have little to do with better decisions. Planning information, for example, could undergo a great improvement in accuracy that would have no impact on decision results. We might spend a considerable sum of money to learn that the originally projected product-demand level three years out was off by 20 percent. Yet many long-range decisions are known to be subject to so many uncontrollable external variables that accuracy, beyond a certain point, is meaningless.

6. *Managers need the information they request.* This assumption relates to the first we looked at—that is, that managers know what information they need. A request, in many cases, is made with a knowledge of what is available or what can readily be made available. This, however, may fall far short of being complete. Additionally, some managers ask for a lot of information

hoping to discover something in browsing through it. This can be a consequence of being uncertain about what is needed for problem solving.

7. *Managers get too much information.* A great many managers are faced with this problem. But this assumption may be specious when viewed conversely: "If managers received less information, it would help." We can see it does *not* necessarily help. At the very least, the answer is in giving the manager the same message with less information.

8. *Executives need to get information faster.* On its face, this assumption is valid. Yet everyone should realize that "faster" needs to be related to something, and it is here that the assumption can fall apart. Consider the question of whether the salesman on the phone with a customer needs inventory information faster than the president. Most would vote for the salesman. Most of us have also seen days and weeks go by before an executive can review information in his in-box. Notwithstanding certain conveniences, higher-level executives have, in general, less of a requirement for faster information than do lower-level executives.

In making one (or more) of the foregoing assumptions and proceeding on the basis that it is true, we run the risk of wearing blinders that keep us from seeing needs and opportunities as they really exist.

Some Results of Bad Assumptions

Almost by definition, the persistence of false assumptions leads to improperly defined aims. In due course, emphasis is focused on the wrong areas; and, as momentum builds up, it becomes less and less likely that the emphasis will shift. At the end of the dead-end street may be found many good answers, but to the wrong set of problems.

Going down dead-end streets in MIS development is likely to be incredibly expensive, so much so that what looks like an attractive possibility at the beginning can gradually degenerate into a disaster. This can happen because an impossible project has been undertaken. It may be impossible because of what it is trying to do, the money allocated for it, the talent available to work on it, the contemporary state of the art, the timetable for implementation, or any combination of these reasons. It can also be a disaster when the MIS simply does not bring about the benefits needed to justify its existence.

More than a few companies have suffered disasters because they were not working on the right problem or the right mix of problems, encompassing a balance of short- and long-term payoffs. Selecting the right mix entails a procedure whereby the functional modules of a planned MIS can be identified and ranked as to their benefits to management, cost-effectiveness, and other values.

The Nature of Management Information

Over a hundred years ago the Danish philosopher Soren Kierkegaard anticipated the main difficulty with management information when he said, "Life can only be understood backwards; but it must be lived forwards."

Management information systems have the common problem of dealing with the past in order to arrive at symbols or ideas that will serve to help make the future turn out the way we want it to—or tell us what the future will be so that we can plan and make adjustments accordingly. It is no accident that these things happen—or do not happen. Modern organizations that force a forward direction, but that keep sharply in focus an understanding of what they see in the rear-view mirror, accomplish this by design. Other organizations see but do not understand, and still others do not see.

FIGURE 2-1
Levels of Management

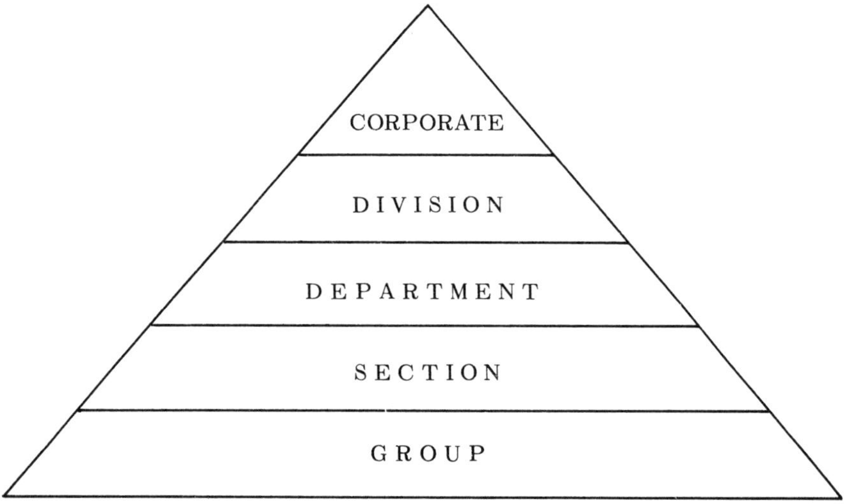

Improvements in management information are sometimes thought of as being limited to the area or level of immediate impact. If, in the organizational hierarchy levels shown in Figure 2-1, the information processing is improved at the group level, the impact is sometimes improperly conceived to be as shown in Figure 2-2. Actually, the effects of an improved information system are felt throughout the management hierarchy as shown in Figure 2-3.

Evans and Hague[1] emphasize a somewhat similar concept with respect to

[1] Marshall K. Evans and Lou R. Hague, "Master Plan for Information Systems," *Harvard Business Review,* January–February 1962.

FIGURE 2-2
Assumed Level of MIS Impact
(Group-oriented System)

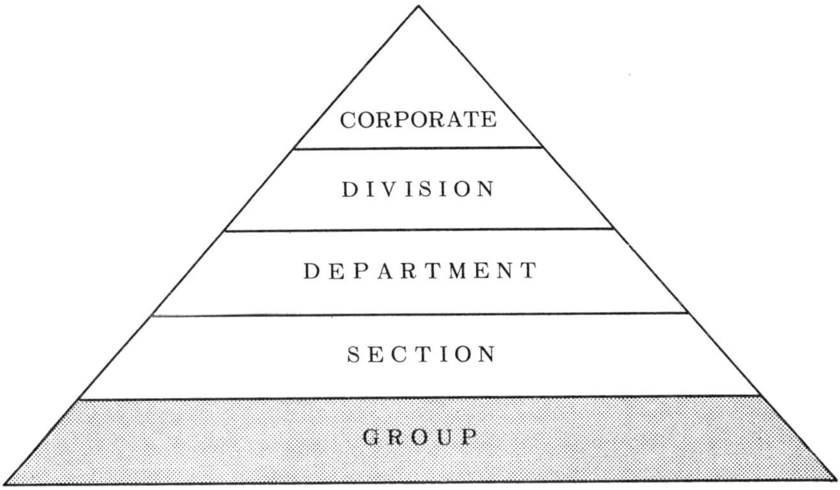

the education of employees when introducing MIS. And Head[2] uses it to describe the uses of data bases.

Active Versus Reactive Information

Everybody knows that history cannot be changed, yet nearly all computer applications developed in the past share a common deficiency in that they report history in a way that would have us believe something can be done about it. At best, historical information elicits reactive decision making. At worst, it has no value for decision making as is the case with a high percentage of existing systems. Top management usually finds decision information totally lacking, and middle management typically finds its value insignificant.

In looking at the positive extreme concerning the role of historical information, we have to appreciate that some conditions would worsen rapidly, were it not for reactive decision making. Some businesses seem to do

[2] Robert V. Head, "Management Information Systems: A Critical Appraisal," *Datamation,* May 1967.

quite well just reacting. However, they undoubtedly have timely access to accurate and appropriate historical information, and they know how to use it. On the other hand, we have all seen many businesses, large and small, that have not mastered this art and are now in trouble. For some, the mastery of reaction would have helped if it had come early enough. For many others, reaction, mastered or not, did not work and will not work. A great deal depends on the specific situation. Consider, for example, how seriously Japanese imports affected numerous American businesses not too many years ago.

Today this particular threat still exists, but the difference is that the companies that could not meet it when it first came do not have to worry about it any more—they lost. But other American companies stepped up to the firing line and hit the problem areas with deadly precision. Sufficiently motivated, they cut operating costs by trimming fat and finding better and cheaper ways to do things.

The production vice-president of an electric motor manufacturer, explaining how badly his West Coast firm was hit by Japanese competition, said: "It didn't take us long to find out that we had to do something right away or fold up. We were lucky that our engineers stayed with us and worked out changes in the manufacturing process. Besides this, our computer system's production and cost distribution reports helped us pinpoint places where we had quality

FIGURE 2-3
Actual Levels of MIS Impact
(Group-oriented System)

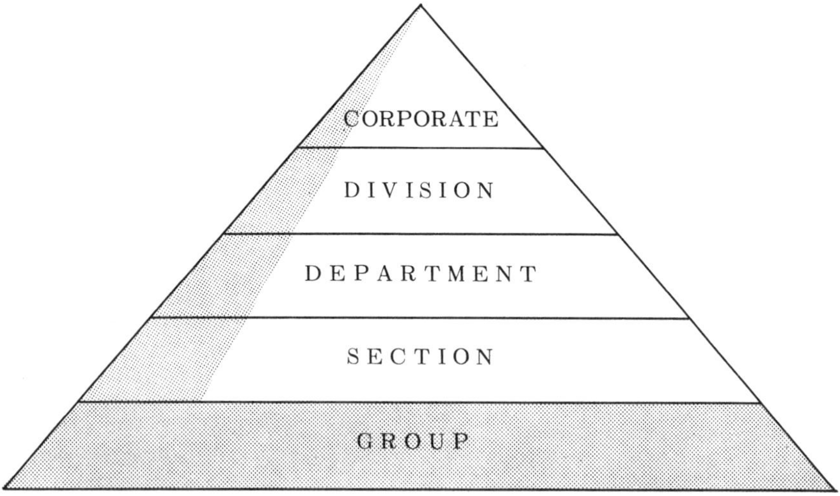

problems and showed where some of our costs were out of control." He said his firm was now doing better than ever, and plans were on the drawing board to develop a computer information system that would do trend projections, among other things. These will help his company analyze future markets. "We've had about all the reacting we can take," he emphasized.

Levels of Sophistication

Not only is sophistication a dirty word in many companies, but it is also subject to broad interpretation. To the medium-size bank that is hearing about its possibilities for the first time, linear programming is sophisticated. To the petroleum company that has been using it for years, it would probably not be. The same kind of relationship holds where MIS is the subject.

Very often, agencies or departments of the federal government do the most sophisticated work on computer applications, including MIS. Government activities, especially the military's, are frequently the forerunner of industry developments, and one can learn a great deal by staying informed. For examples of the government as a leading indicator, we have only to consider the first uses of the computer, operations research techniques, and PERT.

The need for sophistication grows as the complexity and scope of the problem become greater. If we agree that the ultimate in MIS sophistication is that point at which it can examine all appropriate information and alternatives, make the right decision, and take action, it should be evident that the ultimate also becomes increasingly more remote as the business problem becomes more complex. Conversely, a simple business can approach the "ultimate" more easily. However—and this is the point that must be understood—your ultimate is *not* the same as mine.

The sheer complexity of a business problem is not a sound basis for deciding whether it can be solved with sophisticated methods. Solving the problem has to include much more than coming up with the right answer. Right answers can go unheeded simply because no one is listening. Prerequisites for being listened to include management's keeping an open mind and participating in MIS. Participation, however, does not mean pacifying managers or making them believe they had a hand in putting together MIS.

Everyone knows that participation is a good mechanism for gaining psychological support. With MIS, real participation is the only means by which the program *can* be successful. The relevance this has to the question of sophistication is this: The participating managers control the level of sophistication that can be used effectively. MIS represents a step toward higher levels of sophistication. How big the first and subsequent steps will be depends on management's open-mindedness, its desire to improve effectiveness, the quality of the education it receives, and on its ability to learn.

Sometimes, MIS is viewed as a threat to a manager's empire, status, and influence. He will generally protect his hard-earned position, however, not by overt resistance to change, but by limiting the sophistication of the system. A great deal has been written on this phenomenon, much of it blaming the protective manager for MIS limitations. Although it is a genuine and important phenomenon, to credit the claims about its magnitude is not easy. Too much is made of it, and far too little is made of the faulty education of management and the lack of bona fide management participation. Shifting the burden to management resistance, as some MIS literature would have us do, is both inappropriate and useless.

Raw Data Versus Information

The main ingredient of MIS is raw data, but, as is true with so many other ingredients, much of the data's ultimate usefulness is dependent on how they are processed and mixed with other elements. It is common to find raw data employed to help with routine clerical functions. For example, the balance in a checking account is used to direct a bank teller to cash or not cash a check drawn on his bank. Or a notice of shipment arrival will be sent by the receiving department to accounts payable, which will then proceed with payment.

Data-collection systems can often be classified as raw-data systems in that they deal with basic, low-level data. A given data element can be useful only to the extent that it "speaks for itself." It rarely happens that data as data mean much. Let us take three pieces of raw data from an incoming order to illustrate the point: 312 units of product 2701 for customer GD4-411. These data have no significance to us because they have not been *evaluated.* This fact, more than any other, can be used to define them as raw data as opposed to information. To show what we mean by "evaluated," let us take the raw data from the incoming order and make them say something.

Raw Data	*Partial Evaluation*
Customer GD4–411	This is a U.S. Government (G) order for a defense (D) contract, it receives highest priority, and it is subject to federal purchasing regulations. The order was placed by the Navy (4) for project No. 411.
Product 2701	Sells at $100 for first hundred, $90 for second hundred, and $80 for all over 200. Its profit is better than average. There are 70 units in stock, the reorder point is 50, re-

Raw Data	*Partial Evaluation*
	order lot size is 100, lead time is 10 days. The average order size is 30, maximum to date is 50, total last year was 90.
External	Annual sales of our business is $400,000; average order size is $400.
312 units	This order is 10 times bigger than the average for this product; 6 times the previous maximum; it is 7 percent of our annual sales and has better than average profitability; it is 70 times bigger than our average order.

From the evaluation, we may find ourselves needing answers to questions, drawing conclusions, making decisions, and taking action. Some of these might be:

- This is probably the biggest, most profitable order we've ever had.
- How soon does the customer need the product?
- Will the customer take 70 units now and 242 in 10 to 15 days?
- How fast can our vendor get 342 units to us (242 + 100 for replenishment)?
- Should we increase the number of units we usually have on hand?
- Call Joe and have him give this order personal attention from start to finish, full time if necessary.

This hypothetical set of circumstances is meant to illustrate how raw data must be related, compared, extracted, summarized, and evaluated if they are to be useful for management purposes.

Ratio Management Information

MIS developers have repeatedly told of having encountered key executives who insisted that the developers tell these top managers what they need to run the business. In some cases, an executive was no doubt pressed to explain his problems and information requirements and was unable to do so. In at least one case, the executive was really looking for a fresh point of view as to what a systems analyst thought the president of a large company's medium-size division should be using. Further discussions between the MIS analyst and the president set the stage for what was later described as a top management information system. Proposed on that basis, the information that this system provided became the framework for what we call *ratio management.*

Factors such as rate of return on investment, growth, and profit margin are, of course, calculated from ratios. A lot of what business management is about has to do with making ratios change. In fact, one of the essential features of almost every top manager's survival kit is his table of ratios. After decades of use, ratios continue to represent one of the most serviceable staples of successful managers. So, while there is really nothing new about ratios themselves, it might prove worthwhile to view them in a new context.

Our friend the MIS analyst was quick to recognize the acceptance of ratio information and its suitability as a foundation for a top management MIS. Using a little ingenuity and a great deal of common sense, the analyst focused his energies on the twin needs of top management: (1) to deal as much as possible with only the key variables affecting performance and (2) to identify new key variables as fast as possible and assess their impact.

MIS can go a long way toward satisfying both needs, provided that a carefully executed professional systems-analysis job has been done. Top management ratios seem to come in two general varieties: (1) those that tell how good or bad a shape things are in, and (2) those that tell us approximately what problem exists and where it is (or where we are doing well).

MIS can be built to do more than just speed up the function of bringing these ratios to management. A well-conceived system can permit more effective use of more ratios and can also be designed to find out what relationships (using statistical methods and multiple correlation techniques) exist between two or more ratios. In this latter connection, management may discover fairly accurate indications of regularly occurring situations. To take an unsophisticated example of such a circumstance, let us consider a consumer-goods manufacturing company that has been maintaining a weekly ratio of *value of orders shipped* to *direct labor payroll* and a weekly ratio of *finished goods inventory* to *value of orders shipped.* The latter ratio will be more sensitive and will change before the former. An inventory buildup may be revealed, in which case management can start in earlier to cut down production by lowering direct labor payroll; or it can increase production if inventory is being reduced at a faster-than-usual rate. On the other hand, there would be marketing and sales indicators that would show up a decline in advance of an inventory buildup; perhaps one of these might be the ratio of sales-office overhead to value of current orders. To go further, we would expect to have indicators concerning competitive activity and those pertaining to factors in the nation's economy. These would give us even greater advance notice.

Troubleshooting, which is part of management control, is one use to which indicators are put. For example, if all the ratios but one seemed to be in line, we would obviously be alerted to an exception situation. If the relationship of the value of orders shipped to direct labor payroll began to change, for instance, we might find that the payroll has been stable but that scrap and rework have been going up. Records may also show an increase of customer complaints about late deliveries. At this point, we may have a raw-material quality problem or an industrial relations problem (slowdown or careless work). Here we might look at grievance indicators and current vendor quality ratios. Perhaps we might want to know about personnel turnover in the quality control department.

Ultimately, we may find that the entire problem is the result of using an off-standard machining oil. Certainly, it is highly unlikely that top management itself would have discovered this kind of root cause. But this then raises the question of what level of detail MIS will go to. Very simply, the answer has to be: whatever top managers want to get—so long as they judge that the value is worth the price of having it. All information systems have cutoffs, at which point the "put" system goes into effect—pick up the telephone.

Ratios fall into four main categories: (1) financial, (2) productivity, (3) external relative performance, and (4) miscellaneous.

Financial ratios are well known and include indications of liquidity, leverage, profitability, asset activity, and investor evaluation. Examples of the ratios themselves are:

1. Current assets to current liabilities (known as the acid test or quick ratio).
2. Current debt to total assets.
3. Operating expense to gross sales.
4. Per share price to per share earnings.

Productivity indicators can be of many different types, depending on the line of business. One example is salable units produced per man-hour.

External relative performance indicators are of any type that may be compared, usually to company averages within a business line or particular industry. Standards for particular industries are available from government agencies, trade associations, banks, and such companies as Dun & Bradstreet, Robert Morris Associates, Accounting Corporation of America, and NCR.

Miscellaneous indicators could relate to employee relations, government, public relations, market position, law, customer relations, service, demographic trends, national data, competitive situations, world economics, race relations, vendors, stockholders, unions, and others.

Most books on financial management and management controls cover the topic of ratios rather thoroughly. One book of particular interest, devoted almost entirely to ratio management, is Paul M. Stokes's *A Total Systems Approach to Management Control,* published in 1968 by AMA. *The Handbook of Business Administration* (H. B. Maynard, ed.), published by McGraw-Hill, discusses the use of ratios in a number of sections. Also, the Spring 1967 issue of *The Price Waterhouse Review* carried an informative and well-illustrated article on key item and ratio management.

GOOD
* REF.

The following quotation from Stokes's book offers sound guidelines for developing a key indicator or ratio management system.

1. *Select as few key indicators as possible.* When someone was asked how long a woman's dress should be, "Short enough to be interesting and long enough to cover the situation" was the reply. This holds true for key indicators also. There should be as few as possible, but there should be enough to give full and balanced reporting in a key performance area.

2. *Select the key indicators that will help in both present conditions and future projections.* Reporting is needed not only for the present but also for pointing out the direction to be followed in the future. Reporting is history; it deals with past events. The chief value of studying history is to help plot the future properly. We look backward to see where we have been, hoping to operate in the future without repeating the mistakes of the past. Key indicators should be geared to help us plot our future course.

3. *Select key indicators that lead to worthwhile ends.* The health and continuity of a business are the constant concern of the effective manager. Key indicators should be selected which are capable of providing feedback helpful to the organization or the business and which do not merely reflect the hobbies or personal interest of the manager.

4. *Select key indicators that lead to progress and innovation.* A business must progress in order to survive. Key indicators should stimulate better performance in the future. As one American executive has declared, "The future is my business." He is concerned about being ready for the future before it arrives. Key indicators can and should help in plotting a progressive path and should enable the executive to see a little farther down the road of the future of his business than anyone else.

5. *Select key indicators that permit ready comparisons.* Business is a process; and at any given moment progress must be measured in relation to a starting point, a goal, a standard, or some other fixed point. Key indicators tell the executive where he stands at a given time in relation to his performance standards. Key indicators ideally provide comparisons with standards without requiring complicated interpretation.[3]

SYSTEM CHARACTERISTICS

The architects of MIS need to understand the dynamics of the business and the environment in which it operates. These dynamics can be accommodated in the information system only when the factors that control and

[3] Paul M. Stokes, *A Total Systems Approach to Management Control* (New York: © American Management Association, 1968), p. 54.

provide measures of performance have been analyzed and stated explicitly. This work, if taken lightly, usually results in systems with a high rate of irrevocable obsolescence because the flexibility needed to permit changes has not been built in. If this is not to happen, serious analytical attention must be paid to certain facets of the problem, including the following:

- *Scope.* Defined by the organization and the sophistication of the system.
- *Sensitivity.* Described by the level of detail to be monitored.
- *Exterior variables.* Information not generated within the business.
- *Service levels.* Levels of management the system is geared for.
- *Channel relationships.* Characteristics of the information flow, both input and output, especially between functional areas.
- *Selectivity.* Data that need to be maintained by the system.

Taking these areas of inquiry and synthesizing the answers will often suggest a more or less formal description of MIS characteristics.

Getting Information Where the Action Is

Shortcomings in management uses of historical information can be intensified in a computerized system. Many miss the mark because of faults and oversights in the design of important system characteristics.

One common weakness of many present systems is their failure to report on exceptions. Consequently, any manager who needs information has to pore over thick computer listings to find the exceptions. Many managers and nearly all executives refuse to go through this agony, even supposing that they had time for it.

Another common fault is the way in which information is presented. The format of reports is often poor, which makes the interpretation and identification of vital data onerous.

Another problem is that the quality of the data upon which management relies is often suspect and sometimes just plain no good. In addition to this, it is not uncommon to find that the vital data needed for management decisions is not present. Then, of course, if nothing else goes wrong, a manager can depend on getting his information too late to do anything about it.

When all the problems of data, exception reporting, format, and timing deficiencies are considered, and when it is realized that the original systems analysis job was rarely approached from a management-information point of view, it is not difficult to understand why many systems in operation today have little or no value as providers of management information. Attempts to pass off a system to management as something it can use has resulted in more disillusionment than anything else, which helps explain why there may be abnormal prejudice against new systems promising help to management.

Even the existing system problems, which have already been referred to, have by no means disappeared in newly developed systems. That 30 percent of the systems now developed are flops, whereas the figure used to be 60 percent, is hardly comforting. Even where MIS has been considered a success, major efforts are devoted to such familiar problems as data accuracy, standards for systems and programs, uniform data identification, and information codes.

Putting It Down in Black and White

A solid MIS development program must be predicated on knowing the dimensions of the system as early as possible. It is unacceptable to permit the system's key characteristics to emerge as more and more work is done on putting it together, unless, of course, you want to view the program as a research or experimental project.

One of the greatest benefits of a competent systems analyst is that he does not start digging the foundation till he knows what needs to be done. Since competent analysts have been spread thin because of the growth of computing, it is more important than ever to document the findings. This serves two purposes. First, it helps insist on the clear expression of concepts. Second, ideas committed to paper can be understood, evaluated, and reviewed as often as needed by management and systems personnel.

Documentation does not prevent flaws in thinking, although it can reduce their number considerably. What it does do is to provide the opportunity to detect flaws. Intensive reviews of MIS documentation will of course be needed.

Deciding the Scope of MIS

Some of the most ardent promoters of MIS are managers who expect too much too soon from it. Ultimately, they will be disappointed if they expect MIS to solve a lot of their problems. Both the potential and practical limitations of MIS must be understood, particularly with respect to time and scope.

Scope is mainly concerned with the contemplated uses of information. Everyone is interested in getting better information; many managers want more of the right kinds of information; and it is common to find that managers want information faster. But we have to know the uses of information to begin to answer the question of scope. Here is a sampling of such activities: policy making and setting objectives, long-range planning, organizing and defining relationships, specifying and coordinating resource use, short-range planning and decision making, directing and administering planned operations, measuring and controlling performance.

MIS uses are concerned with those activities directly related to what the business is doing to reach its goals. Continuing success is a function of the responsive and effective management of these activities. The informational variables that go into the success formula have distinctive effects on business activities, some having many times the impact of others. A ranking of these business information variables, in order of impact, is one of the first things that needs to be done in order to deal with the question of scope and selection. Such rankings show different sequences of critical items for different kinds of businesses, and they can differ in businesses that are quite similar. What it turns out to be for a given organization depends on circumstances at a particular time. For example, if the price of salt goes from 12 to 24 cents a pound, the housewife probably will not care. Even to the restaurant owner, it will make little difference. But to the chemical company that uses salt as a major raw material, it can mean the difference between success and failure—especially if the price of a competitive substitute for the salt-derived product should suddenly become attractive. On the other hand, a toy-manufacturing company is likely to be about as concerned about the price of salt as the typical housewife.

Focus on Key Variables

If we can classify and rank business impact factors, then it should be possible to relate them to management information needs, thereby helping establish certain ground rules for MIS project selection and scope.

The following guidelines have been found helpful in beginning a survey of the functional possibilities. They should tie into major business functions and important management activities.

1. Adopt a contribution or value-added orientation when examining potential applications.
2. Identify the critical factors within the high-contribution items that have been defined.
3. Isolate high-opportunity possibilities.
4. Define high-cost areas.
5. Examine the profitability of existing business areas.

6. Specify the decisions most critical to performance.
7. Enumerate what data need to be available for important decisions.
8. Identify the origins of the data needed.
9. Assign a risk or probability of success number to the applications identified.
10. Analyze what decisions are made in reacting to conditions and which in acting independently. (This may help isolate areas where action instead of reaction should prevail.)
11. State which decisions are made on the basis of internal measurement and feedback and which come from external sources.
12. In each general decision area, project what adaptive qualities the MIS application must possess.
13. Look at the relative dependence or independence of human contributions on the system's potential effectiveness and value.
14. Try to get a feeling for the relationship of complexity to practicality of development in order to strike a balance.

Providing management with intelligence is another part of the question of scope. At one time or another, everyone has been in the situation where facts have been plentiful but conclusions have been nowhere in sight. Indeed, the facts may have been too plentiful, while the organization needed to make sense from them was lacking.

Selectivity

An important feature of intelligence, as opposed to data, is that it is *selective*. Selectivity means that the manager gets to see net instead of gross—conclusions instead of random facts. For many managers, the proper use of intelligence is a skill yet to be acquired. In the first place, it is often unique to the man who has previously had to look through dozens or even hundreds of pages of computer printout to find what he wanted. Occasionally, in fact, a manager must turn to another well-known "management tool": the adding machine. You can imagine what he must be thinking about computers if he has to go over a computer printout and add numbers. It is not hard to see why business-magazine writers say that top executives rarely interact with computers for any purpose. Quite a few of these writers think that it will take until the late 1970s before top management itself gets real benefits on a regular basis.

Because the information systems typical today fall well short on selectivity, the managers who do use MIS must take what amounts to a shotgun approach to decision making. As more careful consideration and study are given to the decision maker's needs, we would expect, by way of analogy, that the manager's arsenal will begin to contain more rifles than shotguns.

To press a bit more out of this analogy, we can see that success depends on more than just having rifles and people who can use them. What we really must have are marksmen. Making marksmen out of shotgun managers can be a long process, with no guarantee of excellence. However, we can improve the odds and shorten the time span if the approach is basic enough: Have the managers contribute to the design of the "weapon"; make them take it apart and put it together; make them intimately familiar with its construction and use; and, in short, make sure it is built to their specifications.

Finally, remember that you cannot take the whole armory into battle. Too much in the way of weaponry and ammunition fatigues the troops and hampers mobility. For management, too much information and sophistication has the same effect.

Business Functions and Data Flow

Building an effective MIS starts with an analytical comprehension of the various business functions that it affects. From this point, we can begin to see where the different functions overlap. Next, we can integrate the functional needs beyond the obvious overlap in order to form a conceptual operating mode of an MIS that will be concerned with the overall problems of managing the business.

The functional areas that need to be understood in the project's analytical phase, depending on the particular organization, might include:

- Marketing and sales.
- Manufacturing.
- Engineering.
- Purchasing.
- Personnel.
- Inventory control and distribution.
- Finance.
- Research and development.
- Special projects and new ventures.

Each area may have one or more of the basic computer-automated systems, which keep records and issue reports of an accounting nature. These may be termed cost-distribution or profitability-accounting systems. In general, such systems are concerned with the accumulation of historical information about the receipt and disbursement of money, and provide data for profit and loss statements, general-ledger entries, and cash-flow reporting.

Under the category of MIS, we may find a variety of systems that relate to the basic accounting systems but that are primarily aimed at the decision–information needs of a functional area. Thus we find such information systems being called production management systems, inventory management systems, marketing management systems, and the like.

In such management information systems as these, it is not clear what specific problems they help solve. However, there is no sound basis for the idea sometimes expressed that, for example, a marketing information system provides *all* the information needed for marketing decisions. Most MIS tend to emphasize one of three decision-making areas, although some do attempt to cover all of them—with varying degrees of success. Decision-making areas believed to be logically segmentable, but of course related, pertain to logistics, tactics, and strategy.

Logistics is concerned with acquiring, maintaining, and distributing goods and services. Personnel, raw materials, finished products, and facilities of all kinds are implied. Logistics problem solving is mainly a process of mathematical reasoning.

Tactics are concerned with the short-range organization and use of resources toward satisfying part of a larger objective. Tactics problem solving is both an art and a science and is usually limited to situations of small scope to accomplish more or less immediate results.

Strategy is concerned with long-term planning and includes setting objectives, policy making, organizing all functions, and seeking maximum overall advantage. Strategy problem solving is more an art than a science.

Logistics, tactics, and strategy decision making have a number of parallel relationships to their information systems. The table in Figure 2-4 is meant to show how these systems compare with basic data processing systems on some important points.

In a conceptual way, Figure 2-5 depicts the data flow relationships between the MIS data bases, which include financial and nonfinancial records and (1) corporate strategy and planning systems, (2) administrative and operations systems, and (3) corporate control systems. Notice that data flows represent the availability of any data to all systems, including the nine systems areas shown within administrative and operations systems. In actual practice, not all data would be made available to all systems—first, because the data bases contain records not relevant to all systems; second, because some records would be considered confidential and their availability would of course be restricted.

As you might imagine, the systems shown in Figure 2-5 would contain many subsystems for accomplishing specific tasks within the general systems area. Within marketing systems, for example, you would find order processing, sales analysis, competitive analysis, and many others.

Some of the tasks within the purview of corporate strategy and planning systems would be major problem and opportunity identification and authentication; analysis of stockholder interests; analysis of personnel, public, and vendor relations; and formulation of goals and objectives. Tasks undertaken within corporate control systems include corporate performance analysis, division and profit-center performance analysis, project and operating function reviews, major-exception reporting, and others.

FIGURE 2-4
Advanced System Factor Comparison Table

	BASIC DATA PROCESSING SYSTEMS	LOGISTICS INFORMATION SYSTEMS	TACTICS INFORMATION SYSTEMS	STRATEGY INFORMATION SYSTEMS
IMPORTANCE TO COMPANY'S WELL-BEING	Minor	Significant	Extreme	Vital
DEPENDENCE ON INTERNAL DATA	Complete	Very High	High	Moderate
DEPENDENCE ON EXTERNAL DATA	None	Little	Significant	Great
DIFFICULTY OF PROBLEM DEFINITION	Modest	High	High	Very High
DEPENDENCE ON SYSTEMS INTEGRATION	None	Some	Significant	Essential
VOLUME OF DATA INPUT/ INFORMATION OUTPUT	High/High	High/Moderate	High/Moderate	Very High/Low
SKILL REQUIRED TO DEVELOP SYSTEM	Standard	High	High	Superior
EASE OF MEASURING PAYOFF/ MAGNITUDE OF PAYOFF	Easy/Low	Difficult/High	Very Difficult/ High	Often Impossible/ Very High
PREDOMINANT LEVEL OF MANAGEMENT USE	Supervisory	Operating Middle	Operating Top	Operating Top and Corporate Top
PREDOMINANT TYPES OF DECISION ASSISTANCE	Programmed	Deterministic-Analytical	Probabilistic-Analytical	Heuristic-Analytical
USEFULNESS FOR MANAGEMENT CONTROL	Fair	Excellent	Good	Poor
NECESSITY FOR A FAST RESPONSE SYSTEM	Rare	Often	Very Often	Occasionally a Convenience

Logistics, tactics, and strategy information systems are rated relative to basic systems.

FIGURE 2-5
Conceptual Data Flow in an Integrated MIS

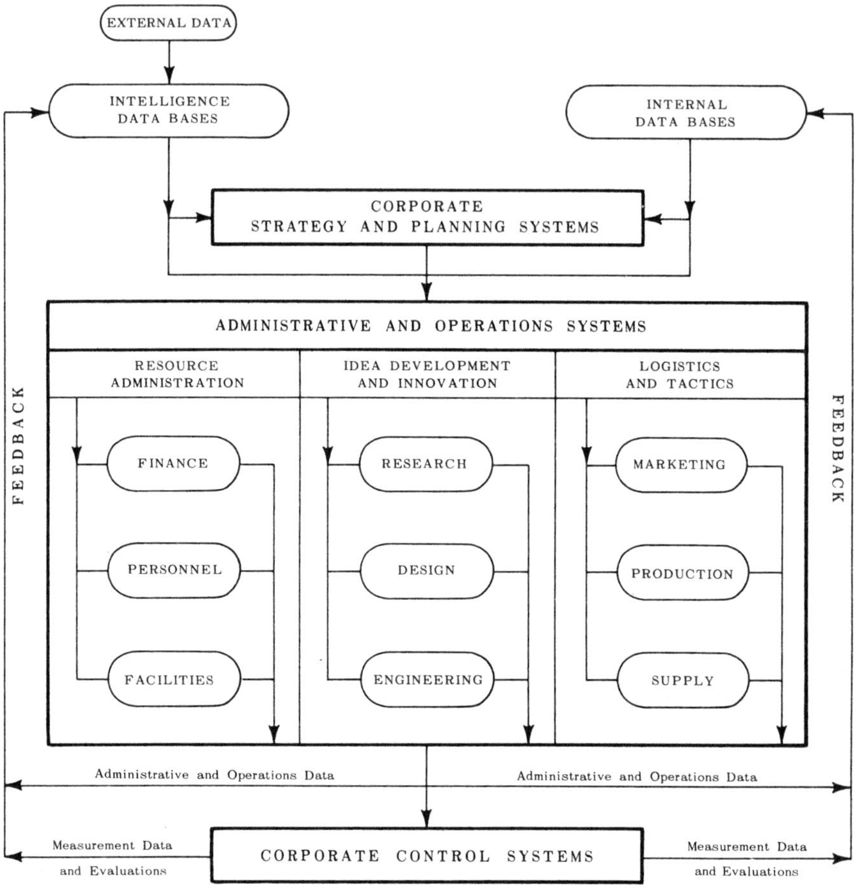

Evaluating Opportunities

Isolating the higher return MIS applications is the first step in focusing on the opportunities you are going to examine more carefully. Risk must next be gauged and applied to what is judged to be a maximum potential return on a given application. The expected value of the return can then be quantified. The application areas that emerge on top after a risk factor has been applied are the ones that should initially be given more serious consideration. Calculating the expected value is easy; whether the answer is valid is completely dependent on the validity of the values established for the potential return and risk. This is the hard part.

To illustrate the calculation, consider a proposal with a maximum return of 50 percent, but a chance of success of ¾. Our expected value of return is ¾ × 50 percent, or 37.5 percent. This is an elementary application of decision theory, a subject we do not intend to get into here. But we have used it to show how judgment must be tempered when considering alternatives in MIS. There is a pressing need to undertake this kind of evaluation for MIS, more so than with data processing and other types of systems. Essentially, such an approach acknowledges that payoffs for some parts of MIS, perhaps much of it, cannot be described in black and white. Who is to say, for example, what return a certain improvement in customer service will bring?

A guess can be made at the value of MIS services, but how good is it, how confident are we about it? Still, we need to ask ourselves whether addressing the tasks of value guessing and risk determination is not better than ignoring them when making decisions on the direction MIS is to take.

The method of going about it so that it does not become unduly complicated consists of asking the company's most qualified forecasters what they think about the potential dollar return of some idea and how confident they feel about their estimates. If the idea is in the marketing area, we might conduct a poll that includes marketing executives as well as front-line personnel, such as sales representatives. It may be appropriate to assign different weights to answers given by each level or person, before striking an average. The weighted average resulting from this study would then serve as the basis for calculating expected return, the system-module-cost figures having been roughly estimated by the computer systems group.

Some people are not inclined to offer a guess, mostly because they are afraid they will be held to it, but partly because guessing is foreign to them. After the fear of being held to a guess has been overcome by repeated assurances that there will be no personal penalty of any kind, the questioners must usually probe for the guess, because the first answer is likely to be, "I don't know." Probing is a narrowing-down process that consists of question cycles. For example, the questioner might begin by asking, "Is the return between $1,000 and $100,000?" Very quickly the range is narrowed to some quantity, which is then recorded. As to risk, the questioner might begin by asking, "Do you feel there is better than a 50–50 chance that the return we just arrived at is achievable?" Once again, the risk is narrowed, and again, the figure is recorded.

If necessary, the system-module-cost side of the return, or cost-effectiveness estimate, can be developed in a manner very similar to that outlined for the return side. While the method described may not be to everyone's liking, it is one of the few means available whereby a fairly inexpensive assessment of alternatives can be made early in an MIS investigation.

Focusing on the Right Problems

R. George Glaser, in his article "Are You Working on the Right Problem?" tells how computer people get off the track and are put to work on the wrong problems. He recommends that a number of things be done to help avoid this. Particularly relevant to MIS is Glaser's warning: ". . . obvious applications are not always the best ones and small companies [in particular] often assign their scarce human resources to development efforts that have a relatively marginal impact on the company's operation."[4]

Cataloging the potential application is recommended as one of the first steps. Successful businesses, Glaser points out, apply the same kind of judgment and economic analysis to potential computer uses as they do to other business decisions. Entries in the catalog, therefore, would reflect answers and imply priorities based on a number of questions the company must ask. The following were suggested by Glaser in his article.

> What are the most important decisions we make? How could these be improved with better information?
>
> Where would a small percentage change in cost have a relatively large impact on profits?
>
> What are our most important resources—plant capacity, raw material reserves, etc.—and are we managing them well?[5]

Once having put together a catalog as a result of answering these questions, we need to learn which of the entries can effectively be meshed with the computer. For answers to this problem we turn to the *feasibility study,* which, according to Glaser, should give management answers to three basic questions:

1. Can the job be done?—a technical question.
2. Should the job be done?—an economic question.
3. Will the system work?—an operational question.

Quantitative Rating of MIS Application Proposals

With the MIS catalog of potential applications in hand, we may find it useful to measure or rate each of the possibilities in some quantitative way. In the October 1968 issue of *Management Review,* Robert R. Renner, in the article "Profit Control: Back to Basics," presents a rating scheme for profit-

[4] *Datamation,* June 1967, p. 22, © F. D. Thompson Publications, Inc.
[5] *Ibid.,* p. 22.

improvement proposals. The method discussed here is an adaptation of the one presented by Renner. Understandably, the modifications are intended to bring the technique in line with suitable criteria for MIS project selection and should not be viewed as a representation of Renner's concepts. Here is how the method works.

Five rating parameters are multiplied together in order to arrive at the weighting of a given MIS application, subsystem, or capability proposal. The higher the value calculated, the higher the implementation priority of the particular item. The parameters are set by management's knowledge, experience, and judgment concerning the proposal's potential, rapidity, urgency, payoff, and investment.

- *Potential.* Reflects, among other things, credibility and confidence.

Fair	1
Excellent	2
Substantial	3

- *Rapidity.* Reflects the value of having benefits sooner rather than later.

Over 36 months	1
25 to 36 months	2
14 to 24 months	3
6 to 13 months	4
3 to 5 months	5
Less than 3 months	6

- *Urgency.* Refers to the level of importance of taking action on one item relative to others of apparently similar importance.

Can wait its turn	1
As soon as possible	2
Highly urgent	3
Critically urgent	4

- *Payoff.* A rating of expected return, or expression of opportunity expectations, or simply a rate of return on investment (result of discounted cash flow calculations for each item).

Under 5 %	1
5% to 10%	2
10% to 15%	3
15% to 20%	4
20% to 25%	5
•	•
•	•
•	•
etc.	etc.

- *Investment.* Reflects anticipated total expenditure to realize the implied benefit. A percentage of annual sales would be appropriate in some cases.

Over 1%	1
.75% to 1%	2
.50% to .75%	3
.25% to .50%	4
.15% to .25%	5
.10% to .15%	6
.05% to .10%	7
.01% to .05%	8
Under .01%	9

Let us take two cases, in a company with $100 million annual sales, to illustrate how the *priority* value (potential × rapidity × urgency × payoff × return) is calculated.

Case 1 is a cash-flow simulation system that has been rated as follows: potential (excellent) = 2; rapidity (8 months) = 4; urgency (as soon as possible) = 2; payoff (12%) = 3; investment ($100,000) = 6.

Case 2 is a purchasing MIS (integratable module) that has been rated as follows: potential (substantial) = 3; rapidity (18 months) = 3; urgency (as soon as possible) = 2; payoff (25%) = 5; investment ($250,000) = 4.

These cases may be recorded in our catalog as shown in Figure 2-6.

Our recipe, as may be seen from the parameters assigned to "investment," penalizes more expensive projects. Hence, larger investments, relative to smaller ones, must be more convincing in every way in order to gain approval. Or, to look at it another way, the "return" must be higher if it costs more, all other parameters being equal. In effect, then, this says that we will risk more only when the rate of return is higher. Whether a company thinks that this is right is for it to decide. Also, as was pointed out earlier, consideration of risk must always enter the picture in some fashion. In our method, it is reflected in "potential."

There are qualitative grounds that must also come into play in project selection. Competitive factors and company image may enter into this, as well as value judgments as to the better quality of decisions. Discussing these matters, M. H. Schwartz of the Atomic Energy Commission, a long-time computer practitioner, points out:

> Visible, estimatable dollars are not alone sufficient, however, for adequate priority determination. . . . *The judgmental weighting of qualitative factors is the best presently available substitute for dollar measures where dollar*

measures cannot be made with confidence but where dollar earnings high in relation to costs may nevertheless be anticipated with confidence.[6]

An Application of Delphi Methods

Depending on the magnitude and scope of the MIS being contemplated, it is sometimes necessary to look well beyond the next few years to shape current designs and philosophical approaches reflecting that magnitude. It might be helpful to mention one way of tackling this problem.

The Delphi method, a recently formalized approach for making exceptionally long-range predictions of technological developments, can be adapted

FIGURE 2-6
Project Rating and Priority and Rating Form

ITEM NAME	RATING FACTORS						PRIORITY VALUE
	Potential	Rapidity	Urgency	Payoff	Investment	Other	
Case 1 Cash Flow System Simulator	2	4	2	3	6		288
Case 2 Purchasing Management Information System	3	3	2	5	4		360

[6] "Computer Project Selection in the Business Enterprise," *Journal of Accountancy*, April 1969, p. 37.

to the MIS planning effort as well. The RAND Corporation is credited with the development of the method in connection with forecasting technological breakthroughs.

In a nutshell, this consists of gathering and regathering the prognostications of many eminently qualified experts (futurists) in the particular area of concern. Following this, the results are tabulated. Those advances mentioned most often are deemed most likely to occur in a given time span.

In MIS efforts, where we are likely to be faced with a poorly structured set of circumstances on which to make long-range decisions concerning the company's MIS, the Delphi method could be used to advantage in getting the MIS started in the right direction. At least there will be some agreement that it is the right direction.

3

Analyzing Management's Information Needs

GROWING prowess at systems analysis accompanied by an increasing inability to synthesize is one of the major difficulties encountered in systems work today. It has become fashionable to speak of "islands of automation," a reference to failures to integrate systems that are, in fact, closely related. Methods and ideas are disassembled and neatly arranged, but few analysts have the ability to put the otherwise isolated pieces back together so that the composite makes more sense and works better than the parts.

Computer-based MIS can provide a focal point. But, there is more to be considered in using MIS as an enabling instrument or tool to accomplish integration. Essential to the realization of value are the skilled and talented men who can use these tools to make things happen. The total packaged result must be created with generous helpings of both business and technical judgment.

Analyzing the Decision Makers

Decision makers not only determine whether an MIS will be undertaken, but also have a great deal to do with its success, through participation in MIS analysis and as users. The importance of selling the decision maker on the advisability of having an MIS is commonly referred to by executives and computer systems people alike, in magazine articles and industry seminars on MIS. Like a lot of obvious things, we sometimes take this for granted, forgetting the nuances and overlooking what is unique.

The "Unselling" Job

The selling job we hear so much about may sometimes have to be an *unselling* job. Perhaps we are addressing a decision maker who is sold on MIS but who may have a lot of misconceptions that cause him to relate MIS to some grand scheme for solving 90 percent of his problems. He may see himself sitting back in a big swivel chair in his company's "war room" directing the "battle" according to the decisions the computer has made, which are being projected on a large-image wall display. This man must be unsold before any conventional selling can be expected to produce the desired result.

An unselling job also has to be done on the executive who may feel, with some justification, that the computer should concentrate on eliminating clerical problems, which it has not done without trauma to date, and which he believes is its only capability anyway.

Then there is the manager who does not know much about MIS but, because it is progressive, wants to jump into it just the same. Here again, we should face up to the task of unselling and, having done that, substitute something that makes sense.

Selling has so many pejorative overtones that it is a good idea to take care in understanding what you really want to achieve when you think about selling MIS. What you might conclude is that management should be given the facts and insights that enable it to sell itself. This is not to say that a proposal need not be organized, or that the facts can be presented without interpretation, or that opinions and matters of judgment must be ignored. Rather, it is a case where the difference between what is fact and what is opinion needs to be spelled out.

Accomplished systems men have suggested that the company president have a display terminal in his office that would give him minute-by-minute sales data throughout the day. One analyst reportedly proposed this, whereupon the president told him such information would not help him. The president went on to say that he was mainly interested in long-term planning and when he did get involved at the short-term operating level he was interested only in those things he could reasonably expect to change. "Knowing today's sales today does not help," he said. "What you can do for me is to tell me today's sales six or more months in advance—*that* would help."

Studying Special Needs

A popular assumption is that MIS would fill what is now a void. The oversight here is in failing to recognize that all managers have information systems of some kind that, while imperfect, do serve them fairly well. And yet occasionally a wholly new system is being contemplated that bears little relation to the existing one. The new system has not been conceived in such a way as to complement or improve the existing one, mainly because the designers have not taken the trouble to learn anything about the latter.

Sometimes competent management analysts and computer people, with the best of intentions, recommend looking at the information problem in terms of what should be happening and ignore what *is* happening. This is a carry-over from systems and procedures work and the computer automation of clerical functions. In those activities, the approach had many merits to commend it.

MIS, however, is a different sphere with new rules and much higher orders of cerebral involvement. There is a lot that is not obvious and a great deal more that is not amenable in the common systems and procedures analytical approach. It is neither appropriate nor wise to look hopefully for practical solutions completely outside of existing management information practices. Such an approach is likely to take more money than anyone is willing to spend and take longer than anyone is willing to wait.

One possible approach sometimes suggested goes as follows: Analyze the MIS functions around organizational positions and responsibilities, not around the man holding the position at a particular point in time. One immediate problem everyone will see is that the organization does not really work the way it appears on paper or the way some executives may tell you it works. If you study it carefully, you can find out how it does work and design the MIS accordingly.

MIS analysis, using an organization chart and job descriptions as the main criteria for information needs, may produce a functionally correct system, but by itself it will not work. Analysts must combine it with two other factors: what really goes on and what the manager wants.

If we are looking at the company president's information needs, perhaps we can arrive at adequate definitions in various areas of interest; for example, marketing, production, finance, R&D. Beyond this we may, as an example, find that finance is crucial. Suppose the company is able to compete because of outstanding time-payment terms. Further, suppose the president's background is almost entirely production. We may very well find our actual MIS needs calling for an adequate production information system, a very strong financial information system, and strong systems in all other areas. Because the president knows a great deal about the production side and has good contacts who can give him the score in a couple of phone calls, he is not going to feel a compelling need to have redundant mechanization of some of the same information. It is not hard to guess that if a marketing man takes over, he may very well want to have the production information system beefed up.

The executive vice-president of a major utility was once heard to say: "I believe I have what I need and get it fast enough for my purposes. However, I would be grateful if someone could give me a system to tell me what a lot of it means." This is not an uncommon reaction. No substitute has ever beeen able to take the place of finding out from the man what he wants. Naturally, you have to understand his problems to do an outstanding job, because he may not immediately be able to tell you what his wants are.

Finally, there is sometimes a tendency to hope for a grand solution just because the problems are also grand. In this we may be overlooking what is real, or what is feasible, or what chances there are for successs. No one denies the need in such instances, but the size of what we will have to bite off to solve the problem may produce indigestion.

Psychological Need to Get Fast Payoffs

In Chapter 1 we discussed several MIS programs that were undertaken as three- to five-year projects. Some of these were implemented on a module-by-module program whereby certain benefits could be realized within intervals considerably shorter than the total project. A number of reasons could be cited to explain why this approach was used, even though such an approach may not be technically necessary. In fact, by virtue of having a series of steps, added expense arises from the need to connect the modules as they are developed. As in adding a room onto a house, the matter would have been simpler and less costly if all the elements had been included originally.

In both cases, the reasons for doing it later instead of now are familiar: We don't have the money to spend now, we don't want to spend money now, we don't recognize the need, we want to wait until we are more certain that the main structure has proven satisfactory.

Since MIS will be a long-term project, we need to pay close attention to the sources of its long-term support in the company. It would appear to be wise for MIS developers to line up this support before going too deeply into the project. But this support may not include explicit guarantees, and it could well depend on the financial performance of the company from year to year. Also, not to be considered lightly is that, over long periods of time, the original supporters may change positions or leave the company or be replaced by individuals not in sympathy with the project. These kinds of things can greatly affect the fate of the MIS program and the people directly associated with it.

A certain amount of faith in MIS on the part of the management that originally approved the program no doubt played an important part in its affirmative decision. To repay management's confidence, the program's promoters must take every measure to insure a good running score. This means that at relatively short intervals it is important to chalk up some kind of credit in the performance ledger. This will substantially reinforce management's original backing and will go a long way toward insuring that the program will be continued if new management should come on the scene. On more than one occasion, the demise of MIS projects has resulted from its overextended credit with management. A project the size of an MIS will stick out like a sore thumb if it is not performing, especially when business is off.

The structure of the master plan and therefore the structure of the MIS design itself will very definitely be influenced by the need to realize some benefits before all the funds allocated have been spent. In doing this, we may not take the most straightforward optimum technical approach to the system. Everyone should quickly recognize, however, that, in planning the project, human engineering is at least as important as system engineering.

Implementing certain kinds of modules early in the project not only gives the company immediate benefits but also helps restructure the approach on such systems as are scheduled for future development. In so doing, we take advantage of what we have learned from the experience with preceding modules. Depending on the kind of system being developed, we may be lucky enough to produce a pilot model. With it, it should be possible to solve many of the problems well in advance of meeting them head on in a fully developed system. Sometimes the pilot system can be used to simulate actual operating conditions and thus discover the critical performance factors.

The psychological benefits of such activities are as important as what we learn in the process of carrying them out and the early benefits realized by management. In performing this work, we need to understand that some of it may take us on an excursion somewhat outside the scope of what had originally been planned. It is also reasonable to point out to management that a limited amount of research must be done that roughly parallels the project's main thrust. This kind of understanding at the outset would seem to give the project more credibility than it would otherwise have. It is especially valuable for everyone to understand that an undertaking having the dimensions of MIS needs to have a commitment to some research.

Many project managers have had good success in obtaining solid management support as a result of special problems they agree to work on in the course of the development program. Some of these projects are actually necessary in order to implement the system, while others are conducted to elicit and maintain executive interest in the larger MIS program. Examples of these could be statistical analysis, simple simulation, and calculation models.

Special studies and the like are not, of course, undertaken casually. They are authorized with a definite objective in mind that goes beyond placating someone who is obstinate about getting on the MIS bandwagon. On the other hand, such studies can play an extremely useful role in allaying a manager's fears that MIS will somehow reduce his importance and expose him to undue criticism. Here we are trying to be as helpful as is reasonable and at the same time doing our best to learn what part MIS can play in helping the manager. It is presumptuous to expect all managers to welcome MIS with open arms. Some of them may have had unpleasant experiences with other computerized applications in the past. Others will be reluctant about, if not openly opposed to, revealing the secrets of their managerial ability and methods. Not the least of the psychological factors that must be overcome is that MIS will turn out to be a "Big Brother is watching you" sort of affair.

Alternative Approaches to MIS Analysis

MIS efforts are significantly influenced by the premises set forth at the time systems analysis begins. Computerizing a payroll system, for example, calls for a systems job that has qualities that set it apart from one undertaken for an MIS. The most salient difference is in the determination of business rules and results desired. In the case of payroll, they have been or can be readily formalized. By way of contrast, MIS cannot usually be subjected to an investigation with the objective of obtaining the absolute, unequivocal truth. To be sure, not every facet of the system will be in this category, but many will—perhaps the most important ones. The first step in understanding the system's requirements is to document them.

One page of the ledger would have an enumeration of what the MIS "must do." Another page would have what it "might do." On a third would be "other" items, which could include subjects for further study—wishes and dreams, poorly defined areas, and the like.

Within each grouping, we need to show where each entry fits within a time spectrum: now, later, much later, and very much later. Corresponding times might be one year, three years, five years, seven years, and over seven years.

A key to success is putting all this into a mosaic that holds all the initial requirements and assumptions. Systems work consists of hacking away at or finding reinforcement for these same requirements and assumptions or uncovering new ones.

There are two basic ways to conduct the MIS analysis: a systems approach or a data-base approach. Each approach, at least conceptually, has its own contribution to make to the systems solution to satisfy management's information requirements. As you will see, no systems job can be all one approach and none of the other.

Systems Approach

Usually, the systems approach follows a distinctive orderly pattern. First among the tasks involved is *requirements analysis,* the most difficult and lengthy part of the whole systems job, if carried out properly.

Requirements analysis begins with gaining a thorough knowledge of the business functions that are of concern. Included would be an understanding of management's objectives, underlying philosophy, attitude toward innovation and change, responsibilities, and plans for the future.

Procedural characteristics represent another side of requirements analysis. Included would be an understanding of the specific work performed, volumes and growth trends of information needs, sequencing and timing of activities, and, in general, the how, when, who, where, and why considerations. An important and problematical area in this analysis of procedures is that of gaining a clear understanding of and agreement on the business rules that will govern MIS operations. All of these rules must eventually boil down to an "if . . . then . . ." relationship. For example, *if* a credit line has been exceeded two or more times in the past six months and *if* the customer is out of state, *then* a go, no-go decision is to be made by the credit department. A method to facilitate the representation of these rules, called *decision tables,* will be illustrated in the final section of this chapter.

Another portion of the systems approach will be concerned with the cost and effectiveness of the present methods and procedures. Once these checkpoints have been satisfied, the requirements analysis turns toward gaining an understanding of what unfulfilled or partially fulfilled information needs are extant.

At the conclusion of requirements analysis, management should be called upon to accept a formalized statement setting forth—

1. What the system is to produce in the form of output information.
2. Description of data that must be collected and specification of sources, in order to satisfy information requirements.
3. The business rules that set forth the logical rules governing the processing of data.

After requirements analysis, the MIS analyst is concerned with *structural analysis,* which is another way of saying "get the facts organized" for systems designers. Structural analysis is the art and science of so organizing elemental requirements that they can be interpreted in order to design a system. Factors that come into play cover points such as what data are needed at what location at the same time; the frequency with which the information is required—for example, account balances every five minutes; and the question of how requirements can be consolidated in order to serve information system users more efficiently.

Following the structural analysis is the *systems design stage.* The design work consists largely of specifying the computer programs, hardware, and procedures that, as a system, will produce the desired results.

Typical data processing systems, as contrasted with MIS, are developed along the lines described here, mainly because a clear understanding of what they must do can be established through some probing and analysis. Certain types of MIS can also follow this pattern, provided that they are limited to fairly narrow functions within a well-defined scope. However, larger and more sophisticated systems seem to demand a dual approach, one that ties together the orthodox with the less orthodox methods of analysis. The thing that makes MIS development tricky is satisfactorily determining how to specify a system, when it is not known for sure what specific tasks it will be called on to perform.

Data-Base Approach

Proponents of the data-base "school" are numerous, possibly even a majority. Basically, the data-base methodology consists of gathering whatever data may be floating around the company and storing those data in machinable form. In time, most of the sources that generate raw data in the company would be sending such data to the MIS data base, in addition to whatever else they do with data.

Thus, at least in theory, we have on tap whatever data may be needed for management purposes. Usually, the data are organized so that they can be extracted and put to almost any conceivable use. Extremely flexible data bases are then at the beck and call of all would-be users.

Much of the data-base approach is justified on the grounds that being prepared for nearly any situation has benefits that exceed the overhead or waste inherent in the excessive storage and other handling it necessitates.

One nice thing about the approach is that it cleverly evades the whole question of MIS application. Because of this, there is some question as to the proper classification of a data-base system—that is, is it an MIS? An important part of MIS is, of course, the data base. However, one MIS manager labeled this sort of MIS as "rigged." But, as was pointed out in the previous section, it is almost impossible to take a pure data-base approach, excluding all systems requirements analysis.

Building a data base is a good way to get an early start on an MIS. It is something constructive that can be done while the application possibilities are studied more carefully.

Naturally, management must be more specific about the kinds of data bases it wants initially, if the data-base approach is to make sense in relation to organizational priorities and values. The choices should correspond to prime application candidates, so that the company avoids setting loose a team of systems analysts and leaving them to their own devices.

The late Sherman C. Blumenthal, in discussing the subject of data bases, appropriately pointed out:

> The desire for information is essentially unlimited, but the necessity for paying cold cash for it will force a scale of relative values to be established. Since the costs of using the system must be compared to the values the user receives, this comparison will be a vital part of the user's thinking during the systems-development process, as he attempts to distinguish his wants from his real needs. The cost-value relationship must be applied by the user to his analysis of requirements concerning the degree of detail, the age of data, the ease of retrieval, and the variety of formats maintained by his information system.[1]

Data-base development efforts could focus on a business function or even on an activity within a function that has limited requirements. Functional data bases could pertain to marketing, personnel, purchasing, distribution, manufacturing, and so forth. Data bases for specific activities may, for example, cover sales, inventory, customer services, cash management, or any of dozens of others.

Companies will inevitably find that both functional and activity data bases could be enhanced if various other kinds of data could be integrated. A good case in point would arise if we chose to develop a distribution data base.

[1] *Management Information Systems: A Framework for Planning and Development* (Englewood Cliffs, N.J.: © Prentice-Hall, Inc. 1969), p. 172.

Here, management could very possibly improve distribution activities through the use of a data base concerned exclusively with distribution. However, we would eventually find that greater benefits could be achieved if production, inventory, and customer services data were included. Likewise, almost any kind of data base will come up short on coordination, if it is too limited as to content. But you have to start somewhere.

It is unrealistic to hope for maximum success when the data-base MIS produces its first services. Nevertheless, the experience evolving from such an undertaking will be invaluable, especially in establishing a foundation to support a more comprehensive MIS in the future.

Fast-moving companies seem to derive more from a data-base approach than more stable organizations, although at first glance it might appear that just the opposite is true. Several factors are concerned. First, the variety and rapidity of new services demanded of an MIS, and therefore its data base, require a highly flexible system. Clearly, the data base's content and "pliability" are the vital elements in this requirement. Second, the rate of MIS obsolescence in a fast-moving company would be unbearable in the absence of a viable data base. Functional extensions to an existing MIS are always needed because of the dynamics of the business. But the more dynamic organization will need more than regular modification and extension of its MIS.

Brainstorming Versus Systems Analysis

Ideally, we might hope to have an optimal methodology for discovering what the MIS should do; that is, what functional problems it should help management solve. The so-called systems approach is a well-known way to take apart and put together the fragments of wisdom and data that result from investigation and review. To start with, analytical work tells us what was, what is, and what should be. From this basis, we then usually proceed to define the functional attributes of the MIS.

Perhaps we also need to try an approach that may allow us to see MIS from a new vantage point. This would call for testing one or more hypotheses once the basic analytical work has been done. Coming up with hypothetical requirements could be done through brainstorming or whatever. What we would be trying to do in this would be to draw much more out of our fundamental analytical work through a point of momentary departure in the hope of discovering something.

This sort of approach is too often overlooked in the everyday world of computer-based systems work. Part of the reason may be the rules we must obey to have the computer do our bidding. The implied constraints and limitations of hardware and software may unduly restrict the imagination in systems analysis. People who have motivation and the ability to deviate from the trodden paths are scarce, but where it is posssible, their talents should be brought to bear.

Where to Begin MIS Analysis: Top or Bottom?

In the analytical work, we are trying to define the relationship between managing and the concept we have of MIS. Seeing how information flows, or should flow, and its effect on the organization and the organization's effect on it, can be a unique revelation. Everyone knows that the informal organization, particularly in big companies, accounts for much of what gets done. MIS developers have to perceive this and shape systems that take it into account.

Many complex relationships exist in the way top management influences other parts of the business. Even more complex are the relationships by which top management is influenced. Going in either direction, we find communications problems—distortion, delay, amplification, attenuation, noise, and losses. But these are not the only problems. W. M. A. Booker, writing in the *Systems & Procedures Journal* of July–August 1965 on "The Total Systems Myth," says the human side is even more important, perhaps the only thing that is really significant. He points out that the systems approach ignores the explanation, prediction, or understanding of why human members of the system act the way they do.

Exponents of the systems approach have sometimes been criticized because their central theme has failed to emphasize or even consider the human element. To this we would like to add that the element of business judgment is usually missing in the systems approach also. Lest the indictment become lopsided, it also needs to be said that the misapplication or faulty use of sound systems approaches is not infrequently to blame. MIS, being a system of systems, requires an amalgamation necessarily harder to accomplish than that of its predecessor systems.

Business executives have to be mindful of the need for business and technical judgment and capable of understanding which is which. Doing this is the only way to insure that business decisions concerning MIS are made when the time comes to make them.

Top-Down Approach

An effective way to obtain relevant perspectives that will serve as guideposts for MIS analysis work is what some people call the top-down approach.

Not everyone agrees that it is best, but there are enough proved and potential advantages to warrant using it for MIS analysis.

Starting with top management, the approach initially seeks to ascertain the broad and long-term perspective. Fitted into this grand overview will be perspectives obtained at each successively lower level in the organization. These are translations of policy, objectives, and problem statements (all business-oriented) into more and more action-oriented procedures. Management's information requirements are extracted at each step along the way.

In effect, the top-down approach first gives us the outline of the MIS mosaic mentioned earlier. In the course of analysis, the individual pieces that should fit within it are collected. If for some reason they do not fit, we clearly have a consistency problem that should be investigated before going much further. Any attempt to superimpose an MIS on an organization where this particular type of problem exists is inviting defeat.

The top-down approach offers more of an opportunity than the bottom-up approach to confront these problems before they make a working system ineffectual. Often, in using the bottom-up approach pieces are collected and pasted together with no relevance to a grand overview. This approach has been by far the predominant one for systems developed in the past. Such systems, when they did get off the ground, rarely got much above the ground floor insofar as their progress concerned benefits to management.

Another significant advantage and another reason for seeing top management first is that many business priorities have been narrowed down to vital matters by the time they reach the organization's upper echelon. The separation of the important from the less important and from the unimportant having already been made, MIS developers can focus their energies with much greater resolution. Because there is so much that could be done, it is especially important to get on the right track as soon as possible. Otherwise, people go off in a dozen different directions, in some cases working at cross purposes and toward objectives invented to cover whatever they happen to be doing at the time.

Bottom-Up Approach

One of the strongest arguments in support of a bottom-up approach is that a great deal of knowledge can be acquired in advance of conducting discussions with upper management. Armed with a knowledge of present conditions and possible future requirements, top management can conceivably be sold on the need others have for an MIS and can also be brought up to date on some of the current problems in business operations.

On the other hand, it is entirely possible that upper management has in mind a vastly different set of needs and requirements; perhaps it even wants to bring about a fundamental change in the business and sees MIS as a key vehicle for doing so.

Another weakness of initially working at the ground level is that the fragments of information gathered may not fit into a mosaic of any kind and as a result may produce misunderstandings and confusion. The absence of a central or unifying theme, with at least some guideposts along the way, may well get a negative reaction from top managers when MIS discussion finally gets to them.

Horizontal Synthesis During Vertical Analysis

The results of systems analysis must make sense to MIS designers. This puts the findings in the realm of formal specifications, where relevant factors are presented in the context of what the system itself is likely to be. Where, for example, management is concerned with inventory control, it becomes a major component of the MIS within which such requirements as marketing, purchasing, and manufacturing are covered. This is distinctly different from looking at the inventory problems within these activities as separate problems. So where the systems analysis may take place vertically, within a function such as marketing, the results from all such studies need to be represented horizontally. Information requirements can then be integrated by a post-analysis that defines how the different functions should work together for maximum effectiveness.

Because the foregoing orientation must prevail in the design stage, there is good reason to believe that significant advantages and better results will be realized if information systems requirements are analyzed with an eye toward synthesis in a new system. A sort of motto for all this might be: "Think design during analysis."

One way to visualize overall systems requirements is through an information flow chart or data flow diagram such as is shown in Figure 3-1. Note that seven major groups of activity in the manufacturing organization are identified: (1) top-level decision making and sales analysis; (2) research, product design, and engineering; (3) inventory control and production scheduling; (4) manufacturing facilities and personnel; (5) purchasing; (6) finance; and (7) sales and distribution. The integrated relationships among these activities becomes more apparent when viewed in terms of data flow. The concept expressed in doing this acknowledges the next level of detail, which concerns systems design.

But how do we lay claim to an objective analysis of business problems if we are thinking about solutions before all the facts are in? The answer is that

FIGURE 3-1
Data Flow in a Manufacturing Organization

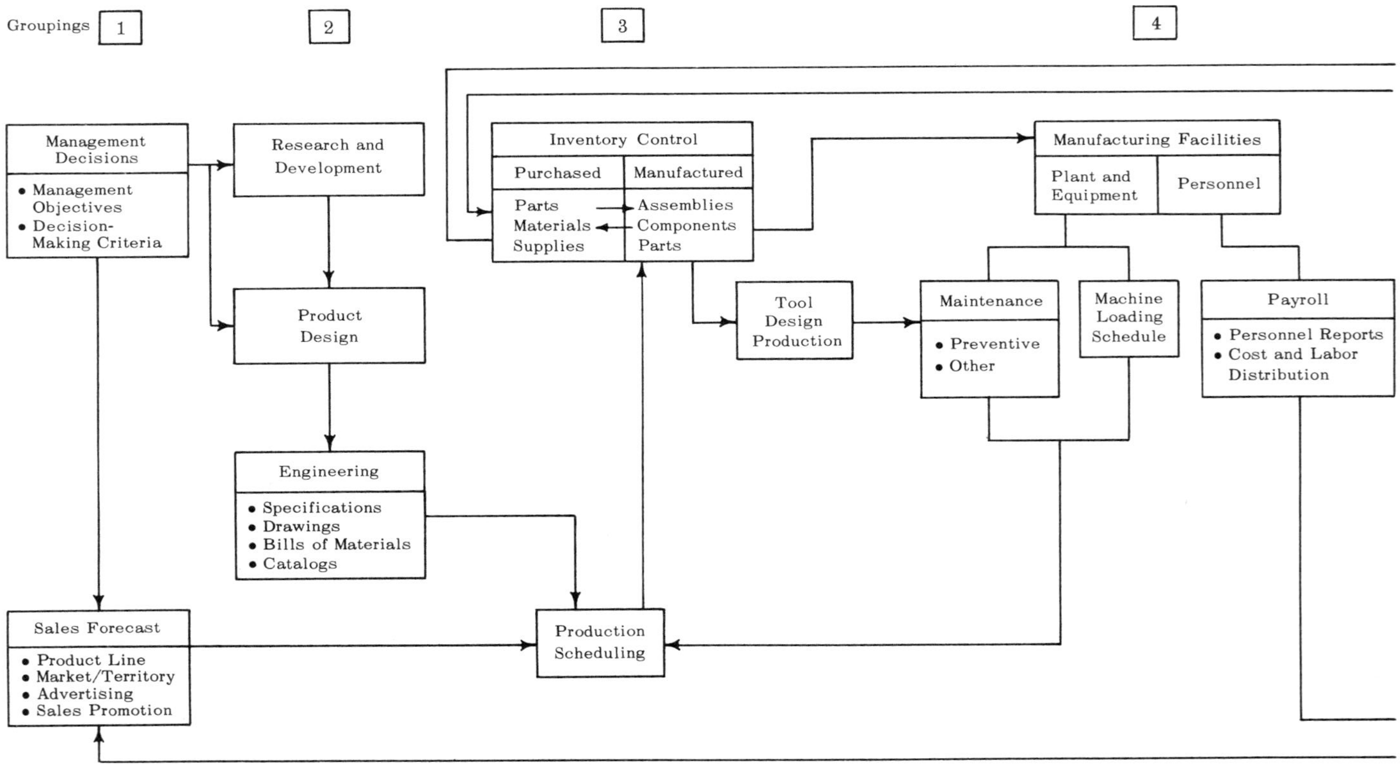

FIGURE 3-1
Data Flow in a Manufacturing Organization (continued)

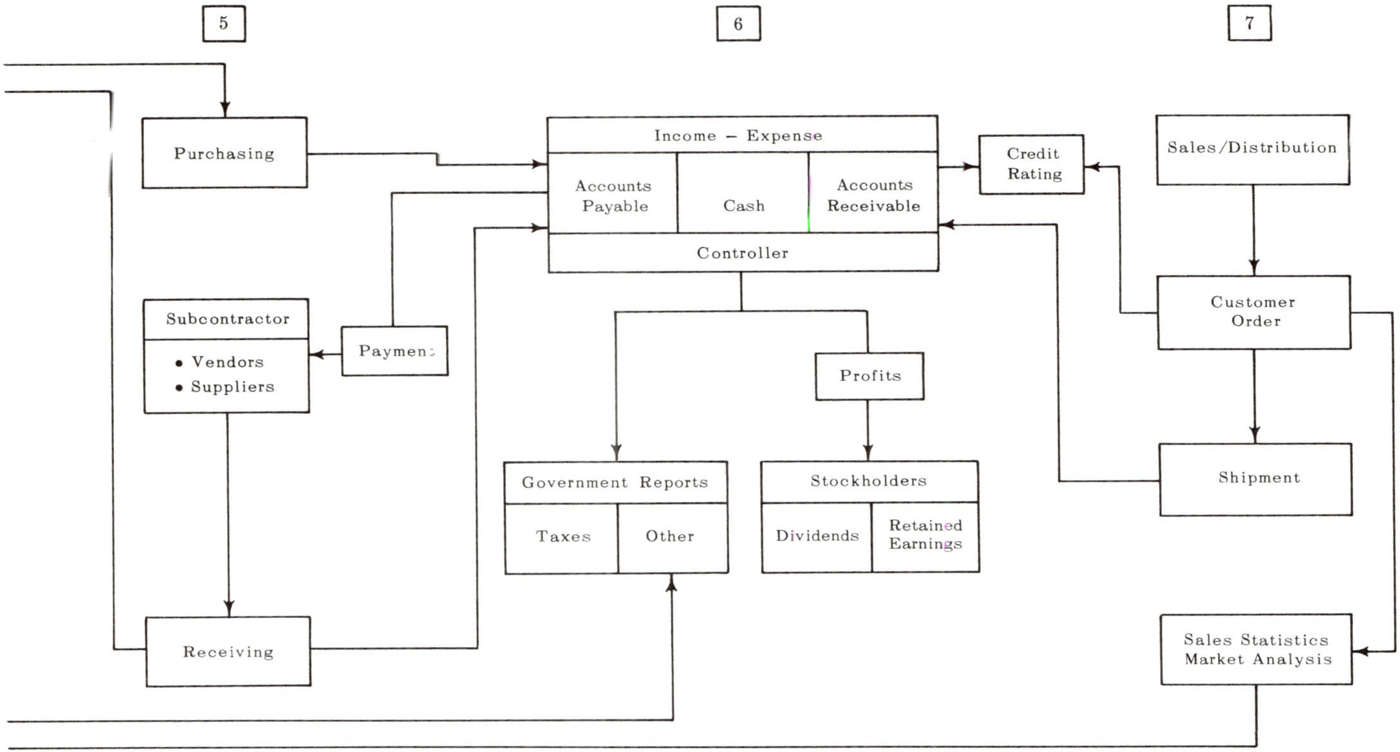

Reprinted courtesy of IBM Corporation.

we do not, that we intend to be prejudiced and subjective. Indeed, it is because we have preconceptions that we can take a businesslike approach. There is no need to apologize for the fact that exhasutive long-term research has not gone into decisions shaping the destiny of MIS. MIS ground rules are, for the most part, the same as those used for other business judgments. In short, management should recognize that there is no particular mystique with an MIS that makes it easier to evaluate than other business projects.

Technological Influences

Confronted with a long list of numbers that you need to sum, and having before you pencil and paper and an adding machine, the choice between the two problem-solving means is not difficult to make. Indeed, the better tool suggests further applications. Thus it is what we call a technological influence, an influence seen quite frequently with computers and related hardware. Many of us have seen jobs, better and more efficiently carried out manually, put on a computer simply because there happens to be idle capacity. Additionally, the existence of technological influences sometimes causes people to go too far or attempt too much in a system. It is therefore important for management to exercise prudent controls to insure the justification of system applications.

Fallacies of the "Black Box" Approach

The fields of communication and information have long emphasized thinking about media first and needs or applications second. Relative to computers, management reporting unconsciously brings out thinking related to paper 11″ × 14″ with 132 print positions across (a standard computer form and print-line width). Until about the middle of the last decade, this approach was not vigorously challenged. Since that time, it has been attacked with growing intensity; in fact, advocates of the "need" approach have gone overboard at times. They say media should be ignored until after the objectives (message or information requirements) have been specified.

While this method has many desirable characteristics, it is a bit too idealistic for the situation we face in the real world. People have trouble working around a nameless, faceless, omnipotent "black box" of unknown dimensions and attributes. These people are managers and executives, who will be trying to define what they want in the way of information from a practical frame of reference.

Developers and implementers think mostly in terms of what is possible—

which is very much dependent on what exists. Tools like computers, graphic displays, audio-response devices, and high-capacity data storage, are possible today, and strongly influence our thinking, whether we like it or not. It is fallacious to assume that we can lock out all thinking about them and ask management to reason in the dark.

A second fallacy is that better systems will be produced if we use the black-box approach. We do not think so, and here is why: People, as a rule, will start to work with what they know about to solve a problem. Innovation begins with that knowledge and goes upward. The higher the level of knowledge at the jumping-off point, the better the answer will be. Hence, it is much better to start with more knowledge and less black box. There is no compelling reason why we should arbitrarily decide to remain ignorant of methodology while examining the problem.

An alternative that is much more to the point is to keep no secrets. Tell all about what is available, and let management's reasoning grow from that higher level of understanding.

Numerous systems analysts say that truly marvelous results have been achieved by discussing with users the concrete rather than the abstract. Suggestions are bounced back and forth between user and analyst as they talk about things they both can see, touch, and hear. One analyst who switched from the black-box approach said his MIS work had been frustrated because two users he worked with would almost always work up information needs based on their experience, invariably designing paper forms. Aside from that, these forms had a maximum width of 88 characters, of which 43 on the left had alphabetic and numeric information, and 45 on the right had numeric only. It was obvious that somewhere these men had been exposed to output from an IBM 402 or 403 accounting machine (sometimes called a tabulator). This equipment goes back more than 20 years, although it is still in use. It reads cards and prints at speeds between 50 and 150 per minute and performs relatively simple logical operations and arithmetic.

System Component Analysis

Valuable as systems analysis is, it is more meaningful when the business problems it addresses can be viewed in the context of those around it. Moreover, it is imperative that MIS requirements, once defined, be understood in terms of their components or subsystem requirements. Structurally, the development of an MIS usually comes in implementable, stand-alone modules. For example, consider an objective such as "all customers placing orders via telephone or teletype will receive immediate verbal confirmation or nonconfirmation and know whether delivery requirements can be met or are otherwise satisfactory." This objective is readily satisfied if there is only one order taker who has the total available inventory in plain view, as when you call your neighborhood hardware store.

But how about a company that has 75 order-taking locations all over the country, 250 order takers, 1,000 salable products, and 10 warehouse locations stocking some or all of the products? Products are in transit from manufacturing locations to the warehouses and for certain size orders are shipped directly to customer locations. There may also be products in transit being transferred from warehouse to warehouse. Exchange agreements may exist, permitting competitors to draw on your inventory in time of need and you to draw on theirs. There may also be conversion agreements where a competitor or other company draws on your inventory for particular products it needs, making available to you different products. Exchange and conversion agreements usually cover commodity products and provide both parties with savings in product movement, warehousing, and other distribution-related expense.

Situations similar to that just described could occur in a $75 million, $100 million, or $200 million company as well as a $2 billion, $3 billion, or $4 billion company. Problems occurring in each company are not necessarily proportionate.

Perhaps you know personally or can see how a centralized information system can help solve such problems. But, in getting back to our original point about specifying the implementable modules, you may also sense or know that solving the problems cannot (or should not) be tried all at once.

The total information systems requirements must be analyzed in light of the objective, which here is to improve customer service. Having done this and having determined what features give you the most for the money, it should be possible to rank specific features as outlined in the previous chapter.

In our example, there are a number of growth steps that may be considered for inclusion in the MIS:

- In-stock inventory only.
- Anticipated arrivals from plant and other warehouses.
- Anticipated additions and withdrawals based on exchange and conversion agreement histories and forecasts.
- Level of service desired; for example, nine out of ten orders for product A can be filled immediately.
- Capital investment decisions concerning old and new warehouses, transportation facilities, and plants.
- Distribution optimization.
- Pricing.
- Competitive analysis.

- Controls to determine whether objective is being met.
- Impact of labor strikes—including those of suppliers.

Tackling the whole list of desirable capabilities all at once is bound to be fraught with much frustration and waste. So you have to decide the order in which each should be developed and implemented.

In fact, the whole matter of analyzing component parts of MIS needs to be examined in terms of system functions, sophistication, and the management problems each proposes to help solve.

Six Facets of Data Transformation

Information, as contrasted with raw data, is in a form suitable for decision making and, more particularly, management decision making. The conversion of data to information, as a computer-automated process, is readily accomplished. Still, to design the system that is intended to provide information, we face the very difficult process of deciding what business rules and criteria are to govern what is to be programmed. Our intended uses for the information generated will offer many clues as to what logic needs to be programmed, but will not often provide us with a complete set of logic. It is at this point that management's intimate knowledge comes into play. This knowledge, along with skill, imagination, and creativity on the part of systems developers, is the source from which the logic will stem.

Let us look at the steps in the conversion of raw data to information and relate each to information concerned with delinquent accounts receivable in a business. With each step, we will show some of the questions that, when answered, will give us the business rules or criteria needed to program the process.

Extracting or selecting. Should we use 30-, 60-, 90-, 120-, and over 120-day-old balances or balances of just 60 days and up? Should we use only those above a certain dollar amount in each category? What other criteria should we use?

Ordering and organizing. Alphabetical sequence by company name? Customer number sequence? Geographic area? Salesman? Alphabetic customer name within salesman number? Customer number within geographic area? Separate by day-old categories? Should we relate other information?

Calculating and summarizing. Compute interest and carrying charges? Totals in each category for each customer? Totals by salesman? Totals for each sales-office manager?

Analyzing and comparing. Should dunning notices be sent with statements for all delinquents? Should notices increase in severity for each category? At what dollar amount and category combination should company representative make a personal visit? What are the write-off-as-bad-debt rules? How should the dollar volume of business from a customer affect delinquency processing? What historical comparisons should be made?

Evaluating. What percentage of delinquents in each category have exceeded a preestablished credit limit? Are some sales offices or salesmen significantly higher than others in proportion of delinquent volume to their total? How do this month's ratios of delinquent to sales compare with last month, year to date, last year this month's, last year? Is there a meaningful correlation between industrial code (or customer occupation) and proportion of delinquents to total volume in its group?

Storing and issuing. What details should be kept about delinquents? How long should details be maintained? Who gets what information and when? What information will be made available for credit reference calls? What reporting media and formats should be used?

Information systems, in general, do not make management decisions requiring judgment but rather carry out routine chores for which a rigid set of logic has been specified. On the other hand, such systems do provide the basis for management decisions. In our brief example, various decision-making situations can be imagined as they pertain to the company's credit policy, sales management, administration and control of accounts receivable, and so forth.

Contributions of Operations Research

There was a time when industrial operations research had two distinct and different factions. One group was composed of mathematical types who were generally regarded as the problem solvers. The other side had mainly business philosophers who appeared to have the mission of thinking about how business operations could be improved without specific orientation to any select set of methods. In fact, it was not unusual to find that this latter faction knew very little about the problem-solving techniques we have come to associate with operations research in more recent times.

One mathematician specializing in operations research tells of having applied for a high-level position at a major company about ten years ago. To his surprise, he found that the OR people interviewing him were "philosophers," with at best a superficial understanding of the mathematical techniques mentioned. He learned that he was to be the first person in the group who understood these techniques; in fact, he was told that no one in the group was able to evaluate his knowledge.

Today, it is probably safe to say that OR is generally thought of as mathematical rather than philosophical, although there are cases where it is strictly a systems and procedures activity. Not too long ago a man with the job title manager of operations research admitted he had not heard of linear programming.

It may be unfortunate that the term "research" has stuck over the years, for this may leave the uninitiated with peculiar notions regarding practical applications. Perhaps the substitute terms that are being used more and more represent attempts to give OR a more suitable name. Two such terms are "operational analysis" and "management science."

For several reasons, management science should be represented and given serious consideration very early in the MIS project. First, its practical application springs from computerization and is a logical part of the decision-making process. Second, it often depends on MIS data to make it work. And third, it can feed back answers to MIS that have been analyzed, evaluated, or optimized. If it is feasible, OR methods should be integrated into the mainstream of MIS operation so that routine benefits can be realized.

Before going further, let us discuss briefly the relationship between OR and the computer. Mathematically, the theory of OR as represented by formulas and algorithms (the logical and arithmetic process rules by which the answer is obtained) exists completely apart from the computer. Linear programming, for example, is over 20 years old, and fairly simple problems have been solved without the help of the computer for a long time. The same is true of other techniques, such as statistics and analysis of variance.

For their practical application, most of the techniques depend on the use of computers. Without them, we would be limited to solving small problems because an impossible amount of calculation and logic is required for solving larger ones.

OR, on the other hand, is of the greatest significance in dealing with problems having a complex array of interacting variables, problems requiring a great deal of computation, and situations requiring complex mathematical manipulation of great masses of data. Business problems tend to be of this variety—that is, complex variable relationships or calculations using a lot of data. Indeed, such problems gave rise to OR methods because they could not otherwise be solved.

Computer simulation is an important technique that may be an integral part of an MIS. More often, though, it depends on the data bases found within advanced information systems. In its introductory material on its *General Purpose Systems Simulator,* IBM describes computer simulation problems as follows:

> Because of the complex nature of modern business systems, data processing aids are increasingly required to assist the intuition and judgment of

management in the evaluation of new methods, concepts, or designs. The practice of experimenting directly on a business and implementing a system before it is fully understood inevitably causes disruptions of normal operations, hasty last-minute corrections, and often personnel or customer resentment. To avoid costly mistakes, the consequences of change must be anticipated before actually implementing a program, and all alternatives should be thoroughly explored.

Computer simulation is a technique that provides an effective means of testing and evaluating a proposed system under various conditions in a laboratory environment. The system's behavior is modeled by a computer program, which reacts to various operating conditions in a manner quantitatively similar to the system itself. Several hours or weeks, or sometimes even years, of simulated activity can be examined on a computer in a matter of minutes. Results help to gain insights, test hypotheses, demonstrate or verify new ideas, establish feasibility, compare alternatives, design systems, or train personnel.

It is appropriate to any discussion on simulation to add a few words of both caution and encouragement. Computer simulation, like any simulation, is not a precise analog of an actual system. What is studied is the behavior of a representation of an actual system. Therefore, careful judgment must still be exercised by the user, both in setting up a good model and in interpreting the results from the simulation.

On the other hand, computer simulation frequently permits measurements which would be impossible to obtain in any other way, and allows the study of environmental situations of a scope far beyond the practicability of experimenting with an actual system. Such abilities as these immeasurably enhance the value of computer simulation in its role as an engineering and management-science tool.[2]

Simulation can be used to study and test many different kinds of situations, including the future MIS operations. This is as valid a problem as production-operations simulation or the simple warehouse system illustrated in Figure 3-2. In the warehouse study, management may be trying to determine the best design of a new facility or improve operations in an existing one.

Sales forecasting, inventory control, and other OR problem areas are enumerated in Figure 3-3. According to many OR experts, past computer capabilities limited what could be done. They especially cite memory limitations and computer speed. An OR analyst in a large petroleum company recently said that as a result of improvements in both areas he can now solve

[2] *General Purpose Simulation System/360: Application Description* (White Plains, N.Y.: © IBM Corporation, 1967), Manual E20–0186, p. 1.

a problem using a new large-scale computer in 4 hours at a cost of $1,600 whereas in the past it would have taken about 24 hours of straight running at a cost of $8,400. This was impractical since the probability of nothing going wrong in 24 hours was too low. In addition, the analyst said, running tests at almost $10,000 a throw was too much of a risk to ask anyone to pay for.

The operations research analyst and computer systems analyst are found working together more and more. In many companies, they report to the same executive. In some companies, the two functions are fully integrated, OR people being considered very much a part of systems development.

One of the biggest problems OR people have always faced is that managers and management-science experts often do not understand one another. Management science appears quite occult, and some of its practitioners seem to delight in promoting its mystique. Managers and executives, by the same token, have often seemed to be unwilling to exert the extra effort needed to comprehend the not-too-difficult but sometimes involved mathematics of OR. In short, the communications gap has to be narrowed substantially before much headway can be made. Someone once said, "Managers would rather leave the problem unsolved or use methods they know than have solutions developed by methods they do not understand."

FIGURE 3-2
General Flow Chart for Simulating a Simple Warehouse System

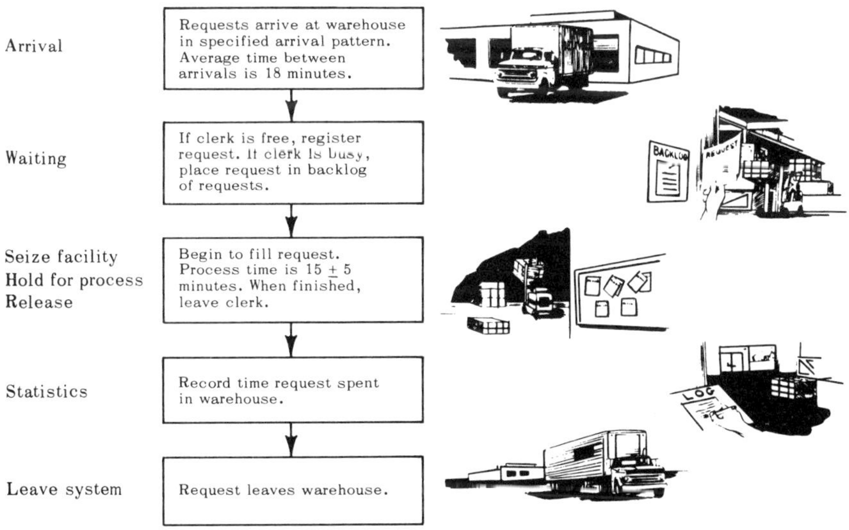

Reprinted courtesy of IBM Corporation.

FIGURE 3-3
Operations Research Application Areas

Area	Existing decision rules	Applied operations research rules	Potential savings and remarks
Requirements forecasting	Requirements may be generally determined by sales forecasting or – in many companies – the decisions of order clerks who must get manufacturing under way in order to keep the company in business.	Use statistical running averages or exponential smoothing modified by sales analysis to make "best" projection.	The "optimum" method will almost always show an improvement. Estimate the amount of savings manufacturing could have made with better information, including reduced obsolescence.
Order quantities	Current order quantities may be periodic requirements, or some approximation of economic order quantities, or judgment.	Analyze setup and order costs, develop sound EOQs or a statistical sample of parts.	Reduction in inventory and setup and order cost will range from 5 to 25% depending on existing rules.
Manufacturing reorder points and safety stock	Existing reorder points may have been reached by judgment or crude averages of usage and lead time, or they may be reasonably sound.	Establish in a sample of items the real lead time, average usage, and the variation in usage and lead time. Compute sound reorder points.	Safety inventory varies from 10 to 60% of the total inventory in a variety of companies; thus this factor will vary widely in importance.
Linear programming	Current production and distribution assignments may be built on past practices or on some nonoptimum rules.	Assign production and distribution by linear-programming techniques for a trial period.	This technique will be of value in multiplant and warehouse operations.
Price breaks of purchase discounts	Additional price breaks may have to be investigated where they are not on published basis. Letter to sample of vendors as to price changes may be necessary if order quantity is halved or doubled.	Make a random sample, compile inventory and cost reduction comparing optimum discount to current.	Where the holding of inventory has not been properly considered or special quantity inquiries not made, this area can be of considerable importance.
Distribution safety stocks	The number of distribution points may be related to conditions that no longer exist and the safety stocks may be excessive.	Determine the real variation in demand and replenishment, and establish statistical reorder points. Complete excess inventory implications of variation in the number of warehouses.	Frequently, in a multiwarehouse operation, the savings are large. In a single warehouse situation, the safety stock decision can usually be improved.
Make-or-buy decisions	Make-or-buy decisions may be based on erroneous data or on incorrect assumptions.	Recompute a sample of make-or-buy decisions, charging purchasing and portions of industrial engineering, product engineering, inspection, etc., and adjusting to equivalent lot size.	Sample should be extended only to amount of business where alternate exists.
Work-in-process inventory	The existing work-in-process inventory between work centers may reflect inadequate control techniques of the past.	Simulate operations for the proper amount of work in process.	The potential saving is proportioned to the number of work centers involved.
Line balancing	Assembly lines may have excess inventory, idle time, and overtime costs because of poor balances of workloads.	Apply line-balancing techniques, either manually or by a computer simulation program.	The potential savings may be important in changing assembly-line situations.
Simulation	In seasonal, cyclical, and style industries, there are current costs related to planning of overtime, inventory, hiring, and firing.	Make Monte Carlo or compute simulation program in sample area.	The greatest impact of simulation comes in testing reactions to potential situations so that better decisions can be made.
Optimization in marketing	Current employment of salesmen and expenditures in advertising may have grown from past practices.	Make a study using formulas that balance marginal income with out-of-pocket costs.	These factors are more important when the coverage of sales and advertising has a significant effect on volume.
PERT and PERT/cost	Current operations may reflect more conventional planning and follow-up procedures.	Use a PERT or CPM program on a sample project.	Of value in defense, R&D, and contracting industries.

Source: Arnold O. Putnam et al., *Unified Operations Management*, McGraw-Hill Book Company, 1963.

To grasp many of the OR techniques well enough to have confidence in them, the executive listener must at least know basic algebra. Many executives have taken it upon themselves to renew their acquaintance with mathematics and to go on from there to read introductory books on OR. Some of the larger companies and governmental agencies hold courses, in hours and after hours, on OR. Consultants can do the same thing for smaller companies. Often the subject matter is taken up as part of an overall computer-education program.

What Price Information?

As a consequence of the often haphazard evaluations of computer applications, users have not had a genuine opportunity to weigh the value of information against its price. No one, of course, is suggesting that this can always be done "scientifically," but there is a middle ground somewhere between the extremes of completely ignoring justification and undertaking a quasi-scientific study. Let us call this the *empirical evaluation.*

To perform such an evaluation, two factors are placed before a potential user: the product (the information he says he needs) and its price. Products of the system are seen as rather distinct types or classes of information services and problem-solving capabilities. It is helpful to think of these as modules that can be, but need not be, incorporated into the MIS.

The empirical approach places the decision-making responsibility squarely on the shoulders of the user. He is presented with the product and its price and must determine for himself whether he wants to buy it. Naturally, if he proposes a modified or different product, this too is priced.

Some systems now in operation tell the user beforehand approximately how much a given run or particular kind of analysis will cost. One system of this sort, which uses a data-communication terminal, gives the user aggregate-to-date costs and tells his estimated job cost at the time he makes a request of the system, at which point he is given the chance to decide whether he wants to proceed. For certain kinds and lengthy jobs he may have the option to have them run off-line in regular batch processing. The cost for this processing is also given in advance.

Master Plan for Systems Integration

Drawing up plans is a fundamental step in the development of any system, but there are some important distinctions between the ways in which we draw up MIS plans and those pertaining to other computer applications. The latter has been widely discussed in the literature. However, it would be useful to examine the specific features of an MIS master plan and try to draw some comparisons with plans prepared for other systems. After this has been done, we will attempt to show pitfalls to beware of.

Comparative Characteristics of MIS Plans

Three characteristics that can be used for comparative purposes are depth, density, and dynamics.

Regarding depth, we find that MIS plans tend to have a tapered format. Very simply, this means that more must be known about subsystems to be developed earlier than about those to be undertaken later. As we have tried to indicate elsewhere, the MIS development process for most companies is a series of discrete steps, each representing the implementation of one or more subsystems. Contrasted with MIS plans, past application systems nearly always had a complete set of plans of uniform depth in detail. In many instances, this meant that a great deal of what had to be done was clearly understood.

Density of content in a given area of former plans had a strong tendency to be uniform, with the level of detailed descriptions about various parts of the system covered more or less equally. For example, if system controls and audit trails were being discussed, everything appropriate about all of them was examined. MIS plans, on the other hand, have gaps in them, where features are planned for future implementation. Under the same heading, some subjects are covered in detail and others are simply mentioned.

Dynamics refers to two properties of MIS as contrasted with former application systems. First, many of the former systems were implemented in a much shorter time than an MIS requires, often in less than a year and frequently in less than six months. Thus the number of changes that had to be accommodated during development was relatively small compared to that for MIS projects.

Second, the application systems of the past were implemented chiefly to automate routine clerical functions. Accordingly, they were not dynamic, especially over intervals of a year or less. Of course, it is true that things like payroll systems do change, but competent systems designers allowed for most changes to be effected easily—changes like new tax rates and new kinds of deductions. MIS, by comparison, has significantly less in the way of routinized processing, or what might be called automated clerical functions. The management part of MIS is subject to change at short intervals and the nature of such changes can be both distressing and costly. Certainly, if we are hoping to have a system to help management manage, it must have many responsive attributes, both in timeliness and functional diversity. In short, the dynamic nature of an MIS demands that a modified approach be taken in planning it.

Avoiding Pitfalls

Let us now look at some of the pitfalls in preparing an MIS master plan and refer to the comparisons that have just been drawn.

To begin with, it was stated that MIS plans taper as the development and implementation of various subsystems extend farther in time. This is to be expected and accepted. However, we can encounter certain dangers in going to either extreme—that is, too much detail or too little on long-range developments. Excessive detailing of far-off work is wasteful because it is usually impossible to know so much about the distant future as to make its detailed description worthwhile.

By the same token, there are those who would have us rush headlong into the immediate development work, never taking time to evaluate or plan for future developments. This usually occurs more frequently than the opposite extreme in most systems work. People sometimes seem to be overreacting to what was bad practice in developing former systems; that is, the quick and dirty systems job. The overreacting we have seen shifts these people to the other end of the spectrum, where they spend all their time planning, but they never develop anything.

Striking a balance between the extremes is not easy, for you must be able to concentrate your attention on the right areas and be on the lookout for the problems that impinge heavily on the more distant developmental efforts. Two vital problem areas in this realm that will be taken up in more detail later are the MIS data bank (or data bases) and subsystem interfaces. Anticipating what will be needed in these two areas is perhaps the most important long-range planning activity in modern MIS development work.

We said that density was another important distinguishing factor in MIS planning. Here, you should be careful that most of the holes are plugged with plausible explanations and specific recommendations. For example, one complete set of coding schemes for an MIS data base included product coding, transportation-mode coding, and geographical-area coding rules, in addition to many others. One important code and its rules were glossed over in the planning: the customer code. As it turned out, this became a very annoying and costly bottleneck downstream in the development work. Apparently the scheme for customer coding was thought to be trivial, if it was thought about at all. And there were many considerations, including conversions from existing systems, changing sales office records, and problems with customers resulting from a number change.

MIS plans, as was indicated, will have holes and gaps. The important considerations, however, center on the question of whether the subsystem can be made operational without working out all the details. Acceptable holes could include data not needed in the subsystem of immediate concern, interfaces to subsystems that have not been fully specified, and possible one-time report requirements that have only general specifications. Other than these and similar areas, a plan for a subsystem soon to be developed must be complete. It is foolhardy to believe that you can make up a lot of these things as they are needed; carelessly thought-out methods typically turn out to be major shortcomings in the system.

Change is the toughest problem area MIS designers face. It is hard to plan for the distant future and harder to translate ideas into systems to tie in with the plans. There seem to be two pitfalls in this area. One is the situation where systems people themselves plan for many possible variations and uses of the system without really knowing whether company management sees the need for them. Consequently, a great deal of the built-in growth potential is wasted because the MIS will never be used in the ways invented by the systems designers. Such cases are almost inevitable, if designers, operating managers, and upper management do not put their heads together on casting the future roles of the MIS.

The other situation, which again relates to a lack of genuine management involvement, is where the system is built to meet today's problems only. As we would expect, obsolescence sets in before the system is off the drawing board. Accompanying this, a great amount of effort is put into changing and expanding the system before and after it goes into operation. However, despite the best forward-looking programs, no one can hope to be even close to perfect in assessing exactly what future functions will be demanded of the system. We now know that some of these functions have to evolve as more is discovered more about how things need to be done, as we observe business changes, and as we learn what management is about in a quantitative and logical sense. This gray area is probably more complex than many of us think.

Modular–Planned Systems

The acid test of an MIS is a successful operational system for the money, effort, and time that have been spent. If we have pursued the MIS program in a businesslike way, chances are that some basis for measuring the system's performance had been specified at the outset. A list of qualitative advantages that are expected is perhaps minimum. Quantifiable measurements are much better and more convincing and should be used wherever possible. Should the rating not indicate that what we have accomplished is a glowing success, we can take stock and find a better way.

Modular systems can be the key to success. First, we can run a test and benefit from what it tells us before we have gone too far. Second, it often proves something about our ability to take the next step. We need to be capable of responding considerably in advance of a crisis, and therefore must have measurements.

Building an MIS on a modular basis also gives us better management control of the project, since smaller entities are involved. At the same time, we can better identify what parts of the system need to be modified or updated to reflect the environmental dynamics of business problems. Each module coming into the development stage from the concept stage defined in the master plan can be tailored to new needs that have emerged and also to more current ways and means of satisfying both the original and newer problems.

Flexibility, adaptability, changeability, and expandability are some of the words used to describe the goals of a modular approach. More often than not we buy these things, although there are times when we can get some of them free. We may have a choice between developing an individual customer-numbering scheme or using the customer's social security number. Here we could reason that the latter has already been established, is usually readily accessible, and can serve as a uniform means of identification internally and externally. Suppose we feel almost certain that someday banks will be handling part of our accounts-receivable activity, directly charging customers' accounts for purchases and crediting the account of our business. It is a safe bet that most banks will use the social security number in the not-too-distant future; and, in line with this, it would be even more advantageous for us to use it.

On the other hand, many features in the modular approach are neither free nor readily accomplished. Data names and definitions loom large as a problem in many companies. This is one of the many *standards problems* that must be effectively confronted in order to modularize. Conventions concerning the use of programming languages are another, audit and control features another, and error recovery still another. And many others exist, especially in communications-based MIS, where very exacting standards are needed.

When we say modular systems, we mean that subsystems of the MIS, developed at different times or by different groups of people, can be readily fastened to one another as the need to do so arises. Since the modular systems approach is being addressed under the general heading of master-plan development, it should be reemphasized that our objective is to have a pay-as-you-go MIS program. This means that integration is taking place in phases or steps that justify the incremental cost associated with installing the subsystem to be added.

Decision Tables for Expressing Business Rules

One of the most difficult things facing those responsible for developing a computer-based MIS is clarifying the business rules that, when programmed into the system, will guide its functioning. Such rules need to be fully defined and documented before they can be programmed. The decision-table concept facilitates both definition and documentation in some important ways. Perhaps the most vital point to remember with regard to decision tables is that system logic must be representable in decision-table form. If this cannot be done, the system cannot be created.

Decision tables can be used to bring together and represent business rules that are to be followed when various sets of conditions arise in the operating environment. A streamlined means of showing alternative actions to be taken under various combinations of conditions, decision tables are one of the most effective methods for showing business logic. They are easily used by persons who have little understanding of computers but who must, nevertheless, communicate their needs so that they can be implemented in a computer-based system. Additionally, decision tables have important applications as a purely technical tool for systems analysts and programmers.

The discussion and illustrations on decision tables that follow are excerpts from an IBM publication[3] and are used here with IBM's permission.

> To begin to see the structure of a decision table consisting of conditions separated from actions, consider an aspect of an airline reservation system.
>
> Expressed in decision-table format, the problem might appear as stated in Figure 3-4, where each column to the right of the vertical double line is regarded as a rule. A single rule at a time is examined, reading from top to bottom. Y and N mean yes and no, and X indicates execute. Actions to be taken for each rule are expressed in rows beneath the horizontal double line. To read this table, examine a single rule at a time in conjunction with the statements to the left. No matter how many alternative rules exist, only one rule can be satisfied in a single pass through the decision table.
>
> The first decision rule (the column numbered 1) can then be paraphrased: *If* the request is for a first-class reservation *and if* a first-class seat is available, *then* issue a first-class ticket. The emphasized words are implied by the table layout.

[3] *Decision Tables: A Systems Analysis and Documentation Technique* (White Plains, N.Y.: © IBM Corporation).

The second rule says that *if* a first-class ticket is requested *and* there are no first-class seats available, *then* place the passenger's name on a wait list.

The third and fourth rules apply to tourist class. Note that where conditions are not to be considered, no entry is made in the rules column. The table considers each condition in terms of "yes," "no," or "don't care."

The information in the above table is shown in an exploded view in Figure 3-5 to indicate the terms that are used to describe the various parts of a table.

The horizontal and vertical double lines serve as demarcation: conditions are shown above the horizontal double line, actions below; the portion to the left of the vertical double line is called the "stub"; and entries are to the right. Each vertical combination of conditions and actions is called a decision rule.

There are three types of tables: limited entry, extended entry, and mixed entry. This table serves to illustrate the format of a mixed-entry table—that is, it combines limited and extended entries. In limited-entry form, the entire condition or action is written in the stub, and the entry is limited to showing, for each case, whether the particular condition is true, false, or not pertinent (Y, N, or blank), and whether a particular action should be performed (X or blank). [In many applications, the *sequence* in which multiple actions are performed is important. Since a particular sequence may not follow the order of the action stub entries, some systems analysts simply indicate execution sequence by replacing the X's with sequence numbers—that is, 1, 2, 3, . . . , n.] In the table shown here, the second and third condition rows and the second action row are expressed in limited-entry form.

In contrast, an extended entry expresses a part of the condition or action in the entry side of the table, as in the first condition row and the first action

FIGURE 3-4
Airlines Reservations Decision Table Example

Rule No. →	1	2	3	4
REQUEST IS FOR	1st CLASS	1st CLASS	TOURIST	TOURIST
1ST CLASS AVAILABLE	Y	N		
TOURIST AVAILABLE			Y	N
ISSUE	1st CLASS		TOURIST	
PLACE ON WAIT LIST		X		X

row of the table shown. Note that this table, being partly limited entry and partly extended entry, is a mixed-entry table. Expressed entirely in limited-entry form, the table would appear as shown in Figure 3-6.

In summary, a decision table defines all conditions (the prerequisites for an action) and separates them from all actions. Further, it relates given conditions to the appropriate actions, with a column of entries which form a rule. Alternative conditions that result in other actions constitute other rules, which are written side by side. Tables may be limited, extended, or mixed-entry form.

Aside from the terms used to describe tables according to the type of entries made, there are two other table types classified by the control they have on the sequence of execution or flow from table to table. Just as actions within a table are executed in the order in which they are stated, there must be similar control over the order in which tables are executed.

Within a set of tables, it may be desired for one table to permanently pass control to another table. This is accomplished by using appropriate terminol-

FIGURE 3-5
Exploded View of Figure 3-4

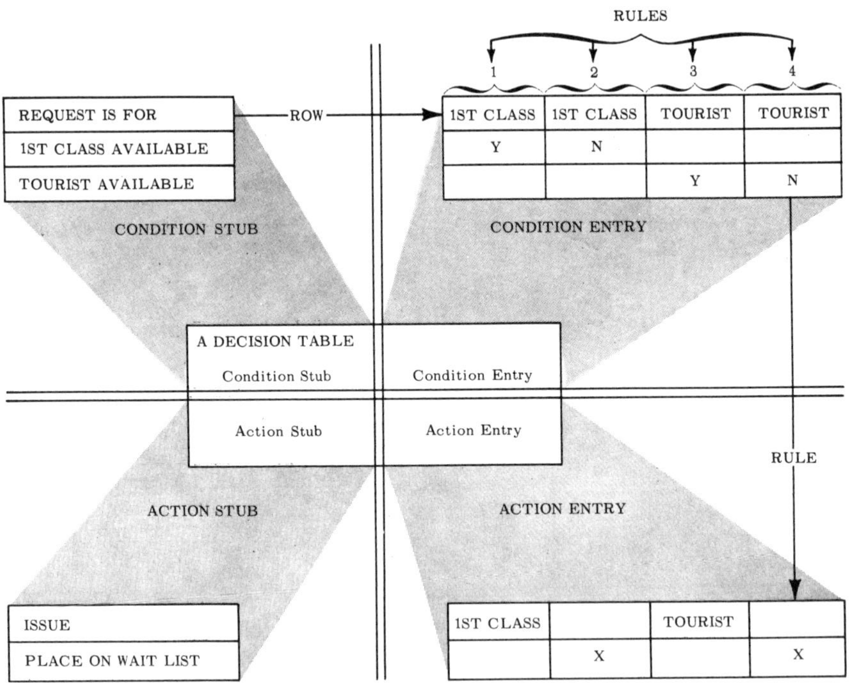

ogy such as "Go To." On the other hand, it is often desirable within one table to execute another table and then return to the original table so that remaining actions can be executed. A notation such as "Do" can be used to accomplish this. For example, in a table it may be desirable to call other tables to perform certain functions, such as determine net price, compute shipping charges, and prepare invoice. Each of these tables can be called and executed by actions in this calling table—for example, "Do determine net price." The tables to be executed by actions in another table with an implied return to the calling table are designated as "closed" tables and may be compared with closed subroutines. Tables that are entered by a "Go To" action are designated "open" tables, and no return is implied.

FIGURE 3-6
Airlines Reservations Limited Entry Decision Table

Rule No. →	1	2	3	4
REQUEST IS 1ST CLASS	Y	Y		
REQUEST IS TOURIST			Y	Y
1ST CLASS AVAILABLE	Y	N		
TOURIST AVAILABLE			Y	N
ISSUE 1ST CLASS	X			
ISSUE TOURIST			X	
PLACE ON WAIT LIST		X		X

Figure 3-7 shows within the numbered circles the sequence of execution of four tables.

Each of the open tables states where to go next. The closed table is referenced with a "Do" command in tables 002 and 004. When the closed table is referenced by table 002, it returns control to the next action row of table 002; when it is referenced by table 004, it returns control to the next action of table 004.

Not only may more than one table reference a closed table, but frequently more than one rule within a given table references the same closed table.

FIGURE 3-7
Sequence of Decision Table Execution

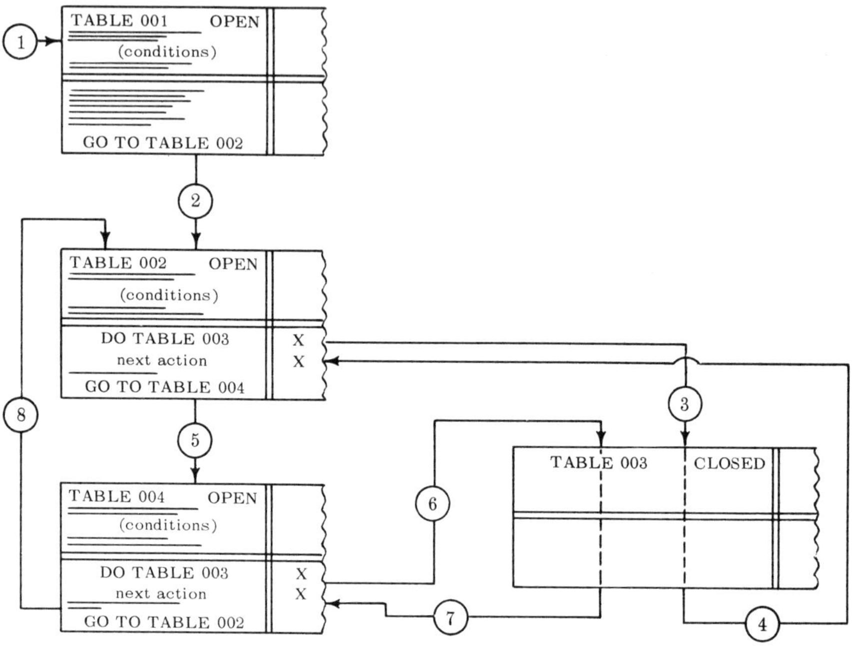

Closed tables make it unnecessary to repeat conditions and actions common to more than one table or more than one rule within a table by abstracting the conditions and actions to form a closed table. Further, they permit reentry to the table which referenced them without starting at the top of the table—the normal entry point.

4

Designing Computer-Based MIS

NUMEROUS business collapses have been attributed to management's failure to develop adequate management information and control systems. In the case of a sizable motor freight company, an improperly designed and programmed accounts-receivable system was one of the problems. In the fall of 1966, a spectacular story broke about another failure—that of a giant West Coast manufacturing firm. Again, management's failure to establish a viable information and control system was one of the problems. This particular company's annual expenditures on computing were in the low eight-figure range. Yet, judging by the news reports, it would appear that management was not directing or was not effective in directing its computer operation. Several brokerage firms on Wall Street have failed due in large part to such shortcomings.

An indictment of systems design work can be made in many cases where systems have ended up in disarray shortly after becoming operational. But that is usually only part of the explanation.

Whatever may go wrong in an MIS project, top management will end up holding the bag if the project is as costly as most management information systems are. Many potentially great situations run aground because executives launch a project and then expect their ensuing contacts with it to be superficial until the time comes to receive credit for the result.

MIS is the kind of thing an executive must get involved in. Granted, there are many pressing demands on his time; but unless MIS will get the attention it deserves, it should not be undertaken.

In this chapter, we will be looking at and explaining the critical areas in MIS design that should receive management's in-depth consideration. Let us see how this work will be judged in the end so that a sound set of criteria can be established at the outset.

Performance Planning Criteria for MIS

Among the most important considerations in designing an MIS is to plan it with an eye toward measuring its performance after it has gone into operation. In this section, we want to discuss 11 key criteria that should be applied during development and that, whether we like it or not, *will* be applied once the system has been implemented. Essentially what we want to do is apply user performance criteria before the system becomes operational and, in this case, before freezing the design of the system. Many questions need to be raised in this connection. The criteria follow.

1. *Relevance*. Is the system addressing significant company problems and those that represent an opportunity to overcome chronic weaknesses? Does the system focus on key variables in the near-term as well as the long-term scene? Are the answers that MIS brings to bear in keeping with management's timetable for the solution to critical problems? Finally, how will the MIS materially assist the company in reaching its objectives and carrying out policy?

2. *Versatility*. Does the MIS allow for growth, and how flexible is it? Are there other needs or problems that the MIS could be designed for at little additional cost? Is the initial problem mix appropriate?

3. *Accessibility*. How easy will it be for management to use, get results from, and interact with? Is the turnaround time realistic from a human standpoint? Will the system be convenient, nearby, and available when required?

4. *Dependability*. Can managers trust their problems and data to the

system? Will they have confidence that the system performs as specified and that it will be up and working most of the time? Have safeguards and appropriate kinds of backup and recovery been examined from the user's point of view?

5. *Security.* Does the design provide for the protection of vital information from access or alteration by unauthorized persons? Has a monitoring capability been built in to detect tampering attempts? What provision is there for auditing authorized access to confidential and proprietary records?

6. *Accuracy.* Are the data and information supplied by the system precise enough for their intended use, and will they be consistent when accessed by all users? Have adequate error checks been planned, and are there practical procedures for quality monitoring and corrections?

7. *Efficiency.* Will the operating cost, both computer and off-line functions, be reasonable in light of the benefits expected? Is it reasonable relative to other systems? And is it defensible in an absolute sense? (Is it providing hundred-dollar answers for ten-dollar problems?)

8. *Sensitivity.* Does the system detect, on an early warning basis, variances in situations of vital concern to management? Or is it passively reporting such situations only when they have reached crisis proportions? Can management get adequate focus on a situation through a hierarchical scheme of information representation? Has the system been designed to isolate and guide management's attention to exception conditions?

9. *Auditability.* Have means of measuring the system's results, and hence its value, been built into the design where practicable? Are there such provisions for logging the payoffs and other expected benefits that top management can know and understand what return the company is achieving on MIS expenditures? Have current operating data been duly recorded and agreed on in order that measurements against them can be made relative to the objectives of MIS?

10. *Sustainability.* If the system depends on the collection of many data from many sources on a continuing basis (which is often true of MIS), what thought has been given to: (a) maintaining the flow of input at an acceptable quantity and quality over long time periods and (b) coping with the inevitable changes in the systems and organizations that support MIS? In addition, what incentives exist for cooperation? Has an assessment been made of MIS performance in the light of company growth and anticipated changes —and how about the long-run continuity of top management support? Technically, can the system be supported at a reasonable manpower and cost level?

11. *Availability.* Is the system designed to get at some of the knotty business problems on a high-priority basis, or must everyone have faith, and

hope for the best until they see a result three years later? Has an appraisal been made of the psychological impact of time to be spent waiting for results? Does the overall design call for a time-staged series of implemented modules?

Companies in the process of developing MIS should ask questions like those just outlined more frequently than they have. The day of reckoning does come, and all those associated with the MIS effort should be prepared for it. Too often, there is a tendency to bury oneself in the fine details of daily chores without putting up the periscope to see whether the original target is still in view.

The Nature of the Design Effort

MIS, the visible product of the project effort, is designed to satisfy the needs uncovered in the course of analysis. "Selling" the right product is in part based on this investigatory homework. It is also based on the conclusions drawn, which will be represented in the design of an operational MIS. Out of the dialogue between management and the systems man come five elemental determinations:

1. *Information* needed for decision making.
2. *Time span* from the origination of information to the point when it is needed for decision making.
3. *Collection of data.*
4. *Processing requirements* and business rules used to convert data into decision information.
5. *Distribution of information* in a form useful for decision making.

The foregoing determinations, of course, are not made by simply asking the questions each poses. It is the conversations between the systems analyst and the manager that typically uncover many of the answers. The systems analyst is learning what decisions, problems, issues, and questions confront the manager, and he is also observing what assumptions are being made and verifying their soundness. He is further observing what contribution the manager is making apart from his information needs. For his part, the manager will be learning what the MIS is being designed to do for him. He will also be learning that being candid with the analyst will yield better results for himself.

Transforming the information gathered in analysis into meaningful specifications for systems design work represents roughly a third of the entire project time. Perhaps another third of the work takes place in designing the system. The remaining third consists of programming and testing the system.

Tangible Design Elements

The whole design problem generally comes apart in eight pieces. All are intimately related, yet each retains characteristics that permit it to be studied independently. They are:

1. *Applications.* Very specific functional uses.
2. *Data base.* Information storage and retrieval techniques and software.
3. *Security and backup.* Protection of confidential information and disaster recovery.
4. *Error and exception control.* The handling of the nonroutine in system auditing and controls.
5. *Inquiry and response.* The input and satisfaction of user information demands on the system.
6. *Communications.* The means of user contact with the system (for example, terminals) and the transmission of inquiry and response information over a data carrier.
7. *Hardware and systems software.* The central processing and peripheral device configuration and the general-purpose programs to facilitate its use.
8. *User education.* Programs that must be established to insure that all authorized persons will understand how to make the system perform.

Less Tangible Design Elements

Pervading nearly every facet of an MIS are human considerations—"less tangible" because so many of them relate to subjective interpretations of user needs in the real world. They involve motivation, persuasion, resistance, semantics, learning patterns, biases, misconceptions, and almost every other human-affairs variable.

MIS Design Stages

Design is usually explained in terms of the tools used to accomplish it. An understanding of what actually takes place is notably missing. This is significant, because more creative energy may be consumed in design than in any other stage of the MIS project. No single approach to design has been universally recognized as best. Some people start designing from the center and work outward. Others design from the outer perimeter, concentrating on outputs and inputs, and work inward. Still others use both approaches concurrently, working from the outside to the center where outputs are involved and working in reverse in the case of inputs. There are also people who seem to design as one might put together a jigsaw puzzle, laying out fragments and then making whatever connections appear to fit.

While the completed design is a statement of the master plan for an MIS, it is not without technical considerations. When implemented, the design should satisfy predetermined objectives and goals as set forth by user management.

The design effort consists of three stages, each resulting in a progressively more detailed representation of the system: (1) conceptual design, (2) subsystem design, and (3) process design. When these steps have been completed, computer programming commences. Programming activities include the logical design, coding, and testing of individual programs or program sections. Program specifications are developed as part of the system design effort. They tell the programmer what the program must do, but not how to do it. The latter is determined by the programmer in the logical design of the program.

Conceptual Design

Many conceptual designs are best represented by diagrams. Depicting the grand scheme of the operational MIS, they focus at a general level on the important components and variables in the system. Significantly, however, conceptual design is not a general concept. Instead, it is a concept or grouping of specific concepts. Hence, it must relate to an MIS solution custom-tailored to your company's needs. Should it appear so abstract that the distinctive characteristics of your company's functions are not in evidence, then you probably do not have a meaningful conceptual design.

It should convey the notion of subsystems or system modules and show how they relate and work together. Further, we should understand how and when these modules should be developed and how they fit into the framework of the master plan.

Figure 4-1 is representative of a general overview of an MIS, whereas Figures 4-2 and 4-3 represent a much higher degree of conceptual detail. As may be seen, each of these three illustrations pertains to altogether different systems.

Subsystem Design

In this second stage of design, subsystems are defined. Logical functions within each subsystem are also identified and defined as they relate to

(*text continues on page 111*)

FIGURE 4-1
Overview of a Manufacturing Company's MIS

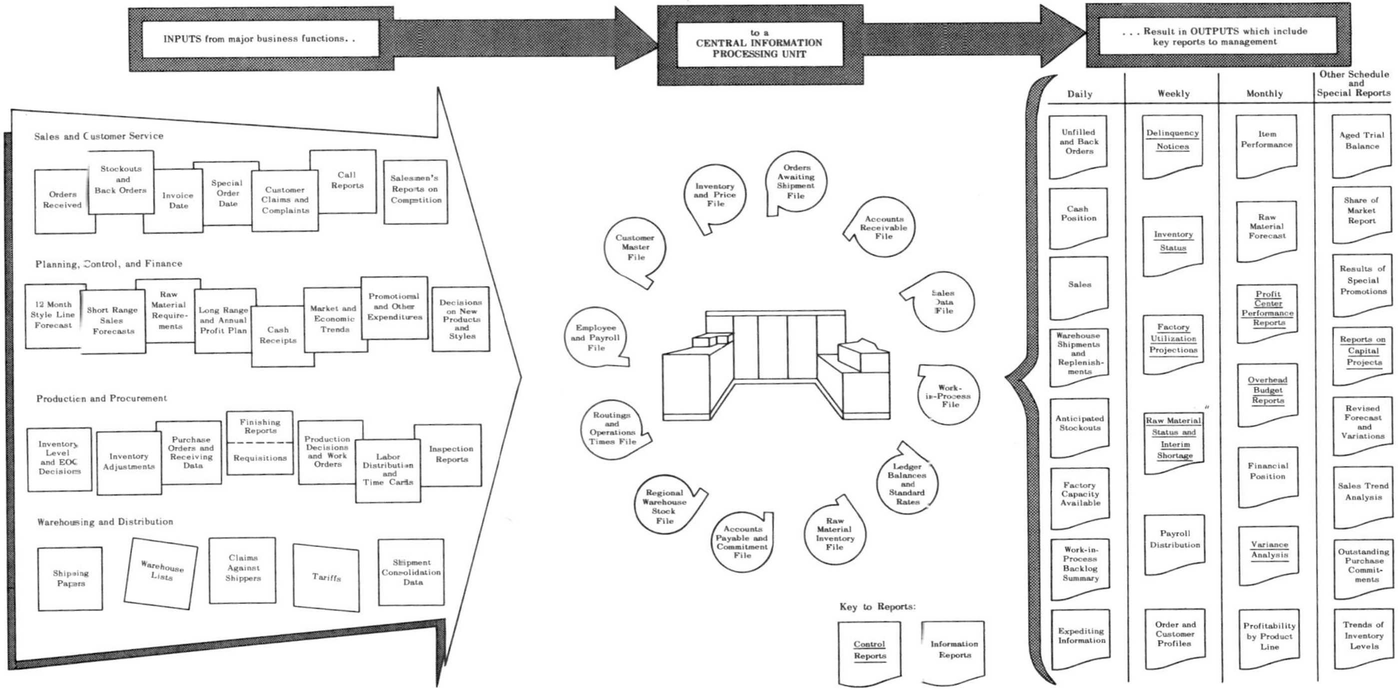

Source: J. W. Konvalinka and H. G. Trentin, "Management Information Systems," *Management Services*, September-October 1965.

FIGURE 4-2
Subsystem Relationships in a Manufacturing MIS

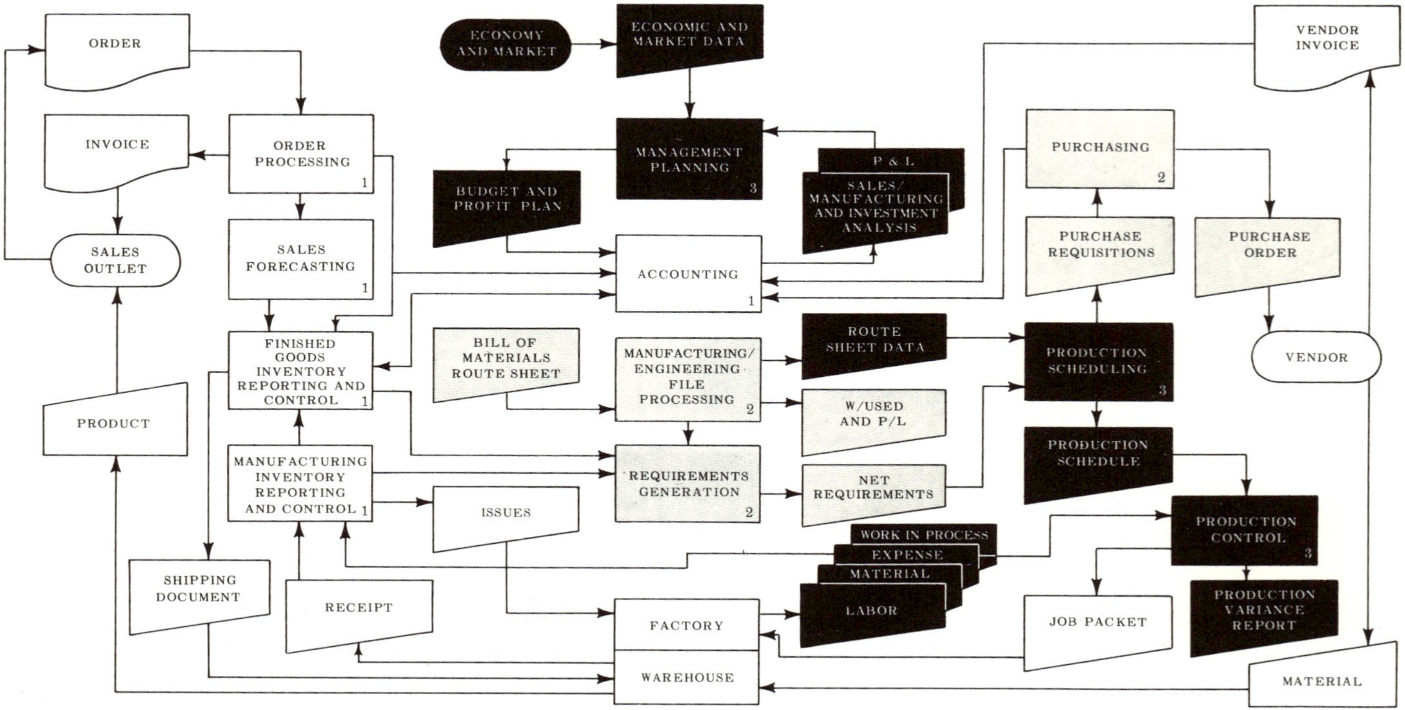

Numbers in subsystem rectangles indicate the phase in which each is developed and implemented.
Used by permission of Honeywell, Inc. © 1968.

FIGURE 4-3
Functions of a Process Control MIS

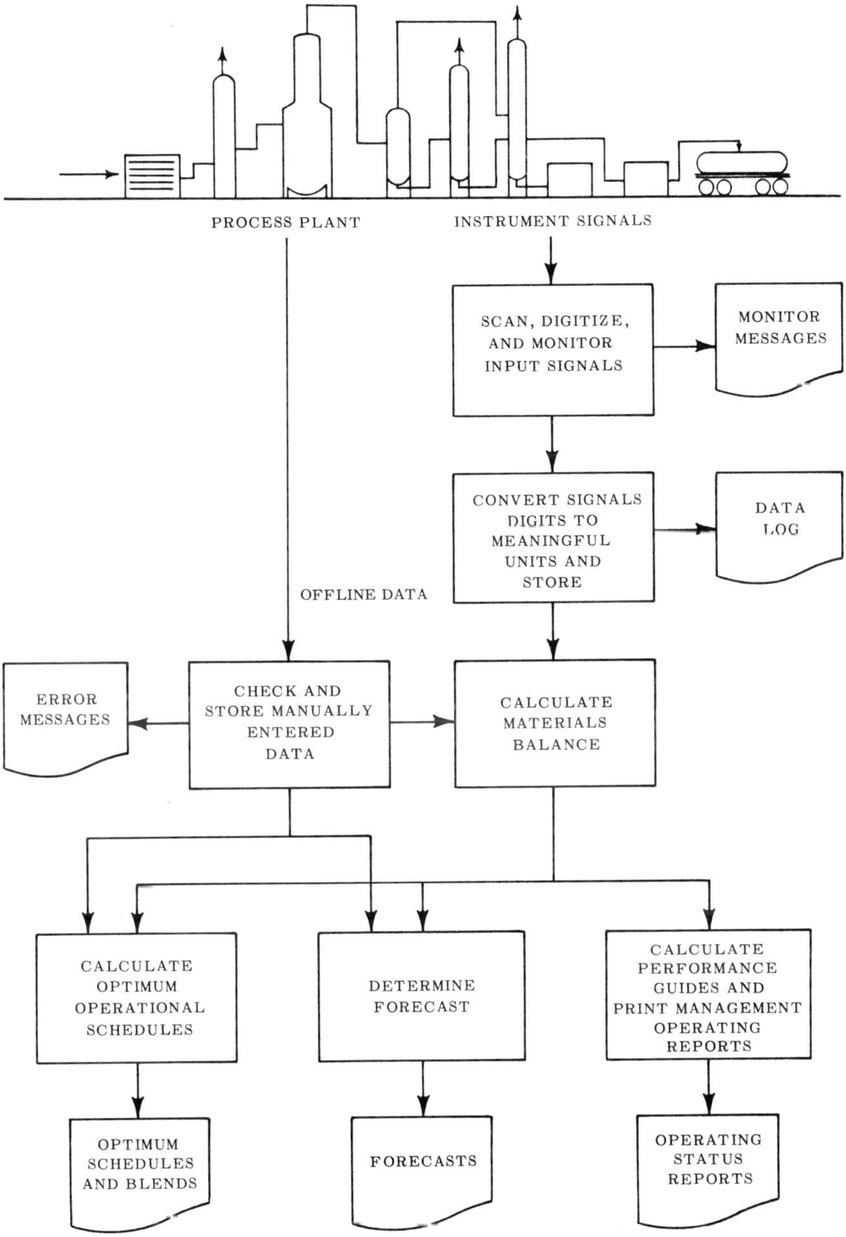

Reprinted courtesy of IBM Corporation.

FIGURE 4-4
Subsystems in an Inventory MIS

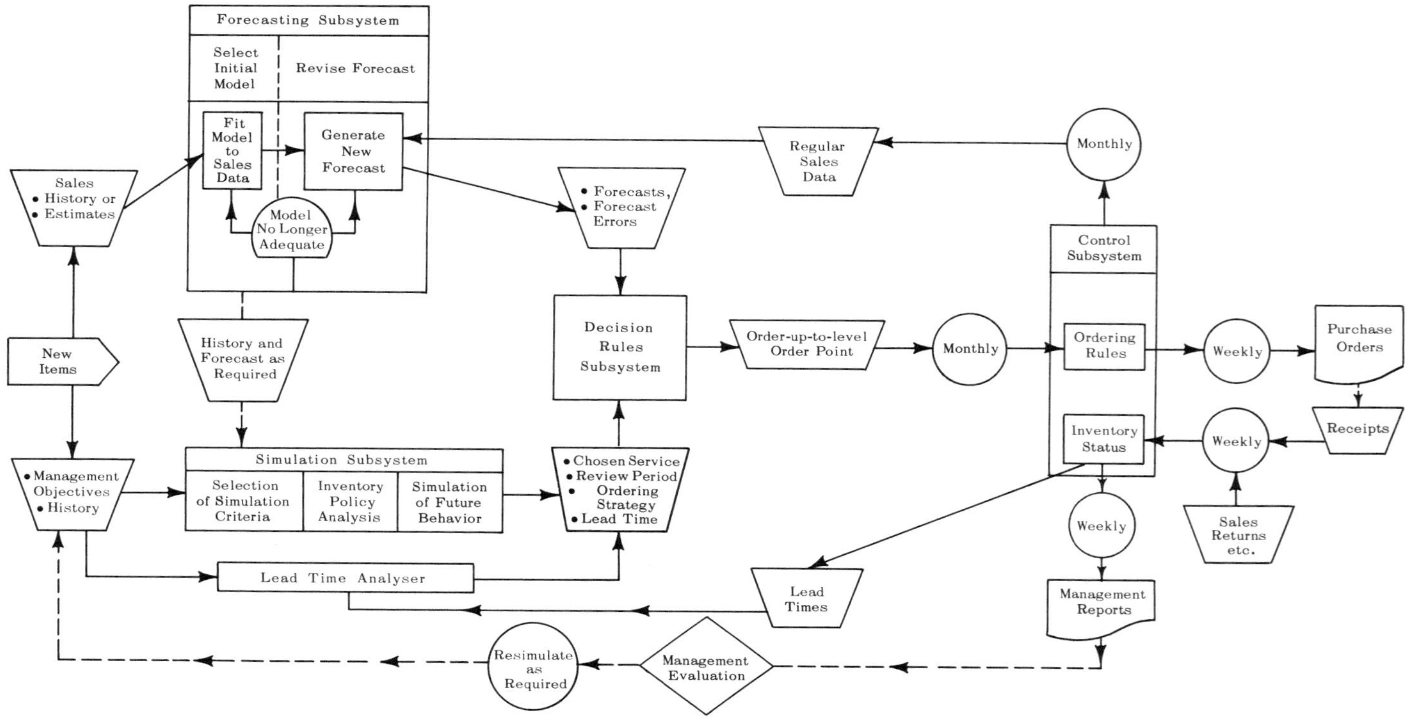

Reprinted courtesy of IBM Corporation.

satisfying the application(s) requirements that fall within the boundary of the subsystem. Details concerning the surface features of the subsystem are examined and specified as they relate to: the flow of information, means and sources of input, appearance and types of output, and the functional attributes. An important task in subsystem design is arriving at standards that may pertain to nomenclature, error and exception controls, or calculation and processing rules. In essence, you are working with black boxes that will accomplish the required functions, knowing in general what each is supposed to do. Figure 4-4 depicts a number of subsystems within a retail inventory management system.

How to delineate and control subsystems. As we have indicated, subsystems within MIS need to be described in terms of the functions they carry out and the key tasks within each function. Systems perspective rather than general concepts is used in delineating subsystems, since concepts do not generally provide the specific problem-solving focus we are aiming for in this process.

Initially, even prior to the point at which conceptual design is begun, rough images of the subsystems will usually emerge. Eventually, these major components are perceived as subsystems to facilitate certain analytical work. However, if we somehow fall into the trap of viewing these as fixed entities from "day one" and proceed under that assumption for the duration of the project, the grand finale will usually be a very poor, if not unworkable, MIS. This can be avoided if you remain flexible on subsystem definition till you really know what you are talking about. In many cases, the pieces of the puzzle will go together nicely, provided we have the pieces. The danger is that either we do not have the pieces or we shape and trim the pieces to fit into a fixed concept.

Even the smallest MIS is too big to tackle as one entity. This in itself gives rise to the need for dividing the effort—preferably, of course, in some orderly and logical way. Two of the most important benefits resulting from a careful and competent delineation of subsystems are that—

1. Sharp distinctions can be drawn as to what each subsystem will accomplish. This is especially critical where they are to be implemented at different points in time or are being worked on by different individuals.
2. Effective planning and control of development tasks are facilitated. Groups assigned to work on subsystems more clearly understand their responsibilities and can relate them to the places where subsystems interface.

As you proceed with delineation, some tasks or responsibilities will present problems that cannot conveniently be disposed of without your first having examined the systems considerations. These generally crop up at subsystem interfaces and often end up being answered through an informed decision by project management as to which subsystem should do what. It may be that the descriptions of some functions are such that a decision cannot be made until the design has been gone into in more depth. In these instances, project management may temporarily assign responsibility until it becomes possible, through more refined knowledge, to make a better, more consistent assignment. In process design, however, a decision must be made. It is essential to keep special tabs on these tasks so that they find a permanent home at the earliest possible time.

Conscientiously applied management controls in packaging subsystems help minimize the chance that tasks will fall into limbo or get lost, as has happened in MIS projects. Occasionally, reappearing at inopportune times, they prove both embarrassing and costly.

Looking ahead for a moment, we will finally arrive at a point where all the pieces are supposed to be assembled. Here we will find, despite our best efforts, that some pieces will not fit together as planned and that others will be missing altogether. This will always happen in large MIS projects, and management should not be dismayed at the need to make on-the-spot extensions to the system.

Process Design

Having gone through the first two stages, in which we drew up the master plan and proceeded from there to define and examine subsystem components, we should now be in a position to be very exact about the information processing required within each subsystem. The black boxes with which we had been working will now be distinctly shaped and molded. In this final stage of design, each program in the subsystem will be explicitly specified. Program by program, the detailed requirements relevant to input, output, and the processing of data are set forth in the form of program specifications. Decision tables, discussed in the previous chapter, would be included in these specifications as they relate to program processing logic.

Operating Mode Design Classifications

Input, processing, and output are common to all computer-based MIS. *Timing* of these actions defines the operating modes of the system. There are three mode classifications in general use: batch, on-line, and real time. Very briefly, *batch mode* means that input data are collected for some relatively long period of time (perhaps a day), then processed as a batch of work. All work is accomplished and inquiries are responded to only during the periodic (once a day) operation of the system. *On-line* has no universally agreed-upon definition. For our purposes, it is the capability to (1) enter input data into the system as they come into being and (2) receive immediate responses to simple inquiries concerning preexisting information. Fairly limited processing is implied. *Real time* refers to the full processing of input data at the moment that data come into being or when conditions arise that call for processing. Further, the input and processing take place parallel to a physical process, such as in a real-time airlines reservation system. In some applications, results of the processing can be used to direct that process in some way. Fairly comprehensive processing is implied.

A given MIS may have one or more of these classifications represented in it, some tasks being batch mode, others on-line, and still others real time.

As we said, the definition of on-line is not universally agreed upon, and the term is sometimes used in place of or in conjunction with real time—that is, on-line real time.

As we discuss some of the salient design considerations for these modes, it would be well to watch for the implications of timing in the design of an MIS. To begin, let us concentrate on the "business end" of MIS: its output, which is almost always triggered by an input of some kind. The generation of output may result from routine processing, from exception processing, or from an external (on demand) request. Let us now see where each of these comes into play in a typical batch-mode processing system.

Batch Mode

In batch-processing systems, input is collected and held for later processing rather than being processed as it becomes available. As part of the routine operation of the system, outputs of certain kinds are always produced. This happens automatically and usually at regular time intervals. Such routine output is identical in form for each processing cycle. For example, a payroll register is produced automatically every two weeks by the payroll system, and there are no programmed conditions that can keep it from being generated.

Routine output of this variety is not generally of interest to management, the content being in many cases too voluminous and the information of little value in the form presented. However, the summarized versions of routine output do provide part of management's information, especially financial performance reports. The usual case is that such reports are historical and neither provide future trends nor tell management specifically what went wrong in the past. Knowing that a sales office's performance is off 10 percent, which is often the kind of information presented, is not really very helpful. MIS, on the other hand, ought to be able to tell management why, or at least help narrow down the possible explanations. Better yet, it ought to provide planning and control information to help management avoid problem situations before they become critical.

Continuing with the batch-processing systems, there are sometimes optional outputs available to the user, as opposed to uncontrolled or nonoptional outputs. Optional outputs may be considered in two ways, both of which coexist in many systems. First, we have program-controlled optional outputs, (for example, a report showing information about those employees whose overtime earnings exceeded 25 percent of regular earnings). In this case, no report would be issued if no one was in the over-25-percent category. This kind of output is called an *exception report,* and its appearance is preconditioned by fixed, programmed logic. Note that the option is controlled by the system.

Another exception-report category within the optional kind of output is what we call externally controlled or parameter-triggered output. These outputs appear only when specifically requested, and may or may not be subject to external parameters that can be changed at each running of the system. So we can have output subject to fixed logic on demand and we can also have output subject to parameters (or variable logic) on demand. For example, we could have an optional exception report with fixed logic that may simply be requested if management wants it (for example, a report showing employees with salaries of over $25,000 a year). *Parameterized reporting,* to use a similar example, would allow management to enter any salary figure as the cutoff point and obtain a report that has been at least partly tailored to their needs. All such reports, however, would have the same form and substance.

Variety in report form and content in many existing routine batch operations is achieved by having the desired outputs designed in or added on as the need for them arises. This has typically meant programmer involvement, with all the phrase says about expenses and delays of one sort or another. MIS specifically seek to overcome such problems. Adaptable characteristics of the design must provide room for growth, perhaps along the lines discussed in the next chapter on general-purpose data-base management systems. These systems can eliminate the programmer as an interface between management and the information system. In this way, management interacts directly and quickly while the expensive programming talent is put to better use.

On-Line and Real-Time Modes

Communications-based systems designed for real-time management promise a great many benefits. However, it will take time to get a company used to this new mode of operation. Overcoming the seat-of-the-pants practices of the past is not as simple as it might appear. Serious consequences can result from seemingly minor shortcomings in design. Some may completely wreck the effectiveness of the system. If, for example, a certain answer to a management question has to be had in three minutes and the questioner must have a fairly good answer in that period, an MIS designed to give him the best answer in ten minutes does not satisfy the need. Vigilant design reviews by management users of the developing MIS must therefore be conducted to guard against both underdesign and overdesign.

MIS analysts and user management sometimes exhibit a tendency to look at the timing question in a single perspective—fast response—which implies expensive communications hardware and software. Typically, this means ten seconds or less, which is the interval between the time when a request has been entered and the time when an answer begins to come back.

Management information in the fast-response mode is frequently a convenience rather than a necessity. How much you are willing to pay for the convenience is another matter. Additional hardware, software, and application programming costs are associated with fast response. Numerous companies have committed themselves to buy a service they could get along without if they understood the problem. Data-transmission networks have sometimes been installed at great cost to speed data to and from various locations. But no consideration was giving to speeding up what went on at either end of the communications link, with the result that three- and four-hour delays were usually experienced at both ends. Rough calculations for one industrial-products manufacturer, with a cluster of locations on the eastern seaboard, showed that the company could save half its communication costs by leasing a Rolls Royce complete with chauffeur, and a small jet airplane complete with pilot, to carry data from point to point. This, incidentally, would have improved the service too.

In another company, over $1,500 a month was being spent to transmit data between New York City and a suburb of Newark, New Jersey, a distance of approximately 25 miles by car. An analytical effort of two days by one systems man showed that a part-time messenger service could easily serve the purpose at a greatly reduced cost.

A communications-based MIS, as compared to batch processing, helps us portray more accurately the MIS operation as conceived by most companies. However, we hasten to point out that you can have a non-communications-based MIS. With the question of how fast MIS can collect information and make it available to management in a useful form, another question needs to be answered, that of how fast management can act or wants to act on the information. Since MIS development and operation costs increase with faster system response or turnaround time, the justification for faster response should be carefully examined. How much more such faster response costs is hard to say, but there are sometimes dramatic differences, where it costs perhaps five to ten times more.

Real-Time MIS Design Considerations

Companies caught up in the exciting world of real-time and communications-based systems sometime fail to anchor the many loose ends that characterize such systems. That the term "real time" is ambiguous is no small part of the problem. When someone speaks of real-time systems, he could be referring to one of half a dozen categories:

1. *Process control systems,* such as those used to run paper mills and steel- and chemical-production processes.
2. *Environment control systems,* such as those found in the military or in the Federal Aviation Agency's air-traffic control.
3. *Management information systems,* such as those encompassing the complete cycle from order entry through billing and accounts receivable.
4. *Time-sharing systems,* such as those used today by scientists, engineers, and others for mathematical computation.
5. *Remote batch processing,* where jobs to be run are entered at remote stations (particularly small satellite computers).
6. *Demand data-collection systems,* such as those to collect job-progress data in manufacturing, hospital patient data, and weather data.

For our purposes, we will be concerned only with MIS. It is understood, however, that elements of the other kinds of real-time systems can enter into an MIS. That includes elements from demand data collection and even process control.

Real-Time MIS Characteristics

A number of characteristics of real-time MIS apply equally well to other systems. Nevertheless, it may be helpful to enumerate some of the more important ones:

- An integral component of an ongoing business activity, the real-time MIS provides information in sufficient time to affect decisions relating to the activity. Shortness of time is implied, often being measured in seconds, only rarely in hours. In general, measurements pertaining to the status of the ongoing activity are available instantly. Inputs affecting these measurements can also be entered quickly and immediately. Acceptable response times of real-time systems may vary only within a small range.

- The numbers and types of users and data sources are known.
- A specific data-transmission network utilizing communications terminals of any kind is implied.
- A finite number of distinct functional capabilities are provided for.
- A specific language or vocabulary is used to communicate with the system in order to invoke its functions.
- Central processing hardware together with associated control programs is often backed up fully and is otherwise designed to permit graceful degradation of service, such that minimal operations can be sustained until an orderly shutdown or repair can be accomplished.
- Structured data bases, the contents of which are well-defined, are implied, as are means of indexing data records, to cut down retrieval time. Data bases associated with real-time capabilities are connected on-line and are updated as events take place during the real-time day.

Real-time systems are basically the same, to the extent that they satisfy the definition. Their application varies, of course, depending on the objective being sought. Airlines reservations, order entry, and bank-teller systems may be seeking better customer service, improved control of inventory, faster management action, and the like. Real-time systems for production control seek to keep on top of the interrelated events and scheduling problems. And, in general, such systems seek to speed the collection and dissemination of data, to limit the impact of human foibles, and to complement human capabilities.

Conversational Mode MIS

The success of a real-time MIS hinges in part on the level of effort a user has to exert. Needless to say, there have been potentially good systems that no one could use because they were nearly impossible to communicate with. In searching for a way to make system communications almost painless, systems developers have tried to emulate human communication. Examples of this are found in computer-assisted educational systems, where the student and system teacher try not to depend on special computer knowledge. In effect, they converse.

In general, people are more mentally stimulated in conversation than in formal or highly individual processes. Conversational mode permits conversationlike interplay between the manager and the computer. In approximating a man-to-man or a man-to-ideas relationship, the system adapts more readily to enhance human thought patterns and to compensate for human failings—as, for example, forgetfulness. The typical alternative to providing conversational-mode capabilities is called *transaction mode,* which requires that the user follow a specific set of rules in order to invoke the powers of the system. Should he forget these rules or make a simple human error, the system provides little if any assistance as to what he should do.

This characteristic, common in many systems, diminishes their value because users find them cumbersome. At its highest state of development, a conversational design would permit a person to engage in dialogue with the system even if he had never heard of it and had no idea as to its area of application. In fact, an individual could encounter the system without having any idea as to what he wanted to do. The system might begin the conversation by giving the man a list of options from which he could pick out items of interest. Having received an answer, the system could tell the man what it knew concerning these interests. The individual would choose something that interested him and the system would proceed to explain the selected item in more detail. If the chosen item should be a method of calculating some value, the system would explain how the capability is used.

The more typical situation in an MIS environment is one in which the user knows what he wants to do. Here, the system would merely ask for certain factors required to solve the man's problem or answer his question. As a consequence of this mode of operation, the burden of external-user training programs is greatly reduced, if not entirely eliminated. Problems that would be introduced as a result of user forgetfulness are caught at the time they are made. Indeed, a well-conceived conversational-mode system demands very little of the user.

Some of the management information systems now implemented are designed for conversational-mode use. Several start the interacting relationship by listing the major functions that may be performed and asking the user to select the processing related to the chosen function, which it then begins executing. To make the process painless, the user is asked multiple-choice questions, the answers to which serve as input data. With multiple-choice questions, it is not possible for the user to enter invalid data in answer to a single question. If the user should know what answers he will be entering, in advance of being asked, some systems permit him to skip the questions and just provide the answers. Since the questions and answers may change from time to time, the system provides that when new questions are put into the system they cannot be bypassed for a short time. This insures the system against incorrect input for that period of time.

One objective in designing the system for conversational mode is to make it responsive to time dimensions in the real world. Busy people often cannot spend the time necessary to learn a lot of rules. Making the MIS easy to use provides the opportunity to have large numbers of people take advantage of it directly. By way of contrast, transaction-mode systems require specially trained personnel capable of translating management needs into an esoteric form acceptable to the system. As in everything else, there are losses in translation when a third party must intervene. Intimate knowledge of the problem that management wishes to solve can hardly be expected of the third party unless a concerted effort has been made to bring it about.

Conversational mode, on the other hand, seeks to put the manager in face-to-face communication with the problem-solving tool without requiring him to be an expert in its construction and use.

Conversational-mode systems cost much more and take longer to develop than transaction-mode systems and use more system time to accomplish the same functions. However, there are the benefits mentioned earlier. Also, since conversational-mode design is extremely flexible, extensions to the MIS can be introduced without upsetting old procedures. This greatly reduces the rate of obsolescence of such systems.

Queuing in Communications-Based Systems

A queue is a waiting line. It may be made up of people, trucks, airplanes, computer inquiries, or anything else. Here we are concerned with messages (inquiries or transactions) to be processed by a communications-based system, the nerve center of which is one or more computers.

The body of knowledge that deals with waiting-line situations is called *queuing theory* and is rich with the mathematics of probability and statistics. Any examination of the subject, beyond providing a few basic notions, makes delving into mathematics unavoidable. Since we are not going to do this, it should be said that the basics we will describe have complex ramifications that must be explored fully if a system is to be designed.

Contention Versus Polling

Real-time systems are designed to cope with demands for service in two principal ways: contention and polling.

Contention means that users communicate with the system whenever they want to do so. The system stands ready to respond to requests for service, presumably whenever such requests are received. However, this may not actually happen because the system may be tied up doing someone else's work. To this extent, the users compete for service on an availability basis where, in a sense, the availability is not controlled by the system.

Polling, on the other hand, services demands by permitting users to communicate only when the system wants them to do so. In polled systems, each terminal in the network is periodically checked to learn whether a user wants to communicate. At other times the user must wait, his turn being controlled by the central computer. In practice, such waits are usually a matter of seconds.

Regardless of the method chosen to deal with service demands, the fundamental problems related to queues are unchanged. There are so many users desiring service and there is a system that has a practical limitation as to how much service it can give over a period of time. Since polled systems provide for better overall control of message traffic, they are predominant.

Queue Characteristics

Characteristics of a queuing situation relate to two basic entities: (1) the service facility (in our case, a communications-based system); and (2) demands placed against the system. The behavior of both entities always relates to time.

In theory, the system can be designed to service any level of demand in practically any time frame. It is easy to see that the economics will not permit the ultimate system, however. (You cannot justify having 100 cashiers at your local supermarket, even though it would mean that no one would ever have to wait in line.) As a result, the system must be designed to give reasonable service. This gives rise to design statements such as these: 90 percent of the inquiries must wait no longer than five seconds, or, the probability that the waiting time will be five seconds or less must be 99 percent.

Real-time MIS are designed according to such statements of probability whereas batch-mode systems are designed according to certainties.

Utilization

A basic problem in all queuing situations involves the utilization of the system. The higher the utilization, the greater will be the waiting time. If messages arrive at the constant rate of one every ten seconds, and it takes two seconds for the system to completely service one message, the utilization is 20 percent. If these messages arrived randomly, they would find the system busy about 20 percent of the time. Some waiting would therefore occur. In most systems, the demands are not placed at a constant rate, and service time is not usually constant. There are also peaks, where a lot of messages are crowded into a short period of time.

Real-time design centers on providing a specific quality of service at maximum-demand concentration. Having satisfied this, service at all other times can only be better. As you may have guessed, specific rates, probabilities, and other data—*not averages*—are used in designing the system to meet response-time requirements. Of vital importance, too, are the considerations pertaining to performance of the system with growth in utilization over time.

Message arrivals are often distributed unevenly over time, and they typically vary in length, content, and the time it takes the system to service them. The behavior of the system under such circumstances is ordinarily described by a statistical model. The nature of the mathematics to describe such queuing situations gives rise to nonproportional relationships between incremental changes in demand levels and expected waiting time. Contention for service causes congestion, so to speak, which increases disproportionately as demand grows proportionately.

In practice, this can mean that an on-line system serving five users at five seconds per message may serve ten users in twenty seconds per message. As the utilization approaches 100 percent, the waiting time approaches infinity. Long before anything like this happens, however, something "gives." In a practical situation, someone seeing a long waiting line does not join it; if he does, but later decides not to wait, he is said to have reneged. In both cases he is lost as a user.

In the computer configuration, provision must be made to maintain message queues in memory or on-line storage so they will not be lost. This will limit the size of queue that can be allowed to form. Should this line become full, the system refuses to accept additional entries. Additionally, provisions to deal with reneging must be provided.

In general, the utilization, as we have defined it, of a real-time system is in the neighborhood of 75 percent. Where peak demands occur over relatively short time periods, utilization tends to be lower. This, as we said previously, is because the system must be designed to provide acceptable service at peak conditions. Further, great variations in service rates for processing messages tend to reduce utilization. Here again, system designers must accommodate users at some level of response-time quality under expected worst-case conditions, which can represent a concentration of lengthy message processing.

Queue Discipline and Priorities

The economics in designing a communications-based system are such that decreasing response time increases cost. Response time includes waiting and processing time. By using more expensive computers (or more computers or both) and data transmission channels, response or turnaround time can be decreased. This approach to the improvement of system service, however, may not be justified across the board.

In many applications, a mix of services is provided. There is also a mix of related priorities associated with these services. Higher priorities for service relate to the higher importance of faster response to the company's welfare. A system designed to give equally good response in all services does not take into account that some things are more important than others. Such systems cost much more than they need to, since every function they carry out is geared to the faster response requirements of the most important services.

To combat these higher potential costs, systems should be designed so as to recognize service priorities. Priorities must be established initially through discussion with company officials. After the system is performing in a "live" environment, it is tuned up by changing priorities to overcome unforeseen difficulties and changes that may occur in business operations.

Priority levels, as reflected in the design, are not usually serviced progressively to the exclusion of all other subordinate levels. This means that a deluge of high-priority messages cannot seize the system full time. In practice, the priority scheme gives lower-priority messages recognition *less often* (for example, three messages in priority-level 2 to one message in priority-level 1). In a polled system, certain terminals may be permitted to transmit and receive more often than others.

The queue discipline, in concept, places messages in their proper priority "stack" as they are transmitted in, and it also stacks outgoing messages. Note that a one-for-one, in-to-out relationship often does not exist. Depending on the nature of the application and the design objectives, input-to-output characters may be in any ratio (4 : 1, 1 : 4, 3 : 1.5, 1 : 3, 2 : 1, 1 : 2, and so forth).

The usual service sequence within a given priority level is generally first in, first out (FIFO). Depending on the number of distinct priority levels (or sublevels), the system may be designed to look ahead in order to identify for processing high-priority messages in the queue. Various waiting-time rules and cycling patterns can be introduced to control the *scanning* of the queue.

Last in, first out (LIFO) is another type of queuing discipline that does not arise particularly often in business MIS. It simply means that the most recent message is processed first. Sometimes called a *pushdown queue,* it is applied where a collection of messages (or readings) all contain the same type of data, which have been collected progressively, and where the last arrival is most important (for example, position of aircraft in an air-traffic-management system).

Random ordering is another infrequently used discipline. In such queues as are here involved, it is equally likely that any message will be selected for processing, irrespective of the time it has been waiting.

In advanced real-time systems, the rules pertaining to the processing of queues can get quite complicated. Priorities, for example, may be set dynamically, within limits, so that the equipment can be more fully used and better overall service provided. For example, if the highest priority transaction in the system cannot be processed because the configuration resources it needs are momentarily tied up, the system will look for something else to do in the interim. In some applications, it may be advantageous to hold and resequence messages to provide more efficient search and retrieval of information from on-line data bases.

Concurrent Message Processing

Systems can partly process a message (to the point, say, where a needed resource is found to be occupied or something more important comes up), then do something else, and later return to complete the processing. Since a number of transactions (10, 25, 50, 100) may be in various stages of completion at any one time, it is necessary that processing programs not depend on finishing part or total processing of a message.

Reentrant modules, or programs, permit blocks of code to be executed in order to process new messages without affecting a transaction that may have gone part way through them. Many high-level programming languages (some of them business-oriented) do not have this capability and therefore cannot be used for real-time programs.

Adopting a Practical Design Viewpoint

As we cross the threshold from analysis to design, several matters need to be studied carefully. The first is the determination of whether the MIS problems that have been analyzed and set forth in a standard form of documentation really express management's wants and needs. It is essential to have the project team conduct a series of *requirements reviews* with selected managers and other users of the MIS. They can then capture the bits and pieces of analysis data that inevitably go astray during the process of amassing the ingredients that make up the statement of MIS requirements. These reviews will help pinpoint places where the analysis was not done in sufficient detail. Also, the original problem may appear in a slightly different light when it has been neatly packaged and explained. Occasionally, this alters the emphasis on one or more points in design and gives rise to afterthoughts that can be conveniently accommodated by modifying the statement of requirements. Should these reviews turn up a great many new and heretofore unheard-of requirements, or reveal that the analytical work proposes to solve nonexistent problems, the need for a thorough audit and review will be apparent. While this would represent an indictment of the quality of the work performed thus far, it is better to know now than later.

Requirements reviews, as described here, are meant to have an air of formality. In point of fact, many more or less informal reviews should have taken place before the design event. In the case of some formal reviews, however, we will be looking at results of integrated analysis, as opposed to individual or isolated problems. This sometimes gives rise to changes.

This checkpoint should be satisfied before going further. So the first practical design viewpoint that should be adopted is to look back before you go forward. Even as you proceed into design, you will need to keep looking behind you. It is a basic truth in systems development that changes of various kinds follow on this point in the project, despite efforts to cap the requirements once and for all.

Staying in Touch with Reality

From the time design work commences, it is important to maintain close contact with the business orientation that was so much a part of the analytical work. At this juncture, it is not at all uncommon to find that computer people go off in a corner somewhere and attempt to link together the hottest ideas inside and outside the state of the art. Here, we can often observe several phenomena, none of which is particularly encouraging.

- Getting wrapped up in technical questions to the point where the real problem and objectives are virtually forgotten.
- Introducing too many new and untried design approaches, resulting in too much pioneering work in too many areas.
- Getting tied up in extensive but often irrelevant hardware and software studies, which may be of academic interest, but which do not bear directly on the question of what practical alternatives we have to choose from.

These symptoms portend grief in the design stage as well as the programming and testing stages of the MIS project. Today, largely because computing attracts truly creative individuals, we need to keep a sharp lookout for ultrasophisticated functional facilities. Some of the literature hammers away at them regularly. We can be misled into thinking that development, because it seems slightly more complex than typical systems work, depends on using known methods or techniques. What sometimes happens, however, is that the proposed approach as reflected in design calls for a software invention of some kind. In fact, the whole justification for the MIS could depend on having that invention, with all the accompanying uncertainties of time and cost.

Invention in systems work appears in some areas much more than others. Generalized software is probably the best example; it includes programming languages, operating or executive systems, data-management systems—especially those having facilities designed to accommodate users directly—and multipurpose control programs to handle advanced telecommunications networks.

Significant management problems, however, can be solved without such inventions. Indeed, there are enough problems of this kind to keep the MIS group busy for years. The solution lies in producing, not promising, as is frequently the case when we say we are developing when in fact inventing is a better way of describing the work.

Against this background, everyone directly concerned with MIS should understand that the state of the art does change rather quickly, at least relative to other technology fields. Keeping abreast of what others have done or are attempting to do is important. Numerous managers concerned with MIS have made comments to the effect that talent is all that really counts. To a large extent, they are right. The real problem, however, is to determine whether staff people who have performed well in the past can be as effective at the next level and whether certain individuals can develop at the pace needed.

Lest our previous comments on inventions be misconstrued, we hasten to add that every company should undertake some advanced research in the systems area. This, however, is not the kind of endeavor that is recommended under the guise of an MIS development project.

A pat formula does not exist to tell us how much money should be put into systems research. Perhaps 5 or 10 percent of the MIS budget is the right number. In the abstract, it is a function of what your organization has as long-term MIS objectives.

Going Through the Motions

Abuses of computing technology abound in American companies. One of these is the quarterly and annual exercise in one prominent conglomerate of producing the "profit plan," or "business plan," as it is variously referred to. Hundreds of pounds of computer printout are distributed as the grand finale to days of processing. Asked what benefits management was getting from all this, one systems executive in the know said "very little." He added: "We call them the 'Dead Sea scrolls' around here because management doesn't look at them." When asked why they were produced at all, the executive replied that they were the most stylish form of "security blanket" and also that many executives believed the system was keeping track of things. Of course, no one really knew until a newly promoted executive had someone take a look. As it turned out, there was a big mess to be straightened out.

Value Analysis in the Design Process

Value analysis is an engineering economics activity that is pinned to the philosophy of seeking the optimum solution to a design problem, where numerous satisfactory solutions or alternatives are open. Often, value analysis is done on existing products in order to achieve cost reductions. Designs for new products in modern companies will almost always go through a value analysis procedure of some kind. As a formally identified undertaking, value analysis is relatively new.

Part of the analysis includes looking at components of a system to see whether they bear a consistent relationship to each other and to the objectives being sought. Let us take a hypothetical case to see what this means. Suppose we have designed an air filter for a furnace that is supposed to last about three months, then be thrown away. As it now appears on the blueprint, its frame is shown to be made of a lightweight metal, and it can be made at a cost of 50 cents. The value analyst might say, after having studied the product and its application, "Why use a metal frame that will last a lifetime for a product that is designed to be discarded after three months? A cardboard frame will work as well, and the savings in material and fabricating will reduce our cost by 20 percent."

Computer systems work has undergone little in the way of real value analysis over the years. Consequently, companies have paid handsome premiums for systems that have been overdesigned in many areas and underdesigned in others. An everyday occurrence in program design is one where analyst–programmers spend inordinate amounts of time and energy polishing up a program so that it will run faster and use less computer memory. However, more complex logic and sophisticated programming tricks almost inevitably are brought into play to polish up a program. This means difficult program bugs and future maintenance problems. The unfortunate part is that often the reduced running time and lower memory requirement for the program fail to provide value. The programmer who spends an extra month polishing up a program so that it runs in 25 percent less time may be wasting money.

In a typical case, one programmer worked on a program that had run at one hour per month and cut the running time to 45 minutes. He also managed to save 10 percent of the memory required. The net result was a saving of about $20 worth of computer time a month. The saving in memory did not allow the user to eliminate this portion of the computer rental, as other programs needed it.

Costs to achieve this recurring annual saving of $240 (12 × $20 per month) were: $1,200 (one month of programmer time plus fringe benefits); about $800 worth of computer test time; and $3,600 (the loss resulting from one month's slippage in schedule—due in part to taking extra time on the program and in part to the fact that the programmer was unavailable to work on other problems for the extra month). Obviously, it will be many years before this expenditure pays for itself. And the system will probably be obsolete by that time.

Human Factors in MIS Design

Paying close attention to the habits and attitudes of managers and others who will use the system for information is certain to make an otherwise good MIS better. MIS developers face two challenges: bridging the information gap and bridging the people gap. The information gap is bridged when MIS can generate the needed information. Whether anyone can use what can be generated is the second part of the problem—the people gap.

Human Affairs

The human side of MIS can no more be neatly confined to some arbitrarily defined part of the system than we can confine its considerations to this particular section of the book. It permeates almost everything in MIS. Some of the human factors are rather pedestrian, and some are related to the advent of MIS, although this in itself does not make them new. On the one hand, we are confronted with the problems of a records clerk who uses a visual display terminal all day—perhaps with the size and color of what he sees on the screen, the fatigue it causes, or the emotional effects of "talking" to a machine for long periods. On the other hand, we may be interested in finding out how to overcome resistance to the "monster" that has been variously described as a fast idiot and a real threat to job security.

Automation has been down some of these roads before. MIS can benefit from these experiences, but must go further, for it is something more than the mechanization of simple operations.

At this point, as we consider the manager, we have to develop an empirical approach. Orthodox or authoritarian managerial doctrine became unpopular many years ago, giving way to more delegation of responsibility and the enlargement of the individual's role within a limited functional area. From this, we have gone to various kinds of team approaches and we are now on the threshold of what is sometimes called the participative management approach. This approach shows a great deal of promise in that it can overcome the tokenism of its alternatives by bringing more individuals into a genuine decision-making role. Now, let us see what all this has to do with MIS.

Because we are concerned with management and how it can be made more effective with MIS, we should endeavor to learn how it ties in with the company's trends in management approaches. If participative management is or will be the desired mode, then MIS needs to be molded to accommodate decision making and policy formulation in this atmosphere. If other approaches are prevalent, MIS must take the form that is most useful for those approaches.

Besides management as an abstract entity, we have to look at management as people. Developers should make every effort to shape MIS to individuals as well as to functions. This may seem like heresy in light of the coveted systems approach, and it may well be. Nevertheless, time and again the systems approach has failed to solve the problem because it has failed to take people into consideration. Perhaps the systems approach was misapplied or was never very strong on human factors in the first place. But the evidence that this portends an MIS flop is unmistakable.

What goes on in the project truly sets the stage for what will happen when the system goes into operation. Although this is so obviously important, it is often glossed over, with disastrous results.

User Information Barriers

People just are not willing to spend the time and energy to undertake a task that they know will be an ordeal unless there is some compelling reason to do so. Therefore, the first rule for MIS designers concerned with user interaction is: Keep it simple.

One of the most interesting and important human phenomena that an MIS designer must deal with is what we shall call the *pattern syndrome*. To illustrate it, let us consider an order-processing operation that predates the arrival of the MIS. Suppose that in this particular company it took an average of one week to receive shipment confirmation after placement of the order, a week and a half being the longest elapsed time and three days being the shortest. The man who, under this system, got three-day confirmation was elated. By the same token, he became annoyed when it took more than a week. This, then, is the pattern.

If you make these same order-processing functions part of an MIS, a new pattern is likely to be created. In it, new levels of service will be matched by the same sentiments. If 15-minute service becomes typical, this is what many people will consider standard.

That the user considers service under the new system bad when it takes 45 minutes to get his answer, whereas bad service used to mean a week and a half, is irrelevant. His way of reacting is the essence of the pattern syndrome.

This issue is being raised under MIS design because there is sometimes a tendency for systems men to make design judgments relative to two or more patterns. This can be a serious mistake. Where a design decision in one part of the system is made on the basis that certain information is provided much faster than it was in the past, you should concentrate on determining whether the service is consistent with the new operating environment. If it is not, you can expect complaints. In one system, for example, inventory information was immediately available in up-to-date form for nine out of ten stocking locations. For the one in ten, a report was issued once a day. This proved very upsetting to managers and was a source of complaints, even though all inventory had previously been reported once a day. As a consequence, MIS designers must view their work with an eye toward consistency and balance *within* the system.

Individual Psychological Considerations

The fine hand of management should be felt in working with or around the psychological side effects that arise in developing and implementing an MIS. No one is opposed to the careful consideration of human engineering at every stage, but in actual practice the attention is spotty. Even where there is hearty endorsement and support by management, the results are frequently poor because there was insufficient knowledge to guide such endeavors. MIS analysts reflect this in designs that fall short in their orientation to people. Habits, resistance to change, and behavioral influences are among the more important psychological considerations that must not be treated superficially.

Individual habits. Habits can be good, bad, or indifferent. But to ignore them is to invite problems. An important advantage of a habit is that creative mental processes can be invoked concurrently. Every systems man wants the users of his system to get into the habit of doing certain things that will make interrelationship as painless as possible. The disadvantages of habits are especially acute when they need to be dropped or changed in the name of progress.

MIS may have to be approached in a new key. Teaching management how to answer the questions that need to be answered is often the first step. The manager who insists on getting a report on every sales transaction may have a real need for it, or he may be reflecting conditions and an operating environment that once made this necessary. Perhaps he only wants access to any given transaction. For the man who really wants the power to get information on every transaction, but needs to be convinced that he can do without his full report, it may be best to provide both. This will permit the man to make a transition when he learns enough to persuade himself that he should.

It is vital for systems analysts and designers to look beyond the stated aims in designing MIS. Sometimes it may be desirable or necessary for the system to have seemingly redundant options.

Resistance to change. It is perfectly natural for people to do things the way they're in the habit of doing them and to resist changing their old ways and adopting new ones. Yet, as with all generalizations, this one does not always hold true. Many people do not change simply because they do not choose to change. In part, this may be because they are suspicious of anything new.

Most situations where resistance is encountered can be handled so as to gain user acceptance. In the case of an MIS, easier and more effective transitions can be accomplished where the system is developed and implemented in a planned series of steps. This fits a dual need. First, people difficulties can be minimized if they can adjust to the change over a period of time. Second, it is a sound way to proceed from a purely technical standpoint.

In cases where the system has been thrust upon users, acceptance of an MIS has been rare. The key to success is to have the people who are involved with the system find it to their liking. Systems management bears the responsibility for seeing that this happens.

Evolutionary psychology. A rejuvenated awareness of human factors on the part of computer managers has brought about a fairly recent change in the approach many companies are taking on massive computer-based systems. Popular now is the *evolutionary approach,* which is supplanting the old approach: freeze it and build it. Conveniently, this fits the several relevant practical aspects of MIS: availability of funds, growth in technical know-how, and the desirability to have users grow with the system.

In the casual view, evolution and the classical systems approach are competitive. In fact, they should be in harmony. One is saying, "Tackle a problem and devise solutions for it when it arises"; the other, "Plan for the problem so that it can be solved." Where there is polarization, progress will be so slow that it can be observed only over long periods of time. Reaction, not action, will often be the main thrust. This is not the brand of evolution that makes sense for MIS.

Influence of Communication on Behavior

> The language and variables of the technological system are quite unrelated in many instances to the language and variables of the social system, but more of us must become concerned with translating from one to the other if organizations are going to maintain the amount of receptivity required to continually introduce change into the existing establishment.

This is the way Lawrence K. Williams wrapped up his article, "The Human Side of a Systems Change," in the July–August 1964 *Systems & Procedures Journal*. The basic idea behind this statement is communication. At least part of the problem, as he points out, is gaining or maintaining receptivity. One receptivity prerequisite is the translation of technological systems language into that of the social system.

Time and time again, it has been proved that the best systems are those that give the people who live with them some say in their design and performance. Obviously, no one can have a say if he does not speak the language. Foremost among behavioral influences is communication. Individual attitudes about computer-based systems are too often founded on misconceptions, incomplete information, and ambiguity. To avoid these, MIS developers must bring new emphasis to the task of communicating.

Security and Privacy of Information

In the following sections, we will be concerned with threats to information privacy and some of the countermeasures to help insure the security of management information. Infiltration into the company's proprietary data bases is undertaken to improve the position or advantages of the infiltrator. The damage can vary greatly, depending on both the information and the person to whom it is disclosed. Among the reasons for seeking out confidential information are curiosity about salary records, a desire to play company politics, industrial espionage, vindictiveness, and fraud. In designing the MIS and relevant procedures, it should be obvious that preventive measures must be seriously considered.

The Problem of Confidentiality

Integrated systems like MIS are made possible by the ability to collect data and keep it stored at a central location. This centralized corporate data bank enables management to pull together the information needed to run the business effectively. Unhappily, having information collected and pooled in this manner can make it easier to secure vital information and use it for improper purposes. Add to this the fact that MIS capabilities will typically be shared by numerous users, many of them with access to various records via query terminals at geographically dispersed locations, and you have the makings of a security breach, or worse—that is, unless the system's design anticipates the threat by providing suitable deterrents and means of apprehension.

As has already been said, there are many reasons for breached security. Stories coming back from auditors, consultants, and private security investigators all emphasize the importance of preventive measures, which usually may be taken with relative ease. In most installations, unfortunately, the preventive steps taken have been grossly inadequate. People tell of cases where strangers off the street come into computer centers and walk off with magnetic tapes containing customer and employee information, including both the name and address files in one reported incident. One man bet an executive that he could even remove a piece of hardware without being stopped, and proceeded to remove two tape drives without being questioned, much less asked for credentials or authorization.

There have been untold instances where confidential credit or employment information has fallen into the hands of someone who had been refused credit or who had suspected that he was turned down for a job because of an unfavorable reference. Where such information was inaccurate, either through willful misrepresentation or through error, some subjects have collected five-figure amounts in out-of-court settlements. Now that certain legislation has obliged disseminators of information to permit subjects to know of derogatory reports and to correct errors in them, the potential liability is much lower except where gross negligence or willful misrepresentation is involved. Still, management should be deeply concerned.

Computer-related criminal acts are now a part of crime statistics. Alarming newspaper accounts of such acts have begun to raise considerable concern over the security of MIS, as in stories about computer embezzlement on Wall Street, in banks, in manufacturing, in a midwestern municipality where computer time was being sold by operators who pocketed the revenues, and the imminent danger of underworld infiltration.

A complaint often heard regarding computerized-information privacy versus the old manual systems is that dishonesty with the latter typically involved collusion between two or more employees, while illicit activity in the former often needs just one person. Detection with computers is therefore more difficult. Still, it is usually possible to devise procedures for checking and verification that, because they would force several people to conspire, greatly reduce the risk.

Kinds of Infiltration Threats

H. E. Petersen and R. Turn of the RAND Corporation have thoughtfully examined a number of types of threats and countermeasures concerning information privacy in their paper "System Implications of Information Privacy." Presented at the 1967 Spring Joint Computer Conference of the American Federation of Information Processing Societies, this paper appears in the *Conference Proceedings: Volume 30* published by Thompson Book Co. The definitions in this section are from Petersen and Turn.

The loss of information privacy is due to three causes: (1) accidental disclosure, (2) passive infiltration, and (3) active infiltration.

Accidental disclosures can result from program bugs, user errors, and hardware malfunctions. Any of these could result, for example, in confidential information's being displayed to an unauthorized party. It is assumed that in an accidental disclosure, the appearance of "interesting" information comes unexpectedly. Now that a person knows something he should not know, the question to consider is whether he can use it or pass it on to someone who can. Chances are that no serious consequence will follow, unless the recipient is dishonest or wants to cause trouble. The odds of the latter would seem to be low, and thus the company has a low risk. But of course there is no guarantee. Certainly, if accidental disclosures happen more than a few times, it may set the predisposed criminal mind to thinking.

Passive infiltration is deliberate. It is "listening in" to learn whether there is some information that might be of interest. If there should be, it may be assumed that the information will get into the wrong hands. This kind of infiltration can arise out of wiretaps or electromagnetic pickups placed on data communications networks. Electromagnetic radiation from terminal devices, particularly cathode-ray tube types, may permit the eavesdropper to tune in through the use of a signal pickup. In such instances, the content and often the user's interest in the communications is disclosed. Reportedly, the noise made by high-speed printers can be decoded. Then there are the simpler matters of physical security of the terminal locations, security of magnetic-tape storage and access, the shredding of printouts and carbon paper, and the proper disposal of typewriter ribbons, lockword authorizations, keys, identification cards, rotation and division of responsibility of personnel, and so forth.

Active infiltration is deliberate, direct entry into the system and its data bases through normal or seemingly normal means. Even though such infiltration may require exceptionally clever approaches, often it depends on an inside contact or uses inside information on how the MIS operates.

Using normal access procedures, an individual may browse in unauthorized data files in an attempt to relate certain pieces of information or to make unauthorized inquiries. Unauthorized access through normal procedures may also result where a spy masquerades as an authorized user upon learning the appropriate security keys through passive infiltration or other sources.

Loss of information privacy can occur through legitimate access made possible by privileged position in the MIS operation. People without a need to know but with the wherewithal to get at secret information may include programmers, operators, and maintenance and management personnel.

Then there are the undercover means of active infiltration where the system's security controls or normal checking functions are bypassed or are otherwise incapable of detecting invasion activities. Such means may involve the use of extraneous or altered programming that permits undetected entry into the system. Infiltration is also possible by virtue of "trap doors" in the system that, when discovered, offer a detection-free corridor into the processing.

Specially engineered terminals hooked into the MIS communication network may permit various kinds of sub rosa information leaks and modifications. Messages could be intercepted for the purpose of modifying or making substitutions for transmitted information. This may be termed a "piggyback" entry. Another kind of entry, called "between lines," arises when the infiltrator uses the idle or inactive time during a legitimate user communication to penetrate the system.

It is possible for the interloper to trap a user's sign-off transmission in order to continue operating, giving the appearance that the authorized user is still connected. Under the conditions where a particular user's transmission is tapped and otherwise used, the possible loss is confined to what the legitimate user is ordinarily authorized to access.

Countermeasures to Infiltration

One fundamental measure that is always taken to help prevent unauthorized access to the system and its data bases is the use of a password or other identification at the time the user signs on. In the more common applications, a user number will usually permit access. A more elaborate type of authorization, one in use on several MIS today, requires the user to give a permanent number (such as employee number) followed by a passkey number. Each user's passkey number is changed periodically in order to provide greater security.

Authentication of the identifying information provided by the user when he signs on may take any number of forms depending on the extent judged to be required. For example, if the individual's identification number and passkey matched those stored in the computer, the system might seek to authenticate this identification by asking the user for his date of birth. Research for more positive means of authentication is well along in one area that involves the identification of the human voice; this relates to earlier work done on voice-print identification.

Since it may be possible for a sophisticated infiltrator to set up an elaborate façade, a user might be required to ask the computer-processing complex to identify itself. That is, the user would be required to be sure "who" he is talking to. Or a hang-up and call-back procedure with special codes might be employed.

Where there have been unsuccessful attempts to gain access to the system, the MIS should provide for the monitoring and recording of such attempts, which may be investigated as they occur or at periodic intervals.

Assuming that the user has gained access to the system, his personal identifying number would indicate (within the system) the information to which he was permitted access and the functions he is authorized to activate. Here again, attempted violation of these authorizations should be detected by the monitoring function and dealt with as may be deemed appropriate. Operations that constitute violations may include illegal attempts to retrieve certain information, employing unauthorized functions such as copying files, attempts to write on protected data files, entering or deleting records on protected data files, and other instances of suspicious activity, such as extensive periods of use.

Having established the computer-to-user connection without difficulty, there are more sophisticated threats that relate to intrusion on the communication link itself. In fact, some of the provisions we will be discussing are used even where the threat of a communication tap does not exist.

A well-known technique used for many years in the military is *scrambling*. Very simply, this consists of rearranging characters of information either on the data file or in the message being transmitted so that an interceptor would not be able to make sense out of the message unless he knew how to unscramble it. Scrambling may involve a simple rearrangement or transposition of characters or may be based on a more elaborate formula.

Substitution may be used to make the message unintelligible to the interceptor. This involves translating some or all characters into completely different characters.

Additive techniques may also be used. Here, numeric data may be modified by adding or subtracting certain values. The message may also be rendered unintelligible through the use of extraneous characters inserted into the text of the message or record according to an insertion plan.

The determined infiltrator will, of course, attempt to crack the code.

Different transformations make it more or less difficult to accomplish this. Made elaborate enough, it may be impossible for the spy to discover the decoding rules, even with the help of a computer.

Ironically, systems designed for elaborate security are sometimes left open to invasion because simple things are overlooked. For example, passwords printed by a terminal have on occasion been left on a form hanging out of a wastebasket in full view. Such information should never be printed in the first place. On occasion, too, people have been allowed to look over the shoulder of a user entering a password, and documentation regarding decoding schemes has been left lying around unattended. Needless to say, it is pointless to spend money on elaborate controls if you do not seek to apply common sense in dealing with basic security provisions.

Figure 4-5, which appeared in the Petersen and Turn article referred to earlier, summarizes some of the points discussed.

Computerized MIS Design Aids

Given the size, scope, and complexity of most systems, designers are finding it increasingly difficult to cope with all the variables. Relationships between the many variables must be understood and brought to bear on design decisions. Even more important is the application of these relationships as they change with the passage of time, the idea being to project future situations so the capability of the MIS to deal with them is planned or built in initially.

Too often, designers have relied exclusively on their intuition for the answers to questions that could be subjected, at least in part, to quantitative analysis. The resultant designs, as a consequence, become less and less likely to be optimum as the complexities in bigger systems multiply. In terms of money and lost opportunities, such mistakes in judgment can be exceedingly costly. Their significance when companies were building systems that cost thousands or tens of thousands of dollars was not too worrisome. But make the same mistake in the MIS world of hundreds of thousands, millions, and tens of millions of dollars, and a whole new set of ground rules and penalties applies.

System Simulators

Simulation has been applied successfully to numerous industrial design problems. With equally impressive results, it is being applied more and more to MIS design problems. It is probably safe to say that no major MIS developed by the larger industrial corporations has been or is being designed without the help of simulation somewhere along the way.

FIGURE 4-5
Summary of Information Privacy Threats and Countermeasures

Countermeasure / Threat	Access Control (passwords, authentication, authorization)	Processing Restrictions (storage protect, privileged operations)	Privacy Transformations	Threat Monitoring (audits, logs)	Integrity Management (hardware, software, personnel)
Accidental: User error	Good protection, unless the error produces correct password	Reduce susceptibility	No protection if dependent on password; otherwise good protection	Identifies "accident prone"; provides post facto knowledge of possible loss	Not applicable
System error	Good protection, unless bypassed due to error	Reduce susceptibility	Good protection in case of communication system switching errors	May help in diagnosis or provide post facto knowledge	Minimizes possibilities for accidents
Deliberate, passive: Electromagnetic pickup	No protection	No protection	Reduces susceptibility; work factor determines the amount of protection	No protection	Reduces susceptibility
Wiretapping	No protection	No protection	Reduces susceptibility; work factor determines the amount of protection	No protection	If applied to communication circuits may reduce susceptibility
Waste Basket	Not applicable	Not applicable	Not applicable	Not applicable	Proper disposal procedures
Deliberate, active: "Browsing"	Good protection (may make masquerading necessary)	Reduces ease of obtaining desired information	Good protection	Identifies unsuccessful attempts; may provide post facto knowledge or operate real-time alarms	Aids other countermeasures
"Masquerading"	Must know authenticating passwords (work factor to obtain these)	Reduces ease of obtaining desired information	No protection if dependent on password; otherwise, sufficient	Identifies unsuccessful attempts; may provide post facto knowledge or operate real-time alarms	Makes it harder to obtain information for masquerading; since masquerading is deception, may inhibit browsers
"Between lines" entry	No protection unless used for every message	Limits the infiltrator to the same potential as the user whose line he shares	Good protection if privacy transformation changed in less time than required by work factor	Post facto analysis of activity may provide knowledge of possible loss	Communications network integrity helps
"Piggyback" entry	No protection but reverse (processor-to-user) authentication may help	Limits the infiltrator to the same potential as the user whose line he shares	Good protection if privacy transformation changed in less time than required by work factor	Post facto analysis of activity may provide knowledge of possible loss	Communications network integrity helps
Entry by system personnel	May have to masquerade	Reduces ease of obtaining desired information	Work factor, unless dependent on password and masquerading is successful	Post facto analysis of activity may provide knowledge of possible loss	Key to the entire privacy protection system
Entry via "trap doors"	No protection	Probably no protection	Work factor, unless access to keys obtained	Possible alarms, post facto analysis	Protection through initial verification and subsequent maintenance of hardware and software integrity
Core dumping to get residual information	No protection	Erase private core areas at swapping time	No protection unless encoded processing feasible	Possible alarms, post facto analysis	Not applicable
Physical acquisition of removable files	Not applicable	Not applicable	Work factor, unless access to keys obtained	Post facto knowledge from audits of personnel movements	Physical preventive measures and devices

Source: H. E. Petersen and R. Turn, "System Implications of Information Privacy," *AFIPS 1967 SJCC Proceedings*, Thompson Book Company, 1967.

As was said with regard to operations research, simulation uses a set of mathematical relationships, called the model, to describe the situation we wish to study. An example of such a relationship in MIS design could be a formula that provides the time to retrieve a record from a data base. Factors that enter into the relationship include time to search the index in which the address of the data record is found, time to position the reading head over the data record, time to transmit the record into main memory, time to execute the instructions associated with the retrieval, time delays because of contention over the device and transmission channel, time delays because of contention over central processing unit services, and overhead time losses of various kinds (such as software allocation functions).

The *variables,* which may be changed for each simulation, could relate to type and model of computer (instruction execution rates and channel speeds); data storage device type and model (head assembly movement, head switching, rotational delay, and data transfer rate times); number of starting entries and growth of the index; starting volumes of access service demands and growth multiplier; or multiplier to reflect additional work in accessing overflow records (if any).

Working with a simulator, it is possible to ascertain what conditions will cause the system to peak out in the event of overloads. Running times at selected points in the future can be obtained and the effects upon them resulting from hardware changes may be seen. Current and longer-range plans can then be made according to expectations relative to these variables.

On-line or real-time systems may be simulated in three parts, as was the case in a $30 million MIS developed by one major corporation. Part 1 was the *data management simulator,* which had to do with the operating characteristics of the data bases. Part 2 was the *communications simulator,* which had to do with the design and load characteristics of the network and the "front end" of the system to which the network was connected. Part 3 was the *processing simulator,* which pertained to the application systems programs, and particularly to expected processing times for various kind of service demands.

Not only were the three simulators designed to work independently for studying the particular parts of the system, but they could also be connected. When operated in concert, one or two simulators were used to "drive" the other. Hence, activity against the system, as described by the communications input, would be fed into the processing simulator, which in turn fed the data management simulator. From all appearances, the $30 million system is a resounding success. And simulation was evidently an important tool in bringing this system to fruition.

At the design stage, the best estimates obtainable are used in simulators where cold facts do not exist. However, the role of simulation does not cease at the end of formal design. Once the system becomes operational, cold facts and known trend data (say, for demand-volume levels) become available and simulation continues to be an extremely valuable technique. It discovers the vulnerable areas that need to be worked on and tuned up so that planned performances (as perhaps measured by response time) can be maintained. Priorities for such work can be established because the simulator tells not only what will happen but also when degradation or failure will occur.

We hasten here to point out that building a worthwhile simulator takes highly talented and specially educated analysts who, in addition to possessing systems knowledge, must be simulation experts in their own right. Among the most highly paid in the computer industry, such talent is rarely found in the average company. Outside consultants who specialize in this sort of thing are often used in such situations. In any complex MIS, simulation is costly. It is hard to even get started unless you are willing to spend in five figures. But it is quite cheap relative to the MIS investment. Depending on the specifics, an expenditure of 0.5 to 1 percent of the MIS budget on simulation studies can pay high dividends. For certain kinds of studies, it may be possible to take advantage of existing general-purpose simulation programs, cutting down the expense somewhat.

Network Design Programs

Aside from the telephone companies, most if not all major computer-hardware manufacturers have programs that will optimally design telecommunications networks. Often, the manufacturer will run these programs with data you supply and will return the results. But he will not allow the program to be taken out of house. The comprehensiveness of the analysis done by some of these network design programs is very impressive. One reportedly gives the best location for the computing center to minimize line and related costs. Data supplied to the programs typically include map coordinates for the locations of terminals, terminal operating speeds, and message traffic statistics.

Data-Base Design Programs

Mainly used to carry out calculations for the determination of data-storage requirements, access times, and breakpoints where additional capacity is needed, these programs have been designed by computer manufacturers as well as computer consultants.

Some proprietary data-base design programs reportedly help compute the optimum design, based on data-element use statistics. Considerations relating to the establishment of multiple records, optimum record lengths, and the use of separate files for batch and real-time processing could enter into the analysis. Hardware characteristics and the availability of packaged software with specified features could also have an effect on the final outcome.

Experimentation in Design Aids

The use of linear programming and its extensions for MIS design work is one of the more promising areas of investigation. Much lies ahead in the effort to describe such design problems as have the properties appropriate for linear programming. For organizations having access to operations research analysts, it could be rewarding to assign a task force the job of determining how linear programming might be used to arrive at an optimum MIS design or hardware configuration or both.

Tools for Evaluating Hardware Configuration

Aids to assist planners in evaluating computer hardware configuration have been developed both by computer-hardware manufacturers and by computer consulting firms. These aids consist of one or more programs that calculate various measures of computing power and relate them to cost. Input to such programs would include variables describing the jobs to be run on the system (for example, number, growth rate, and record size of input transactions), and hardware-configuration identifiers. The evaluation program uses the hardware identifiers to extract speed and cost data from its catalog. Job running times for specific hardware are then computed on the basis of input, output, and processing requirements.

Such analysis is intended to show throughput rates (transactions per minute) and price performance (cost per transaction) at various input-output volume levels. It tells us whether the configuration *can* do the job in the time allocated for its completion. Price performance has relevance for the purpose of getting the best buy only when the throughput requirements are met or exceeded.

Systems measurement programs are also available from a number of independent companies for the purpose of isolating inefficiencies in operational systems and indicating means of improvement.

5

Data-Base Management

DATA-BASE management concerns the record-keeping system of MIS. Exactly what shape a particular data base will take depends largely on what the MIS is being designed to do. For example, if we are developing a communications-based MIS that requires fast response, we will need to design our data base for fast access and in such a way that the system can get to a desired record without searching through half the file to find it.

A data base may be considered a reservoir from which user personnel in the organization, as well as computer application systems, draw information needed for decisions and general operation of the business. The outstanding characteristic of a data base is its design, which permits a wide spectrum of uses to be accommodated. In most cases, a data base will be further identified as to the primary activities and functions with which it is concerned. For example, we might have a customer data base, product data base, physical-movements data base, and personnel data base.

Some of the many reasons that could be cited to explain the growing trend toward the use of a data-base concept, rather than files oriented exclusively to a particular computer application, include the following:

- It minimizes the carrying and updating of duplicate and redundant information.
- It has the ability to pull together and integrate related data from various applications, as the need arises.
- It provides useful indexes and cross-referencing on selected information.
- It improves the accuracy, control, validation, and security of information.
- It eases the burden and expense of programming by taking over common file processing and by making available user-invoked functions.
- It speeds up response to user inquiries and provides direct user communication with the system.

All of the company's data bases go to make up what is sometimes called the corporate data bank. Under this approach, we are attempting to provide the information resources for integrated decisions, which, by definition, require the use of multiple streams of data. Yet because MIS will be built up over a number of years in steps or phases, we need data bases so organized that a thread or multiple threads will tie them together.

Within any given data base, the logical organization of information tends to be uniform in content with respect to the function, the activity, and perhaps the operating division of the company it relates to. The concept of a data base is a logical, and not necessarily a physical, one. Paperwork filing systems are logically as well as physically related, and therein may lie certain difficulties.

Ordinary office files have grouped together those records which are logically related. Suppose we take a typical management request for information, such as "Please bring Mr. Jones's personnel records." Here, the secretary would go to the file identified as Personnel and pick out Jones's records, probably by locating his folder, which would be in alphabetical order. If the personnel file was in employee-number sequence, which had no relationship to employee name, the secretary would have to begin a search. Without other information about Jones and without an index, she would have to go through the personnel records and look at the name in each folder until she found Jones's. At least the search would have been narrowed down to a logical grouping: personnel. Obviously, if we had inventory records and customer records mixed with personnel records in the same file, our secretary would have to spend a great deal more time finding the records we need. This is sometimes true of correspondence files.

All of us have had the experience of filing away information and then, on attempting to retrieve it, finding that we have forgotten just where. Perhaps the needed information is in one of three places, whereupon we face a search. But perhaps we originally had three copies of the information filed away in each of the three locations. Although this means keeping redundant information, we can take comfort in knowing that the file we pick will contain what we need. Thus, if we wanted to see information on all industrial engineers over 50 years of age, we could have one file containing just these records. The same records may be found in the personnel file, the industrial engineers' file, the project file, the bonus eligibility file, the 15-years-or-less-to-retirement file, and so on. Ludicrous as this may sound, there are analogous cases in industry. For example, one aerospace company supposedly has 15 different personnel forms that have to be completed in order to bring a man on board. Over 50 percent of the information is said to be duplicated on each form. It should come as no surprise, then, when systems analysts tell us that 200-odd documents are used in the course of producing and selling a fairly simple product. In some cases, analysts have reported that information duplications exceed 70 percent.

Data: The Vital Ingredient

A manager's effectiveness is a function of two factors: the man himself and the information available to him for the purpose of managing. Certainly, the interdependence between these two factors is strong. A bad manager making decisions based on good information and a good manager making decisions based on bad information will both probably make bad decisions.

Competitive Differences

Almost by definition, competitive businesses have similar capabilities. Let us suppose that it were somehow possible to have the management of Company A take over the running of Company B and have B's management run A. Again, assuming A and B are competitors, the switch in management might have little effect on the competitive balance. In fact, all of us have seen cases where top executives with outstanding accomplishments are lured away by a competitor and within a short time record similar outstanding accomplishments in the new environment. The executive's former company, in turn, vigorously pursues the task of finding a replacement to restore the competitive balance. While this canceling effect does not always hold true, it is nevertheless useful to contemplate as it relates to management information. Now, if we declare that management *potential* on both sides is equivalent, the marginal effect of better management information, on one side or the other, can be dramatic.

Somewhere, every company has the data it needs for improving the basis for a great many decisions. Data that are not now available can be made available after the need has been established, but to start out it is prudent to look at MIS in the light of what you already have.

Accounting systems exist in every company and can be used for collecting data pertinent to management decision making. Although reasonably accurate, data used for accounting purposes are typically concerned exclusively with money activity, and management uses these data at a summarized level.

Inasmuch as accounting is undertaken by every business, we might build on our earlier argument by saying that it does not provide a company with a competitive advantage, but is instead an equalizing device. Another way of putting it is to say that it contributes to keeping the company's position from deteriorating but does not improve it.

Developing a Data Base as a Hedge

Should you develop a data base just to hedge the bet against the unknown? At least one executive has expressed his opinion about MIS in this light. A younger man who at the time was vice-president of marketing for a New Jersey industrial company, he said, "I think we ought to be working on management-oriented data base just as a hedge against competition, if for no other reason." He went on to say that he was not too sure what it would do for him specifically.

"But," he said, "we have all kinds of 'goodies' in our computerized accounting systems, which I could put to good use if I could get my hands on them." When asked what he might do with these data, the vice-president described a general scheme he thought would improve sales and profit margin at the same time. The idea was to use postal ZIP codes (or groups of codes) to define sales territories. Within each area he would distribute nonassignable costs. This would include assigning most of his advertising to each area according to its proportion of the previous quarter's sales.

Doing this, he said, and relating sales costs to revenue in each group, would give him information as to which areas were highly profitable. These areas, he said, would then be given more attention by the marketing force to stimulate the growth of additional high-profit business. He also said that the analysis would be done regularly so that shifts in demand levels and profitability could be acted on as they occurred. Some day, he indicated, profitability analysis on each customer should be undertaken.

Using Existing Systems as Data Sources

"Existing systems," as used here, is a term meaning any or all computerized systems now operational or close to being implemented. Further, the existing systems to which we want to direct attention are ones that have relevance to the MIS you are contemplating. One category in evidence everywhere is accounting systems. In addition to accounting per se, many other systems directly relate to accounting for the purposes of planning and control. In manufacturing, for instance, an accounts-receivable (accounting) system is related to sales analysis and forecasting (control and planning). Having the data generated in the latter system, we can readily see, can serve as a partial basis for a production planning system, which, depending on the product line, can be linked to an engineering system. An elaborate inventory management system could be linked to all the systems we have named so far and others besides.

To take one view of what is happening in the process, there is a sort of cascading action with strong data dependencies between systems. But also observe that each functional area contributes information that is exclusive and unique to the limited purposes it serves. Whether existing systems can be used as data sources for MIS depends to a great extent on whether they were designed to "grow" to accommodate future needs. If they were not, you can expect to get into some messy situations.

Systems currently in operation, in all but a limited number of cases, do not have what it would take for them to be a foundation on which to "grow" an MIS data base. This is not hard to understand, since the development of these systems was fragmented to start with, and no one was really considering whether they would fit together.

Changes in management's philosophy about computerized systems development also must be taken into account. Up until recent times, computer applications were not given the serious thought traditionally given other capital investments. Factors such as useful life, obsolescence, maintenance, and even depreciation, were just not considered. Almost everyone was ignorant about the reality of such things as applied to systems.

Companies that have attempted to somehow fit pieces of existing systems together have met with great complications in the vast majority of cases. More modest MIS, however, developed a little at a time, have been accomplished. But these are in the minority. Those who have managed to get something out of their patchwork-quilting effort have gained certain advantages, but often the original shortcomings have come back to plague them. There is often a low margin of safety working against you in ventures involving existing systems, which necessitates great caution. A certain analogy can be drawn from the concept of a *safety factor,* which, while it increases the cost of the system, buys a lot in return.

Is Your Safety Factor Adequate?

No one would be willing to trust his life to airplanes and bridges with low safety factors, the odds of failure being unacceptable even though low. Obviously, added safety costs more, but it is the only means by which many things become practical.

Application systems and their programs typically have had what we might call a low safety factor to begin with, one that was barely acceptable. Safety factors with such a system decreases with the passage of time because the system is continually being patched and modified to accommodate changes in business requirements. As the number of patches increases, the risk of breakdown grows exponentially. In addition, the difficulty of making each successive patch tends to increase. Soon, perhaps three, four, or five years later, the system becomes impossible to live with and needs to be redesigned and reprogrammed.

This phenomenon is fairly well known these days, and many companies are giving serious study to ways and means by which to combat it. However, the relevance of this to using existing systems to provide the data bases for MIS should be clear: Do not build on something that is on the verge of collapsing of its own weight. Admittedly, not every company has this problem in the same degree. Most do have a very serious problem in this regard and are well advised to steer clear of using this as a foundation for MIS.

Once, for example, a $100 million distribution operation came close to the brink of collapse because the data source for its small MIS—an antiquated computerized accounting system—was malfunctioning every few days. Within a short time, an all-out crash effort, to the tune of $800,000, was put into developing a new accounting system. This system temporarily cured the problems, but within six months, signs of the same old problems began to appear. Why? Mainly because the crash effort made many of the same mistakes that caused the collapse of the system being replaced. The answer is to minimize their occurrence and severity through adequate systems planning, both initial planning and follow-on planning.

Early Thinking About Future Needs

Once there is a commitment to start anew, it is vital to see to it that the shortsightedness and mistakes of the past are not repeated. There will be plenty of opportunities to make new mistakes. A problem already mentioned several times had to do with the growth orientation of an MIS and therefore of its data bases. A major area that should receive early attention is the matter of what data need to be collected.

As a result of studying and deciding on the characteristics and applications of the MIS, certain known data requirements will have to be satisfied in the overall design. The data bases designed will account for three data categories of immediate concern to the new MIS.

1. *Data used now* for administration, control, and decision making.
2. *Data available now* and needed for the new MIS.
3. *Data unavailable now* but needed for the new MIS.

A fourth and fifth category should also be given serious consideration. They are ones that can prove troublesome later on:

4. *Data available now but not needed* for the new MIS, as conceived.
5. *Data unavailable now and not needed* for the new MIS, as conceived.

Since we admit that these data are not needed for the MIS, as conceived, why should we be interested in them? The reason is evolution, wherein we are concerned with the system's flexibility and adaptability to the needs that will become evident as the business changes. In truth, few computerized business systems of any kind are static. Revisions, modifications, and extensions always seem to be needed. One of the factors that enter the picture is data planning.

Data Planning

The data needs and collection problems of the more distant future need to be scrutinized with the idea of planning their solution in the here and now. It is not possible to solve 100 percent of the problems, however. First, not all will be recognized, and second, it is not prudent to solve all those we do recognize. Among those that can be identified, it should be possible to gain a sense of their importance. Of course, a portion of this planning is pure conjecture. Over the long haul, some of the prognostications will be realized, others will not. Here we are thinking about new data requirements resulting from adding new applications as well as upgrading the level of sophistication of the original ones.

The suggestion that MIS provide for some things that "might be" is based on two kinds of experiences. These experiences were with past systems that had been expected to accommodate business dynamics through evolution. First, if needed data are not provided for possible needs in the future, it seems to cost ten times as much to modify the system to include them as compared with building in such data originally. For the most part, it is relatively easy and cheap to put some "fat" on a system when it is being built. Second, a bare-bones system discourages evolution because adjusting it to accommodate new needs usually gets quite expensive and messy. Eventually, this leads to the replacement of the entire system. Obsolescence considerations are especially important when looking at the question of how much fat to add. Replacing systems every four years or so, as has become customary with past systems, is usually an economically impossible alternative in the case of MIS. Data, as we said, are one of the major factors in this.

Doubtless there will be arguments against putting extra data and collection mechanics in the system, if they have no known immediate use. And, to some extent, this is valid. However, the common argument that the system is flexible enough to handle future possibilities and that they therefore need not be built in does not stand the test of experience.

Let us be clear that we are not talking about developing completely generalized systems that will accommodate anything and everything. Even if such a thing were possible, its cost would be prohibitive. Instead, MIS should be planned and built with an eye toward longer-range data needs that, obviously, cannot be perfectly formulated. The fact that imperfection is inevitable need not, however, cause us to turn our backs on the whole matter.

Checkpoints for Data-Base Development

Data-base designers will invariably find themselves faced with a host of considerations common to most management information systems.

The way in which the data base is organized and the specific tasks to be accomplished are predicated upon what the MIS is supposed to do—that is, the nature of the services it is to offer. Whether a service is provided on-line in real time or off-line in batch processing will have an important influence on the data-base design approach taken. The majority of the questions that crop up in trying to settle on an approach revolve around the following 18 points.

1. *Content.* What kinds, levels, and volumes of information are required? What growth and changes must be anticipated?

2. *Service traffic.* How many "service orders" are to be processed per unit of time (average and peak), and what growth is expected in each category?

3. *User turnaround time requirements.* What must the time span (average, worst acceptable) be between user interrogation and system response for the various types of service? (Partly a function of factors other than data-base design and organization.)

4. *Query and response ordering.* What priorities are associated with each type of service order, how sensitive or critical are the requirements, and how will they affect operational efficiency?

5. *Contention for data-base access.* When operating at or near peak traffic rates, does the turnaround time go up to the worst acceptable? How often will this happen, and what effects will growth have?

6. *Input-output device and channel speeds.* Having made the appropriate calculations, will the devices tentatively selected be fast enough to accommodate reasonable growth? What alternatives are open: putting key data on faster devices with remainder on bulk storage? What functions can be accomplished by the channel?

7. *Programming languages and operating systems.* Do the proposed languages and operating system support the data-base management requirements, hardware, and special features (if any)? What decrease in efficiency will be experienced in using generalized software?

8. *Indexes to the data base.* Which of the services should be supported by indexes, and what kind should be used? What special software is needed to create, maintain, and employ multiple indexes?

9. *Inquiry modes and information retrieval techniques.* How does a user inquire and interact with a data base? Should data-base subsets be created for specialized use? Will formatted and coded transactions or conversational-mode input be used? What are the tradeoffs (development costs versus user convenience and acceptance)?

10. *File organization methods.* What alternatives are open (indexed sequential, direct access, combinations)?

11. *Validity checking, input editing, update controls.* What measures will be taken to maintain the integrity of the data base? What data elements may be modified and by whom? How are such updates monitored and checked for correctness?

12. *Expandability.* Are there physical storage limitations, such that in the near future the entire system will have to be redesigned for completely new hardware? What limitations are imposed by software? How flexible is the approach in meeting new demands in a dynamic environment?

13. *User education.* How easy or difficult will it be for the user to work with the system? Are rules few in number and easy to remember? Does the system help the user by providing mnemonic aids and understandable messages?

14. *Data entry and response devices.* Does the system take advantage of the salient features of terminals to obtain effective user interaction? Has the nature of the user's problem been viewed in the light of what capabilities are available (for example, typewriter terminal, video display, audio response, strip printer, or combinations of the foregoing used together)?

15. *Backup, recovery, and controls.* What techniques and procedures are used to insure that, should there be a program error, hardware malfunction, or other event that destroys the data base, there is a means of recovery with minimal interruption and cost? Are there suitable controls to indicate when a malfunction has occurred? Can the system be operated in degraded modes?

16. *Security.* What measures and techniques have been employed to insure against access to data base (directly or indirectly) by unauthorized persons? Have the precautions and security measures (such as passkeys) been designed so they will offer valid protection with the passage of time?

17. *Computer manufacturer assistance.* What design assistance, special techniques, consultation, packaged software, and experiences can be brought to bear?

18. *Requirements for data base interfaces with existing systems.* Is extensive reprogramming or additional programming necessitated by providing existing systems with the capability to access the new data base? Are data quality and validity controls consistent among the systems having updating capability? Where are the weak links?

Data-Base Requirements Analysis

Part of an analysis to determine user information requirements is the problem of determining what all the facts being collected mean. The sheer weight of the information may obscure its relevance to the design of an MIS —that is, unless some effort goes into getting it organized. When all is said and done, you really do need to know what goes in, how it is processed, and what comes out. Seeing clearly the relationships between the three factors is the MIS designer's task. But its complexity can be less of a problem if the conclusions of the systems analysts are logically presented. Some format for doing just this would seem to be advantageous.

User Information Requirements Grid

A user's information requirement is a cluster of information set forth in a way that suits him. At the user's level we are concerned with the uses to which information is put, and we must therefore be concerned with a packaged product that fits the intended use. A monthly balance sheet for the company controller is an example of such a product. We call it a requirement. Many ingredients go into such a requirement, and we will be getting to them shortly. Let us now direct attention to the major characteristics that further define a single information requirement. The codes shown alongside each subfactor will be used in a later illustration.

Requirement Factors	*Code*
1. *User identification*	
President	2
Vice-president–finance	4
Sales manager	6
Salesman	8
2. *Use of information*	
Decision	2
Approval required	4
Review and comment	6
3. *Form of information*	
Printed tabular	2
Printed text	4
Graphic drawing	6
Visual display	8
Audio	10
Microfilm	12
4. *Time demand*	
Scheduled: every X* hours	2
Scheduled: daily	4
Scheduled: weekly on Monday	6
Unscheduled in real time:	
Turnaround time X*	8
Query in non-real-time:	
Response time X*	10
5. *Volume* (projected and keyed to time demand, such as statements per month)	
A demand units	2
C demand units	4
E demand units	6
6. *Location of demand*	
Executive office	2
Branch sales office	4
Customer facility	6
Warehouse	8
Mobile unit	10
Plant	12
7. *Stimulus*	
Inquiry	2
Out-of-control condition	4
Schedule	6
Transmittal request (message)	8
Exception	10
Breakdown or emergency	12

* (Every unique X would have a different code.)

Keeping in mind that the preceding factors need to be understood for each of a number of information requirements, it will be useful to tabularize them in a way that aids in visualizing the total picture. Depending on what factors you want to analyze, there are a number of ways to collate the facts.

First, however, it is wise to establish an all-inclusive representation. We call ours the information requirement–characteristics grid; its form is shown in Figure 5-1. Entries in the grid are codes previously listed alongside requirement factors.

Having set up this grid, it becomes possible to do a certain amount of systems analysis by selecting and extracting for further examination those requirements having characteristics in common—as, say, a particular time demand (perhaps all queries with ten minutes or less response time).

Note that the grid in Figure 5-1 provides for a unique set of characteristics for each requirement, which is usually adequate. However, there may be a question in certain cases where requirements are identical in all respects but one. For example, the president and the vice-president in charge of

FIGURE 5-1
Information Requirement — Characteristics Grid

		USER INFORMATION REQUIREMENT						
		R_1	R_2	R_3	R_4	R_5	. . .	R_n
CHARACTERISTICS	User Identification	6	6	6	8	8	. . .	4
	Use of Information	2	4	4	4	2	. . .	6
	Form of Information	6	2	2	2	3	. . .	6
	Time Demand	6	4	4	10	4	. . .	6
	Volume	2	2	2	2	2	. . .	2
	Location of Demand	4	4	4	6	10	. . .	2
	Stimulus	6	10	4	2	2	. . .	6

finance may receive the same report. Such cases are treated as separate requirements during analysis.

Once the requirements have been assembled in grid form, you should have a clear and comprehensive picture of what the system has to be able to produce. The next question you might want to ask is how to get there. Certainly, one part of the answer has to do with source data.

Data-Requirements Grid

An examination of any information requirement will show that it is composed of one or more pieces of data. In unearthing MIS data requirements, we will be concerned with every unique data element that shows up on an output. If unit price, quantity, and total were on the output, we would consider this to be three pieces of data, even though we know one was calculated from the other two.

Among the tasks related to the analysis of data is the construction of a reference table showing what data appear on which information output. This would be a true input-versus-output table, were it not for the fact that certain of the data are calculated or otherwise developed.

FIGURE 5-2
Data Element — Information Association Grid

		DATA ELEMENTS						
		D_1	D_2	D_3	D_4	D_5	. . .	D_n
INFORMATION REQUIREMENT	R_1	1	10	0	30	0	. . .	0
	R_2	1	3	0	0	20	. . .	4
	R_3	2	0	7	0	0	. . .	0
	R_4	0	0	0	50	0	. . .	50
	R_5	10	0	8	0	1	. . .	0
	. . .	. . .	. . .	. . .	. . .	. . .	. . .	. . .
	R_n	3	8	4	0	0	. . .	10

Entries in grid are number of appearances.

Figure 5-2 is an example of such a table, which is here called a data element–information association grid. The box entries indicate the number of appearances of the data element shown at the head of a column. One use of this table is in searching for possible redundant information requirements and also those that might be combined into a single requirement. The grid in Figure 5-2 shows that the data elements used to satisfy R_3 are identical to those for R_5, except that R_5 has one additional data element (D_5). Where such conditions are in evidence, we would examine the information requirements–characteristics grid to see whether a combined requirement could be created. In the case of R_3 and R_5, a cursory examination of the requirements of each seems to rule out the possibility.

Another use for the grid in Figure 5-2 is in finding out how data elements rank in terms of demand—that is, based upon number of appearances in requirements rows.

With movable rows (cut the grid apart), it is possible to arrange them so that the greatest density of appearances shows up around the upper left-hand corner. After the rows are fixed, the cut-apart columns can be moved to make the upper left-hand corner even more dense. When this arrangement has been accomplished, it is possible to focus more easily on the problems previously mentioned: possible redundancy, opportunities for combination, and the question of which data are in heaviest demand.

There are any number of ways to integrate and relate the rows and columns in the two types of grids discussed so far in order to answer the specific questions that arise during analysis—for example, the question of which data are required for a particular time demand characteristic. The answer could be part of the basis for determining which data should be directly accessible on-line.

Source-Data Analysis Grid

Previous sections have more or less assumed that the data needed to satisfy a particular information requirement will somehow be made available. But without proper analysis this may not be so.

If the manager of engine overhaul at an airline wanted a weekly report of flying hours for each engine in service, he would assume that flying hours would be reported at least once a week. If it happened that the data were available only once a month, he would have a problem: wanting information before it was available. Actually, the problem would be that of the MIS analyst, whose responsibility it would be to reconcile the situation by appropriate means. The same would be true for a situation where the information was generated faster than it was used—for example, collecting all flying hours daily when they were needed only weekly.

There is also the question of methods by which to get data from their point of origin to their users. In fact, there are a number of attributes of source-data elements, the major ones of which are included in the following list. Codes appearing alongside each are used in a later illustration.

Attributes	*Codes*
1. *Source*	
Input: business form	1
Input: user making request	3
Observation or measurement	5
Another computer or business machine	7
Data base	9
Table	11
Resultant of processing	13
2. *Time availability*	
Scheduled: every X* hours	1
Scheduled: daily	3
Scheduled: weekly or Mondays	5
Unscheduled: availability time X*	7
Unscheduled: always available	9
Unscheduled: only when demanded	11
3. *Volume* (projected and keyed to time availability, such as number of savings account deposits—dollar amounts—per minute or number of account balances always on file)	
B available units	1
D available units	3
F available units	5
4. *Location of source*	
Data base on computer	1
Executive office	3
Branch sales office	5
Customer facility	7
Warehouse	9
Mobile unit	11
System	13
Plant	15
5. *Processing required*	
None—used as available or as entered	1
Summarization	3
Logical and/or arithmetic	5

* (Every unique X would have a different code.)

Attributes	*Codes*
6. *Field size (maximum)*	
5 characters	1
10 characters	3
15 characters	5

In exploring the source-data needs to satisfy information demands, it once again becomes advantageous to represent this in the form of a grid. The version of this shown in Figure 5-3 is identified as the data element–attribute grid.

Construction of this kind of grid permits many of the relationships between attributes to be studied. As was the case with the grids previously discussed, the rows and columns of the data element–attribute grid may be arranged to show more clearly what serves our purpose. We might, for example, want to know what data originate from customer facilities and how they relate to time availability attributes. As a result, it may be appropriate to

FIGURE 5-3
Data Element — Attribute Grid

		DATA ELEMENTS						
		D_1	D_2	D_3	D_4	D_5	. . .	D_n
ATTRIBUTES	Source	3	9	9	9	13	. . .	13
	Time Availability	11	9	9	9	11	. . .	11
	Volume	1	5	5	5	1	. . .	1
	Location of Source	5	1	1	1	13	. . .	13
	Processing Required	1	1	1	1	3	. . .	5
	Field Size	3	1	5	3	3	. . .	3

examine ways of consolidating data, or planning the use of certain kinds of terminals to facilitate data transmittal.

A number of important factors can be studied by combining one or both of the two grids described previously with the data element–attribute grid. For example, if we were to position the time availability attributes (for each data element required to satisfy a particular requirement) alongside the time demand characteristics, we would be able to see whether the availability can satisfy the demand. A similar kind of verification can be made to see whether there are a sufficient number of data elements available to satisfy appearances on a particular output requirement. For larger MIS, computer programs can be developed to manipulate these grids in order to facilitate analysis.

The Question of Demand Priorities

Not all demands are of equal importance in the typical organization. A rule for determining priorities that is valid some of the time is to base them on the time demand. This assumes that the more frequent a requirement, the more important it is. Certainly, there will be overriding conditions, such as the once-a-month demands of a board of directors in session.

The priorities of most concern from the standpoint of designing an MIS to satisfy them are necessarily those that are most time-sensitive. Summoning the needed data, which also have time factors related to their availability, is admittedly just as big a problem. However, the methods illustrated in the preceding few sections can be used to help overcome such problems by helping systems analysts focus on prime issues.

To reiterate, it should be the function of the systems analyst to nail down the characteristics of the required results and determine the attributes of the source data to satisfy those results, as well as to define the processing that must take place in the middle. Many of the important conclusions drawn, with respect to the properties of the MIS in the offing, should be readily discernible to any interested management.

The next section hits the highlights of designing the data base. It assumes as known quantities the information demands to be satisfied, the processing required, and the source data to be collected.

Designing a Data Base

Conceptually, a data base is designed in three phases (assuming you have decided what the MIS is to accomplish): (1) data-base identification, (2) data-base content specifications, and (3) data standards development.

Data-Base Identification

Data-base identification means specifying those data that belong to a logical grouping and naming each such grouping, as customers, stockholders, products, sales, distribution, employees, vendors, production, and so forth. In identifying data groups, it is often helpful to think first in terms of the resources the MIS is concerned with and then identify the major functions under those headings. In many instances, the activities within the major functions automatically imply data bases. Looking at the money resource of the business, we can see many major functions and therefore data-base requirements: accounts receivable, accounts payable, securities and debt investments, real estate, capital investment, and so on.

From this rather painless start, the task of identifying data sets becomes progressively more difficult as you try to decide what goes with what. Does inventory, for example, enter into distribution and marketing as well as product information? The best advice here is to ignore possible overlaps and redundance for the moment. They will be resolved later. Again, try to think mainly about logical collections of data about resources, things, and functions the MIS relates to. It should be noted that the design of a data base is an iterative process, meaning that we will have to return to and go through this phase a number of times.

Data-Base Content Specifications

The next phase is to define the contents of each data base. The truly formal definition of each data element is reserved for the third phase; for now we are concerned with a much less rigorous definition. Very simply, the idea is to name each data element that you believe belongs within a given data set.

Partitioning information in a data set is a useful way to view the hierarchical relationships that exist in most data bases. For a particular data base, there are four major breakdowns that may be used: (1) logical record, (2) segment, (3) field, and (4) subfield.

To illustrate what this means in an *employee data base,* let us assume that all information concerning an employee is pulled together. In the category of *logical records,* we might decide on the following:

1. *Indicative record.* Descriptive information about the employee.
2. *Work history and evaluation record.* Information pertaining to jobs the employee has held in the organization.
3. *Payroll record.* Payroll accounting information, such as taxes paid year to date.

4. *Skills inventory record.* Skill codes, years of experience, and dates of last contact.

To show what a *segment* means, let us use the indicative record. Examples of segments within this record could be name, address, education, social security number, and date of birth.

The name segment would include last name, first name, and middle name. In this case, these three *fields* would be the lowest entities with which the MIS would be concerned. However, if we consider the education segment, we might have, in addition to other information, dates attended for each institution. The fields pertaining to dates attended would be "from" and "to."

From and *to* might have the subfields *month* and *year*. In this case, these two *subfields* would be the lowest entities with which the MIS data base would be concerned.

One way to show these hierarchical relationships in defining the contents of a data base is to prepare an indented list, where each indentation position defines one of the four levels within a data set (logical record, segment, field, and subfield). Such a list would have the following format:

Data Base Name 1
 Logical record 1
  Segment 1
   Field 1
    Subfield 1
    Subfield n
   Field n
    Subfield 1
    Subfield n
  Segment n
   Field 1
    Subfield 1
    Subfield n
   Field n
    Subfield 1
    Subfield n

 Logical record n
  Segment 1
   Field 1
    Subfield 1
    Subfield n
   Field 2
    Subfield 1
    Subfield n

Segment n
 Field 1
  Subfield 1
  Subfield n
 Field n
  Subfield 1
  Subfield n

Data Standards Development

Although data standards are here said to be the third phase in designing a data base, there is a valid argument to the effect that this is a continuing task and does not occur at any one point in time. And it may be equally valid to insist that standards be fairly well developed prior to the actual designing of the data base. As we mentioned earlier, the design of a data base is an iterative process, where standards and specifications grow into being in the course of recycling. However, if, for whatever reason, you should happen to have such standards and specifications beforehand, this is ideal.

Often standards arise out of the effort and discussion that go into data-base design. MIS analysts and users will either come to an agreement or negotiate one as to what should prevail. Because consensus gives rise to the most practical standards, discussion is a must. A warning: No matter how you go about getting standards, they must be complete when the data-base design is complete. If you do not have this matter in tow by now, the odds are that you never will. And it will plague the programming and all subsequent systems work.

Though the need for standards is universally conceded, they do not always get a really serious review. Few of us care that shoe sizes in Italy and the United States are not the same unless we are buying and selling shoes internationally.

In MIS, we cannot afford the conversions from one system to another, even supposing that uniformity and conversion rules existed. For the most part, uniformity does not exist in company nomenclature; indeed, we are fortunate if we find standards within an operating area of the company.

Since MIS implies integration of some kind, we have to provide a means of conveying facts that will insure that the meaning at the point of departure is the same at the arrival point. In one company the terms, "location 28," "plant 28," "Pittsburgh facility," "flat work mill," "sheet mill," and "Sampson Street factory" all meant the same thing. Even in the limited environment of the division concerned with these terms, there were people to whom "location 28" meant nothing (it was used in accounting) and others to whom "Sampson Street factory" meant nothing.

Another difficulty is the resolution of ambiguous terms, such as "shipping location." Does it mean origin or destination? In one company it meant either, depending on who was using it.

Integrated systems, where marketing, production, distribution, planning, finance, accounting, and other functions come together, need standards if there is to be clear communication. In computer work this is especially critical because terms are often abbreviated. One insurance accounting system, for example, used "ACTNO," "ACT#," and "CUSTNO" within a single system to mean the same thing. Past systems could get by with this because the physical location of the data within a record was always known. More modern systems are using data bases to achieve integration, and the programs that access the data are written without referring to physical location. Instead, they use a label or data name only. Using a standard label is the easiest and least expensive way to enable everyone to use the data, although we could cross-reference the current vernacular. Then, we have to accommodate "CUST#" and dozens of others as they are used.

MIS can be built, at great expense, to make translations of information labels from one form to another. Sometimes called "filtering," this translation is provided for in some conversational-mode designs through the use of an automated glossary of synonyms. However, if people and not computers need to communicate with one another, we face significant hardships resulting from variations.

Let us now examine the issue of data standards and specifications in terms of a format and certain ground rules. The scheme illustrated in Figure 5-4, a data standards glossary, encompasses the important points, so no further comment is necessary.

Data-Base Structure

Predictably, the efficient handling of large masses of directly accessible information has become an important area of study for MIS developers. Some years ago, when most systems used only magnetic tape as the mass storage medium, the possible approaches to data storage were quite limited. Since, at that time, the storage of data was not particularly critical, any of a variety of simple methods could satisfy the need at a fairly low cost. These methods still exist and are completely valid under appropriate circumstances. However, we face new and significant challenges concerning the organization of directly

FIGURE 5-4
Data Standards Glossary

DATA STANDARDS GLOSSARY

DATA FIELD NAME:	PAGE	REVISION NO.	DATE
	BY:		Date Last Revision

MNEMONIC LABEL: ________________ SECURITY LEVEL (circle): 0 1 2 3 4

CHARACTERISTIC (check):

☐ C – character (8 bit)	☐ E – floating pt. (fullwd.)
☐ Z – zoned decimal	☐ D – floating pt. (doublewd.)
☐ P – packed decimal	☐ A – addr. value (fullwd.)
☐ F – fixed pt. (fullwd.)	☐ Y – addr. value (doublewd.)
☐ H – fixed pt. (halfwd.)	☐ V – addr. (external symbol)
☐ B – binary	☐ S – addr. (base displace.)
☐ H – hexadecimal (4 bit)	

BIT TRANSLATION (check): ☐ ASCII-8 ☐ EBCDIC ☐ Baudot ☐ Other________

FIELD SIZE:________ ☐ Numeric ☐ Alphabetic ☐ Alphanumeric ☐ Text

DECIMAL PLACES:______ ☐ Truncated Result ☐ Rounded Result

OUTPUT EDIT MASK: ________________ PICTURE: ________________

OUTPUT HEADING: ________________________________

VALIDATION:

Range of Values Permitted ________ min. ________ max.

Allowable Codes: ________________________________

____

Zero-Filled: ☐ Yes ☐ No Right-Justified: ☐ Yes ☐ No Align.:______

Other: ________________________________

Error Action: ________________________________

____

____

AUDIT and CONTROL PROCEDURES:

FIGURE 5-4
Data Standards Glossary (continued)

WHERE MAINTAINED (data base, logical record, segment names):

VOLUME on FILE: ________________ As of: ________________ Annual % Growth: ________________

DEFINITION:

INTERPRETATION of ALLOWABLE CODES:

NONSTANDARD SYNONYMS:

retrievable data, particularly in an on-line MIS. Occupying large amounts of expensive storage media—as compared to a reel of magnetic tape stored on a rack in the tape library—these data have a fixed hardware cost associated with them. For example, if a disk pack containing information for inquiries is on-line at all times, we have the expense not only of the storage medium but also of the disk drive (the peripheral device that reads and writes data on the medium), the portion of the control-unit hardware that is allocated to the peripheral device, and a portion of the cost of the data-channel hardware.

Expense is only part of the picture, however. Speed, which is often vital, should cause us to use care in exploring possible data-structuring methods. The methods open to us will generally have a variety of information-access speeds. Faster methods usually cost more, and as a result, we are always looking at tradeoffs in making an evaluation. Innovation in this area is of prime concern as well. Here, the systems designer will be thinking up new techniques to help make the system more efficient.

Data-Base Access Methods

Let us turn our attention to the matter of data-base organization, also known as data-file organization or simply data management. The data-base files with which we are concerned here are stored on one class of media known as direct-access storage devices (DASD). Other classes include paper documents, microfilm, punched cards, magnetic tape, and paper tape.

In Chapter 1 we discussed the specific hardware differences between the types of DASD. For the purpose of this discussion, we need know only that all DASD are capable of being used to access records both sequentially and directly. The two most popular types of file organization are sequential and indexed sequential. Less popular, but important for certain applications, is a third type called random-file organization. A fourth method, least used, is called direct-file organization. Predominant characteristics of the four methods follow.

1. *Sequential.* All records are read no matter how many are of interest. The records are physically recorded in sequence by an identifier, which is part of the record itself—as, say, customer-number sequence. Magnetic tape is the principal medium for this type of organization, although it is also widely used for DASD.

2. *Indexed sequential.* Records are physically arranged in some sequence, as in the sequential method. However, as the file is recorded (and updated), indexes to it are created. These contain the DASD fixed address of the physical location of the records, so that a particular record can be found

directly later on. Indexed sequential, as its name implies, permits direct access to a specific record (by having its identifier or key—for example, customer number) through the use of indexes, or ordinary sequential access, where every record is read. DASD are the only media used for this method.

3. *Random.* Records are in no particular identifier or key sequence, in contrast to the previous two methods. Typically, the key or keys are mathematically converted to the fixed DASD addresses, which are used to place records on the file and to access them. This method permits direct access only and uses DASD only.

4. *Direct.* DASD fixed-hardware addresses are used as the key or identifier. In contrast to random organization, no mathematical conversion is done. Assuming that the fixed-hardware addresses have been adopted as the numbering scheme for, say, customers, which is what is sometimes done, the file can be accessed both sequentially and directly. DASD are, of course, the only media that can be used.

Each of these access-method options has its advantages and disadvantages relative to the others. The requirements of MIS operations, for some functions, will limit if not dictate the selection of the method.

The table shown in Figure 5-5 highlights the major considerations affecting the selection of each of these methods. In several applications a combination of two basic methods, indexed sequential and direct, is used to meet the particular needs. This combination has been termed DISAM (direct-indexed sequential access). The data records on the data bases where DISAM is used are never accessed sequentially, and there is a very low daily activity ratio—something like one in 10,000 records. And, once on the data base, a record is never removed.

Indexed sequential is used to find the physical addresses of the data records that were stored by the direct method. New data records are simply added to the end of the direct file, with an appropriate physical address entered in the indexed sequential file.

The indexed sequential file simply provided the index to the direct file that contained the data. Since the index was comparatively small, it could be reorganized frequently. If only indexed sequential had been used, reorganizing the millions of data records would have been expensive and could have been done much less frequently. In short, this combination permitted extensive manipulation of the keys (or indexes) without carrying along the data. Additionally, it is possible to provide for more than one index using this approach.

Equipment manufacturers support most of the basic access methods in varying degrees by providing the necessary software. Sequential and indexed sequential, as standard methods, are often fully programmed. Other methods

FIGURE 5-5

Comparison of Data-File Access Methods

RELATIVE FACTORS → / ACCESS METHOD ↓	RECORDS DIRECTLY ACCESSIBLE	SPEED OF DIRECT ACCESS	ADAPTABILITY TO EXISTING PRACTICES	VERSATILITY FOR APPLICATION	KEY CONVERSION PROGRAM REQUIRED	SEQUENTIAL FILE USE	ADAPTABILITY TO GROWTH AND ADVANCED TECHNIQUES	UTILIZATION OF FILE FOR DATA STORAGE	SIZE OF SUPPORT PROGRAMS
SEQUENTIAL	No	DNA	Easy	Limited	No	Yes	Good	Complete	Modest
INDEXED SEQUENTIAL	Yes	Moderate	Usually Easy	High	No	Yes	Good	Fair to Good[1]	Large
RANDOM	Yes	Fast	Difficult	Poor	Yes	No	Fair	Fair[2]	Modest[3]
DIRECT	Yes	Very Fast	Difficult	Modest	No	Usually Yes	Fair to Poor	Fair to Good[4]	Modest

Notes: [1] Storage space is taken for indexes and overflow reserve.

[2] Storage can have unused gaps and also reserve for overflow.

[3] Depends upon the sophistication of the key conversion program.

[4] Depends upon whether "open" numbers are provided.

are only partly programmed. If you want variations on the standard method you have to either program them, have an independent software house provide them, or purchase or lease the desired programs—assuming they exist.

Types and Storage of Records

The processing requirements of the MIS, together with the hardware device characteristics, will guide some of our thinking as to how data records should be stored. In general, systems people refer to four generic types of records: master records, detail records, index records, and table records.

Master records usually contain low-volatility data—that is, relatively static data. In addition, they generally provide high-level data that are used for reference purposes and affect processing in some special ways. The most common example of this is a customer master record, which may contain the customer's number, name and address, credit limit, discount rates, and other indicative information. In addition, it might also contain summary information, such as account balance, total purchases during the year to date, and other financial data.

Detail records, sometimes called working records, are usually associated with the master records but are of a more transient nature. For example, a detail record commonly in use contains some of the information needed to calculate an invoice line item: part number, quantity, and so forth. It would also have the customer number and perhaps the customer's order number. If detail records are accumulated, in most cases the size of the detail file containing all such records builds up rapidly compared with the growth of master-file records. Taking weekly payroll processing as an example, we would find one employee master record per employee and perhaps, at year end, 52 detail records showing data pertinent to each work week.

Index records are primarily used to tell the system where particular records are located. Like the catalog card in a library, index records are examined first to locate the records of interest. (There may be an index hierarchy. For example, the Dewey decimal classification narrows the search by subject, the labels on the card catalog drawers narrow the extent of the possible cards to be looked at, and the separator cards in the drawers further narrow the search. All are indexes.) Clearly, the efficient use of an index file depends its being used in a way that corresponds to the way in which it has been organized—that is, what search criteria it is keyed to. For example, if in a bank we want to access the account information of John J. Jones, we would use an index keyed to account name. The system locates Jones's name in the index and picks up the exact location of his master record. Suppose we now want to retrieve the master-record information for all bank accounts with average balances of more than $50,000. In the absence of an index keyed to average balance, the system would be forced to look at all master records, picking out only those that meet the stated criterion, a long and costly procedure. Yet creating and maintaining an index is also costly. The decision, therefore, is based almost entirely on cost and time considerations. Cost will necessarily be computed on the basis of number of inquiries.

Suppose inquiries without benefit of index cost $100 each, whereas inquiries with an index have a fixed cost of $2,000 a year and a single-inquiry cost of $10. Here, it can be seen that an index is advisable if we expect to have more than 22 inquiries per year. Time is the other important factor, and, as is pointed out elsewhere, cost is very often a function of it. Using the cost figures just referred to, we might find that time, not cost, is the overriding factor. Suppose that the turnaround time was overnight without the index and five minutes with it. Assuming we needed five minute turnaround, our choice is obvious regardless of the number of inquiries. Naturally, there should be justification for any such expenditures, regardless of marginal cost differences between various approaches. Businessmen will want to watch for and evaluate the absolute merits of such marginal comparisons.

One more point about index records deserves mention. In some applications, they will contain information other than merely the location where a complete set of data may be found. For example, in a banking application we may want to have the available dollar balance of a checking account stored with the index, since tellers will frequently use and update only this information when cashing checks; the master record would be updated at the end of the working day.

Table records are found in applications that have a need for large amounts of reference information as part of the information-processing activity. The tables typically contain calculation data and factors that control or otherwise enter into processing. Examples would include price tables, insurance mortality and premium tables, freight rate tables, ZIP code to alphabetic city and state name, conversion tables, and others.

By way of summary, a record, being made up of logically related contiguous information, can be segmented in several ways. It may be broken up into a series of records that follow one another on a file. Or a hierarchical arrangement may be used where records of one level of detail are segregated from those of another level, each being a separate but related file within a data base. For example, we may have a file with regional sales records, a file with district sales records, a file with branch office sales records, and so forth. Further, there may be a variable number of records to a given logical set. And each record may have a variable number of data fields, or data fields of varying lengths, or both. The choice depends on the functional requirements of the MIS. Requirements aside, our objective is to do the job at the least overall cost.

APRIL 3 - P. 277-84 ✓

10 CH 1 ✓

(30) 37-66 (22) 255-76

17 CH:2 ; 8 MON & TU PM ✓

67-101

24 CH. 3 P. 101-12

MAY 1 112-31 131-36 136-40

141-186 (45) 187-217 (30)

8 CH. 5 CH 6

Techniques for Record Association

In the last section, we said that logically related records could be segmented in various ways. For quick access to index records that have something in common but that are not stored in a group we had the option to scan all records, picking only those of concern. Sorting all records, on the data fields containing the keys that correspond to our search criteria, is another means of grouping together records of interest. In this section we are going to explore two other important record-association possibilities and the subclassifications within them. They are chains and lists. Both techniques have more elaborate file structure and record-design ramifications than indexing, but can be much less expensive and faster than sorting or scanning. It should be noted that various terms are used to describe these techniques.

Chains and Chaining

Chains are used to logically (not physically) link records that have characteristics in common or are otherwise related. Chaining is accomplished by way of *pointers,* which appear in the data records themselves. A pointer is actually the address of another record bearing the same selected characteristics as the record in which it appears. The selected characteristics are determined by the functional requirements of the MIS. For example, a systems designer, faced with the need to relate and have access to inventory records showing values on hand exceeding $50,000, may use a chaining concept.

Chaining is a technique that allows the MIS to leapfrog from one record to another without being concerned with the records that physically reside in between. This technique, and variations of it, are programmed to access a series of noncontiguously recorded information directly rather than sequentially. In most cases, the need for chaining arises when information is stored in a sequence other than the one that facilitates the type of retrieval we would like to make. As a result, from a practical standpoint, we have four options for accomplishing our objective: (1) We could have the computer look at every record on file and select only those in which we are interested; (2) we could establish and maintain a duplicate file containing only those records that meet our selection criteria; (3) we could maintain an index; (4) we could use a chaining technique, which obviates the need to either examine all records sequentially or maintain indexes or a separate file of duplicates.

On the surface, chaining is the most attractive of the four. That does not mean that its use is always advised. As outlined earlier, there are tradeoffs to be considered. Unlike the other three, chaining requires additional and somewhat more complex program logic and also increases the size of the data records because additional fields, called pointers, are stored with them. In addition, a *list of starting locations*, showing the first record of each selection classification, usually has to be built and maintained. The points in favor of chaining include faster retrieval, less computer time, and fewer files (less duplicated information), serving multiple purposes.

Through various illustrations, let us now see how chaining works. Here, imagine that the records are stored in a direct-access device of some kind, say a disk pack. We will assume, in these examples, that a list of starting locations has directed processing to record 1.

In the following example, the selected characteristic is average balance of $25,000 and over. As can be seen in Figure 5-6, the pointers (P_1) give the system the ability to leapfrog through the customer master file, picking up only those records meeting the criterion and ignoring those in between. Note that no logical or physical sequence with respect to the selected characteristic has been assumed and that we are working with a single chain.

FIGURE 5-6

Single-Chain Illustration in a Customer Master File

RECORD AND LOCATION NO.	ACCOUNT NO.	ACCOUNT NAME	AVERAGE BALANCE $	P_1
1	104375472	SMITH R L	27000	6
2	104375609	ADAMS B R	150	
3	204304791	BERG W W	33370	4
4	220116711	JONES S A	71001	*
5	250179891	ABLE O	10	
6	251180035	DOE J D	25550	3

Key: P_1 – Pointer to records with balances of $25,000 and over.
* – Indicates last account record in chain.

Let us now look at an example of a multiple-chain file. Here we have two selected characteristics, using pointers P_1 and P_2. The first, the same as the one in the preceding example, is average balance of $25,000 or more. The second chain links all accounts affiliated with other accounts in the file. Here we are concerned, not with the specifics of the affiliation, but only with accounts that have this characteristic. In Figure 5-7, we have illustrated how these two pointers would show up in records on the file.

The previous two examples of chaining were shown as part of a single file of records that had no hierarchical relationships. That is, customer master records, all of the same form, were used. In the next two examples, we will introduce multiple files and hierarchical relationships to explain two other types of chaining: the tree chain and the circular or ring chain. Our illustrations will show conceptually how each type of chain (or file structure) works.

Tree structures involve the use of parent and subsidiary files or master

FIGURE 5-7

Multiple-Chain Illustration in a Customer Master File

RECORD AND LOCATION NO.	ACCOUNT NO.	ACCOUNT NAME	AVERAGE BALANCE $	P_1	AFFILIATION	P_2
1	104375472	SMITH R L	27000	6	Y	4
2	104375609	ADAMS B R	150		N	
3	204304791	BERG W W	33370	4	N	
4	220116711	JONES S A	71001	*	Y	6
5	250179891	ABLE O	10		N	
6	251180035	DOE J D	25550	3	Y	*

Key: P_1 – Pointer to records with balances of $25,000 and over.
P_2 – Pointer to records showing affiliated accounts.
* – Indicates last account record in chain.

and detail files. Note that the files are separate because of the frequent need to use them individually. What we are doing here is tying together information contained in multiple files when a request has been placed against a parent file. As may be seen in Figure 5-8, we have oriented the illustration to a vendor-keyed inquiry into the purchasing data base having a tree structure. In a typical system of this type, we may want to cross-link relationships between three master files containing: (1) vendor records, (2) order records, and (3) item records. We may wish to do the same between two detail files containing: (1) item-list records, and (2) order-list records.

Circular, or ring, structures provide for the association of master with detail-type records. This technique tends to eliminate the carrying of redundant information and facilitates information access, utilizing multiple keys. Our next illustrations shows conceptually how this technique works and the *closed loop* of records that gives rise to the terms circular and ring. This example relates to a bill of materials application. Using a ring structure, Figure 5-9 shows that we can enter the system at *any* record in *any* file and find all other related records.

There are many applications for this chaining technique besides bill-of-materials applications. In education information systems, for example, we might have a student master record with the semester and course records associated by a ring structure. In an information system for criminal justice, a ring structure may be appropriate to link conviction and mode-of-operation records with a criminal master record, thus giving rise to more elaborate and efficient suspect searches. Note that the principal feature of the ring structure is its ability to associate all related records if any one record turns out to be of interest. As you might expect, the number pointers contained in the physical-data records to accomplish the linkage can grow rapidly in more sophisticated systems, and in certain applications, pointers can take more space in a record than data.

Lists

When chaining was discussed, we tried to emphasize that its purpose was to extract only those records that met prestated criteria, ignoring and skipping over all others. Lists, like chains, are structured to accomplish the same purpose.

A list, as opposed to a chain, may be thought of as an external index to the data records we are interested in. List structures have external tables containing pointers, whereas pointers in chain structures are contained with the data, as may be seen in the previous illustrations. Still, the concept of

FIGURE 5-8

Tree-structured Data Base in a Purchasing Application

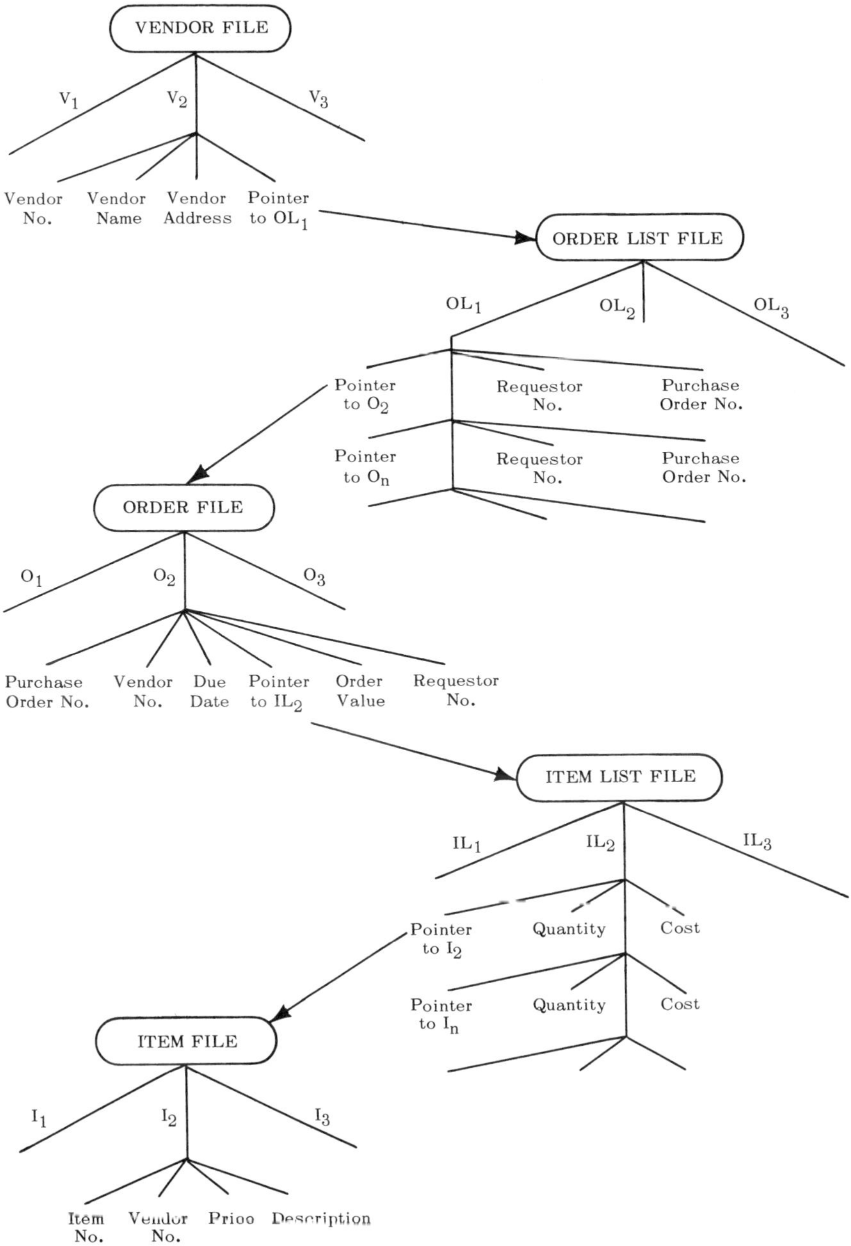

Inquiries keyed on vendor number.

FIGURE 5-9

Ring-Structured Data Base in a Bill of Materials Application

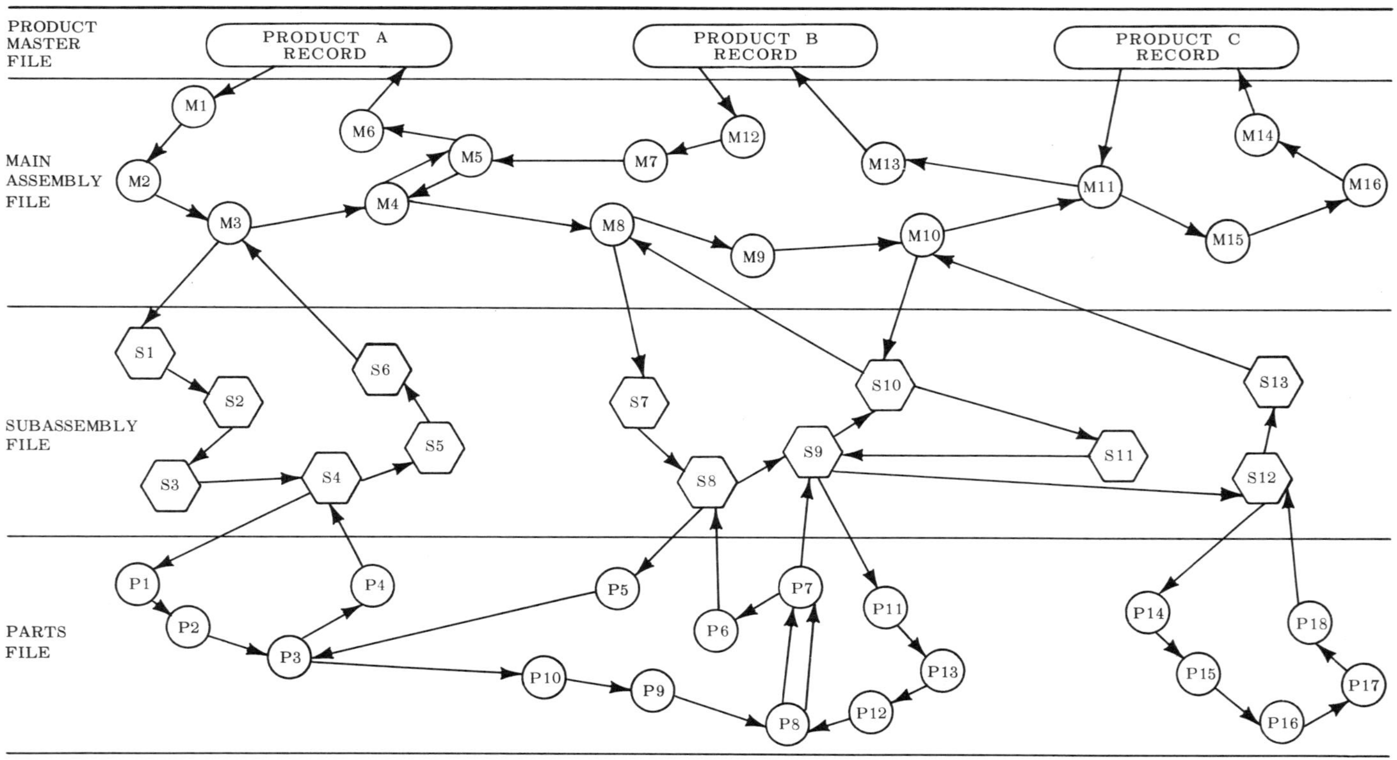

chaining does arise in certain types of list structures described here. This is one of the semantic problems we alluded to earlier.

In this section we will look at three types of lists: (1) simple (or threaded), (2) inverted, and (3) involute.

Simple lists contain only the entry-point addresses for records bearing some common characteristic. This table of entry points allows us to restrict the number of records having something in common. An entry point is, in actuality, the first record in a chain of records.

As in chaining, lists have pointers in each of the data records, starting with the first, that allow the system to skip around in the file, picking out records that have common characteristics. A simple list, then, provides entry-point addresses for particular series of chains.

By way of contrast, some applications require data-management software that provides lists that include the addresses of *all* the data records associated with a particular chain. We will discuss this shortly, but for now let us concentrate on simple lists (entry points only).

As a point of information, a number of *list-processing languages* are in use today. They are designed to handle list-structured files and have special application for large information-retrieval systems as well as certain MIS requirements.

Figure 5-10, an example of a simple list, shows entry points for certain skills in a personnel skills inventory file. The personnel file itself is assumed to be in order by social security number, and thus its sequence bears no

FIGURE 5-10
Simple List Illustration

ADVANCED PROGRAMMING SKILLS		
SKILL NAME	CODE	ENTRY POINT*
Artificial Languages	AP 110	31
Compilers	AP 112	2
Computational Arts	AP 114	30005
Information Retrieval	AP 116	918
List Processing	AP 118	77
Natural Language Processing	AP 120	10310
Operating Systems	AP 122	412
Pattern Recognition	AP 124	22346
Sorts-Merges	AP 126	14

* Physical device addresses of records.

relationship to type of skills. If we were looking for people with sort/merge experience (AP126), the system would look up the entry point—in this case 14—and begin retrieval there.

We may wish to have *nested lists* to give us the ability to retrieve records that have more refined characteristics than a single simple list. For example, in Figure 5-10, compilers (AP112), one skill was in the list of advanced programming. Since it would prove worthwhile to know of specific compiler programming experience, we might nest a list within the category of compilers. Such a list might appear as shown in Figure 5-11. As a matter of interest, note that the entry-point address of 2 is shown three times, meaning

FIGURE 5-11
Nested-List Illustration

COMPILERS (AP 112)		
TYPE	CODE	ENTRY POINT*
ALGOL	C-008	58600
ASSEMBLER	C-010	2
BASIC	C-012	4056
COBOL	C-014	2
FAP	C-016	18932
FORTRAN	C-018	12
JOVIAL	C-020	21777
LISP	C-022	21777
MAD	C-024	81
PL/1	C-026	2
RPG	C-028	4056

* Physical device addresses of records.

that the individual whose skill records are located there has experience with the three compilers shown.

Inverted Lists

Inverted lists are simply indexes that, under a given heading in the index (list)—for example, COBOL—include the addresses of *all* records belonging to a set. Chaining is not used with inverted lists, and therefore there are no pointers in the data records. It is noteworthy that the inverted list represents the farthest development of a simple list concept—that is, the number of entries in a particular list fully equaling the total number of records that would be in a chain having just one entry point.

As in the case of all list or indexing approaches, the decision to use selected lists must be based on MIS requirements and the economic and other justification for satisfying them. We would most likely want to use inverted lists in cases where regular access to large massses of data is required to retrieve a low percentage of records.

Building on the skills-inventory example discussed earlier, let us take a hypothetical instance to illustrate the use of an inverted list. Suppose that inquiries to our file were such that very frequently we had to produce the records of all programmers who had developed COBOL and PL/1 compilers. One way to make these records readily available is through the use of an inverted list for each category. The lists could be arranged for the least amount of access time—that is, in direct-accesss-device address sequence.

Figure 5-12 shows the construction of an inverted list for an application requiring frequent access to COBOL and PL/1 compiler programmer records.

FIGURE 5-12
Inverted-List Illustration

COMPILER PROGRAMMERS		
TYPE	CODE	RECORD ADDRESSES*
COBOL	C-014-1	2
		28006
		30937
		31412
		32655
		43118
		51624
		51625
PL/1	C-026-1	2
		39
		32655
		43118
		44206
		44309
		51001

* Physical device addresses of records.

Involute Lists

Before getting into the subject of involute lists, it should be said that some data-management specialists consider this merely an extension of the inverted-list concept, and do not use the term "involute." However, involute lists are quite distinct in that individual data values themselves appear in the lists rather than the addresses where they may be found.

Taken to its extreme, the involute approach does away with logical data records as we know them. Thus we may have a completely generalized data bank, one permitting the information to be used without requiring the system to be built to handle specific MIS problem data requirements. In effect, it can now handle any request for which the system has data. No prior assumptions are made as to how the data will be used. A problem submitted to the system collects from among the lists only those data elements relevant to it. The involute-list concept has some interesting parallels with the circular structure discussed earlier, one of which is the idea of associating information.

Our illustration of the involute-list structure, Figure 5-13, displays conceptually how it might be used to relate pieces of data by means of a simple identification number (ID). In this case, we have made up a partial set of lists for a personnel MIS. Restrictions to the access of certain lists could be established through the use of security or passskey codes, whereby a user would have available those data he needs but no others.

The potential users of the kinds of lists we have illustrated are afforded the opportunity to inquire into the data bank on the basis of any criteria desired. For example, if the information were on-line, he could receive rapid responses to unusual questions and inquiries like this: "Give me the middle initials of all individuals at company location 307 who have a master's degree." Without this structure, such inquiries might not be answered quickly unless they had been preprogrammed. This kind of structure opens up great opportunities. Consider its use in a criminal-justice information system, for example.

Paging

As you might imagine, the buildup of indexes and lists in an MIS can quickly put an ordinary hardware (and software) budget out of line, as significant storage capacities begin to be needed. Creative software specialists have devised interesting ways to help hold down these costs. Paging is one technique that falls into this category, and it has several nuances in the esoteric world of the software man. As we use the term here, it is a means by which information is grouped and always accessed as a group. This cuts down

FIGURE 5-13

Involute-List Example

LAST NAME		FIRST NAME		MIDDLE NAME		SOCIAL SECURITY NO.		AGE	
LISTS	ID	LISTS	ID	LISTS	ID	LISTS	ID	LISTS	ID
ABLE	1	ALBERT	11	NONE	4	137113465	11	20	3
	2	ALFRED	1	A	8	140601712	10		1
	3	DAVID	10	B	5	151221130	8		2
BAKER	4		3	D	3	193498745	9	22	11
	5	MARY	8	E	7	201735511	7		4
	6	ROBERT	6	R	1	210013942	1	25	9
DOE	7		4	W	2	220991007	3		10
	8		5		6	225917072	2	27	7
	9	WILLIAM	2		9	225927111	4		5
SMITH	10		9		10	230010333	5	33	6
	11		7		11	235671246	6		8

WORK LOCATION		HIGHEST EDUCATION		SEX		MARITAL STATUS		SALARY/MONTH	
LISTS	ID	LISTS	ID	LISTS	ID	LISTS	ID	LISTS	ID
303	5	COLLEGE-2 YR	7	FEMALE	8	SINGLE	11	600	3
	1		1	MALE	1		10		4
	11	BS DEGREE	2		2		9	700	11
	2		3		3		8		2
	10		4		4		7		1
307	3		5		5		1	850	6
	9		6		6		2		5
	4		8		7		3		10
	6		10		9	MARRIED	4	1000	7
	8		11		10		5	1100	9
	7	MASTERS	9		11	SEPARATED	6	1600	8

COMPILER EXPERIENCE		MANAGEMENT EXPERIENCE		YEARS WITH COMPANY		APPLICATION EXPERIENCE		LAST EVALUATION	
LISTS	ID	LISTS	ID	LISTS	ID	LISTS	ID	LISTS	ID
ALGOL	8	1 YEAR	9	1 YEAR	3	NONE	1	EXCELLENT	3
COBOL	8	2 YEARS	5		1		2		5
FAP	7	3 YEARS	6		2		3	GOOD	8
FORTRAN	9		8		11		4		11
LISP	9				4		5		7
PL/1	6			4 YEARS	9		6		9
	3				10		7		4
	2				7		9		6
	7			5 YEARS	5		10		10
					6		11	SATISFACTORY	1
				8 YEARS	8	1 YEAR	8		2

the number of entries and therefore the storage requirements of index lists, since they would show a group and not an item entry. The group is called a page; once retrieved, it has to be scanned by the system in order to pick out the specific data item needed. Hence, the index or list would contain one entry for each page, indicating the range of records on the page.

A Note on Record Association

Recapping what we have said might best be done by reflecting on where we have been in MIS work and where we are going. It needs to be understood that capabilities both in hardware and in software to accomplish the kinds of things discussed here are rather new. There is as yet no widely used programming language in general use that has facilities for automatically handling all the ideas presented here. That is not to say they have not been done; they have, by large companies and governmental agencies that have spent considerable sums of money building the software capabilities themselves. Indeed, a recommendation has been placed before the CODASYL (Conference Data Systems Languages) COBOL Committee to include list-processing techniques as part of the standard COBOL. The Center for Computer Sciences and Technology at the National Bureau of Standards has undertaken major research projects in the area of data management: (1) file organization and segmentation and (2) generalized data-base management aids. A book of interest in this area is D. Lefkovitz's, *File Structures for On-Line Systems* (Spartan Books).

General-Purpose Data Base Management Systems

In the latter half of the 1960s, more than two dozen different general-purpose data-base management systems appeared on the computer scene. Some were developed by computer hardware manufacturers and related to the capabilities of third-generation hardware being produced at that time. However, many more of these systems are being developed by independent computer consultants and software companies. (Such systems have also been developed by companies for their own internal use.)

Seven common functions found in varying degrees in all general-purpose data-base management systems are as follows:

1. Data-base and file creation.
2. Data-base and file updating.
3. Data retrieval.

4. Logical and arithmetic processing.
5. Sorting of records.
6. Merging of records.
7. Report generation.

All seven functions are invoked and controlled by parameters supplied to the system by the user. For example, the user (often *not* a programmer) "tells" the system, by means of parameters, what information he wants printed out (or otherwise output) and in what form when the reporting function is activated. Some systems translate user statements into an intermediate language such as COBOL.

The Data-Management Environment

As we mentioned earlier, until recent times data files were set up individually to serve specific applications and the programs within them. Applications such as accounts receivable, inventory control, and production planning had individual data files that, in numerous instances, contained redundant or duplicate information. Often, the current status of a particular piece of data that was needed in more than one application differed from one system to the next. Thus a data file might be kept up to date in one system and be out of date in another. Tying business plans and controls together under such conditions could be impossible.

The same data was usually found in differing formats from system to system, in some cases to comply with particular input-output requirements or package programs. However, despite these differences, all data in all systems had a great deal in common with respect to fundamental processing logic.

For example, substantially the same program logic is required to update a salesman's home address as is required to update the business address of a vendor or a customer. In fact, much of the updating of data files is nearly identical from the standpoint of programmed logic, and it can be generalized so that updating of all kinds can be accomplished with substantially the same type of program logic.

Past applications repeated this and other kinds of file management and report-generation logic. And a significant portion of all processing costs was attributable to the handling of redundant information. In addition, the maintenance of the same logic in many different programs added to the overall cost of computer services.

For many years, systems analysts and others realized that a more practical approach would be to have an integrated data file containing data for more than one application. However, computer technology, in hardware as well as in software, was not generally up to the task of providing this capability, and only within the past five years has this approach become feasible. Early attempts to generalize file processing were not generally considered too successsful. However, the coming together in recent times of more advanced hardware and software with more sophisticated application requirements, has served to popularize general-purpose data-base management systems.

Why the General-Purpose System Is Gaining Stature

Reasons for the growing popularity of general-purpose data-base management systems are many, but all essentially boil down to time and money. Many people have concluded that the best way for a user to get his job done is, in effect, to command the computer to do it. In other words, take the programmer out of the picture as an intermediary, thereby putting the user and the system in face-to-face communication. But there is more to giving the user the ability to use this new tool directly than meets the eye. And, as every serious practitioner knows, the crux of accomplishing direct communication is the language that is used to command the system.

Programmers use a programming language—COBOL, FORTRAN, or Assembler, for example—but the management user could hardly be expected to master these languages and the general art and science of computer programming. But general-purpose data-base management systems represent a means of communication more akin to the one that the user now understands. What differences and conventions exist in the new system are easy to learn. Hence, the tool has been designed to accommodate the user rather than being a burden on top of the problem he is trying to solve. Other reasons for the growing use of general-purpose data-base management systems include the four that follow.

1. *Skyrocketing programmer costs and scarcity.* Demand for competent computer programmers often has made it impractical to wait until one becomes available to do a job, or unjustified in terms of cost, or both.

2. *Complexity of modern computing equipment.* While modern hardware is more versatile and usually has lower per-unit operating costs than older equipment once a system is operational, it often costs much more to develop and program systems than it did in the past.

3. *Management's need for flexible systems.* Programming is a well-known bottleneck in keeping up with the information needs of a dynamic business. Seemingly simple program modifications are often disproportionately expensive and take an incredibly long time between request and realization.

4. *Increased demand for simple systems.* Reacting to the presence of the computer and the availability of data, managers find themselves wanting

one-time computer reports and analyses for various purposes. Computer departments sometimes view these as nuisance jobs, and responsive service (especially to middle management and below) is often denied. But a simple function can be done with ease if the manager uses a general-purpose data-base management system. As a result, he gets what he wants pretty much when he wants it.

What a System Costs

Systems developed by computer manufacturers are available to their hardware users at no additional cost or are leased at a monthly rate. Privately developed systems have price tags running from about $10,000 for a fairly basic system to an advanced system that reportedly costs more than $500,000 to purchase outright. The sophistication and number of available options within the seven function categories listed earlier are the main reasons for the difference in price of general-purpose data-base management systems.

As a base purchase price, a typical system might cost in the neighborhood of $20,000 to $30,000. Extra or special features might boost this to $35,000 or $40,000. Depending on particular suppliers, there may be a modest annual maintenance charge beyond the first year. In addition to the purchase option, some systems may be taken on long-term, short-term, or trial leases; some leases have conversion benefits that provide for applying all or part of past rental payments in the event a user wishes to purchase the system. Nearly all independently produced systems are covered by a form of noncompete and nondisclosure agreement. This means that the buyer may not use the system in a way that competes with its developer, nor may he disclose any of the program logic and documentation to outside individuals. With the recent advent of patentable software, the need for these explicit restrictions may soon become questionable.

User Knowledge Requirements

Many so-called general-purpose systems (not necessarily data-base management) have been developed for use by individuals with rather extensive technical qualifications. For example, a general-purpose system for simulation might be effectively exploited only by someone who is already an accomplished operations research practitioner.

General-purpose data-base management systems, for the most part, do not require the typical user to have extensive or even moderate experience or knowledge of computer methods. Sometimes, in fact, prior computer knowledge can be a hindrance in taking advantage of what these systems have to offer.

Several systems have been designed for use by individuals with varying degrees of technical experience. The typical management user of such systems need know practically nothing along technical lines. Yet a wide range of powerful operations can be had by following some fairly simple rules. The available functions that can be put into action in this way include those required to handle most user requirements.

When the user's problem requires that the more sophisticated capabilities of the system be invoked, a programmer may be required to help the user over some of the tougher parts of his problem solving. The amount of programmer time and talent required for this kind of help is well below what it would have been in the absence of a general-purpose data-base management system.

An especially complex problem may require that an experienced programmer devote much more attention to the programming solution. Even in this case, however, the system will provide many of the functions that would otherwise require expensive custom-tailored programming.

If the company desires to extend functionally the capability of a general-purpose data-base management system already in operation, an experienced computer programmer will accomplish this with very little user involvement as such. The need for extended capabilities will be determined in large measure by the general level of sophistication in user-problem requirements. Where one company may find a simple-inquiry capability perfectly adequate, for example, another may find that it needs certain kinds of complex logic to govern an information retrieval process or preparation of special-format files for operations research problems. On the other hand, a company may find that there is a significant volume of substantially identical problem-solving requirements which may not be beyond a user's ability to invoke, but which could be done lesss expensively and more quickly if they were professionally programmed just once and then made available to all users as a standard capability of the system.

Thus we have three or four levels of usage. First, there would be a majority of problems that could be handled by the user alone; a programmer's help would not be required for any purpose. Second, there would be problems requiring only a relatively small amount of time on the part of the programmer; these would need some complex processing logic. Third, there would be the complex program requiring that a programmer handle the job pretty much on his own. And fourth, there would be the case where the company wishes to extend the functions of the system to make it more versatile, or to reduce overall operating costs, or both.

Examples of General-Purpose Data-Base Management Systems

Under the category of general-purpose data-base management systems developed by a computer manufacturer, the following eight are representative:

1. *BEST* (Business EDP Systems Technique for NCR 315).
2. *FORGE* (File Organization Generator for Burroughs 5500).
3. *GIS* (Generalized Information System for IBM System/360 and System/370).
4. *IDS* (Integrated Data Store for General Electric 215, 225, 400 series, and 600 series).
5. *IMRADS* (Information Management Retrieval and Dissemination System for Univac 1108).
6. *IMS/360* (Information Management System for IBM System/360 and System/370).
7. *INFOL* (Information-Oriented Language for CDC 3600 and 3800).
8. *MANAGE* (General purpose data file Management System for SDS [now known as XDS] 900 series and 9300).

These systems, for the most part, require larger-scale hardware configurations, although it may be possible to run a less-than-full version of a few on medium-scale hardware. Software houses and other systems development organizations have devised numerous other general-purpose data-base management systems that can be leased or purchased. Among the independently produced systems, the following 12 are representative:

1. AEGIS (developed by Programatics Inc.).
2. ASI-ST (developed by Applications Software Inc.).
3. COGENT (developed by Computer Sciences Corp.).
4. DM-1 (developed by Auerbach Corporation).
5. GRS (developed by Information Science Inc.).
6. Mark IV (developed by Informatics Inc.).
7. MULTI-LIST (developed by Computer Command & Control Co.).
8. 101 (developed by Computer Corporation of America).
9. PDQ (developed by Applied Data Research Inc.).
10. RAMIS (developed by Mathematica Inc.).
11. SCORE (developed by Programming Methods Inc.).
12. TDMS (developed by Systems Development Corp.).

This list is expanding significantly with the introduction of new systems. If the current trend indicates what the future holds, the use of such systems will be widespread.

We have chosen not to set forth a specific set of characteristics of these or other systems because it is apparent that such information is subject to rapid change. This information can be solicited from developers, if a full set of specifications is desired. Two surveys of interest are "A Survey of Generalized Data Base Management Systems," (Association for Computing Machinery); and "Data Management Systems Survey," (Publication No. AD–684–707, U.S. Department of Commerce Clearinghouse).

6

Data-Communication Concepts and Facilities

MODERN business, with its increasingly complex organizations and its mountains of paperwork, has had to search for new ways to cope with the information explosion. In recent years, computer-based systems have helped business keep abreast of business activities through the generation of more and more working paper. But this has had its drawbacks, and a way has had to be found to collapse time and distance in providing information to management and in exchanging it between decentralized company locations. Modern data communication, still in its infancy as a component of business computer systems, promises to solve these problems. Within a few years, 50 percent of the computers installed are expected to have data communications, whereas in 1967 the figure was 7 percent. American industry will soon be sending more business data over long-distance telephone lines than the equivalent number of spoken words. And this will be only the beginning.

The advent of data communications has brought an entirely new dimension to the use of computers for MIS implementation. A properly designed data-communication system can make it posssible to transmit information practically instantaneously almost anywhere in the world. Let us consider the fundamental concepts and various services available for data transmission.

Spectrum of Uses Today

A data-communication system may be defined as an electrical transmission system for the moving of encoded information. Such a system must include input devices, transmission media (often telephone lines), and output devices. Note that this definition does not exclude voice communication. The telephone is still one of the best data-communication devices available. Telephones are used in conjunction with data-transmission equipment for setting up schedules and for verifying that the proper connections have been made before data transmission is begun. With Touch-Tone service, the phone instruments themselves can be used to transmit limited amounts of data.

Card and tape systems. One of the earliest applications of data communications, and one still in wide use, is the transmission of data stored on punched cards. At the sending end, a deck of punched cards is inserted in a card-reader and a corresponding deck is produced on a card punch connected at the receiving end. The duplicate deck may then be further processed in a unit-record (card) system or used to enter information into a computer. A more sophisticated system records the data, sent from a magnetic tape, on another magnetic tape at the receiving end. While this can be done with or without the aid of a computer, in most cases the tape at the receiving end is used to provide computer input for further processing or for printing out its contents. Punched paper tape is also used for data transmission and computer input. However, other systems do not employ any intervening media and rely on computers communicating directly with each other in a digital language over the same communication channels designed for human voices.

"Talking" computer systems. Computer-controlled audio data communication can have a number of practical applications. The usual situation is one where a person sends a coded inquiry to the computer and receives a spoken reply. One such system is used in banking. A banker wishing to learn a bank balance uses a Touch-Tone telephone to "dial" a special number. Upon receipt of a tone signal, representing the "lifting of the receiver" at the bank's computer, the banker taps out the account number on the telephone's keys. The computer retrieves the balance in the account from on-line direct-access storage and converts this information into a code to be used by the "voice" answering device. Usually these devices have stored vocabulary segments consisting

of a recorded human voice. Voice segments are assembled for transmission back to the inquirer in accordance with the "answer code" generated by the computer. Such a spoken message might say, "The balance in account four seven eight eight is one thousand five hundred thirty six dollars and forty nine cents," each word representing an individually recorded segment.

Some work is being carried out with machines that do not employ recorded words and phrases but that will generate many different voice sounds synthetically. Development work is also being done on a computer that would understand spoken words. In fact, equipment having very limited capabilities of this type is available. But major problems must still be solved because of the variety of voices and accents that would have to be recognized by the equipment.

Airlines reservation systems. The Sabre system, used by American Airlines for making reservations for its flights throughout North America, is a prime example of a very large, complex, real-time data-communication application. Before it was implemented, flights were often either undersold or oversold—it was almost impossible to update the reservation files with the situation changing from minute to minute.

With the Sabre system, the airline's 1,000 or so ticket agents are in instant contact with the central computer, where the up-to-the-minute files are stored. When a reservation is requested, the agent enters into his remote-terminal device the data representing the flight requested. He then punches a series of buttons on the associated keyboard to indicate the date of the flight and the class and number of seats wanted. A light on the terminal is turned on by the computer if the seat requested is available. The agent operates a "sell" key to make the reservation, and the files are updated in the central computer. Cancellations and other reservation-related requests are also handled by the system, which processes 80,000 to 90,000 inquiries a day, each within three seconds.

Plans are now being developed by the Civil Aeronautics Board for a system to provide a means of connecting the computerized reservation systems of the various airlines—a clearinghouse concept.

Hotel-motel reservation systems. Examples of smaller-scale data-communication systems in everyday use are numerous. Some motel and hotel chains now make and confirm reservations in distant cities via teleprinters or other keyboard terminals. Inquiries may be sent to and from a central office where a manually updated "status board" is kept, but, for large chains, the status and reservations data are likely to be stored in a computer, to permit immediate retrieval. One such system, installed for the Holiday Inn chain of motels, reportedly processes more than 140,000 inquiries per week.

Business information systems. Business MIS should provide for the timely transmittal of relevant information to the manager who must make the decision. This concept is being realized today in the purest form with on-line data communications. Instead of generating great volumes of sales analysis figures, for example, the computer is programmed to output only those that fall outside the normally expected limits. Also, instead of being printed in the computer room and placed in the company mail to eventually find its way to the man who needs it, the information can be made to appear in his office, home, or car on a teleprinter or visual-display terminal. Moreover, the manager's terminal provides a means of inquiry so that he can ask the computer about production figures or what the day's sales were in the company's branches.

Basic Data Communications Applications

The variety of applications for which data-communication systems are being employed now, and for which they will probably be used in the future, is limited only by the designer's imagination and his employer's willingness to part with money. Fortunately for the business executive who must be prepared to deal with creative people in this field, there are certain fundamentals that, once learned, are applicable to the understanding of any data-communication system.

New equipment, promising more automation and increased transmission capabilities at lower cost, is offered for sale with increasing frequency. But the basic concepts change little. Virtually every application concept involves one or more of the following: (1) computer load-sharing, (2) computer facility time-sharing, (3) inquiry processing, (4) collection of data, (5) distribution of data, (6) message concentration, and (7) messsage switching.

Computer load-sharing. A business organization having two or more computers in separate locations might find it desirable to join them by data-communication links to take advantage of the enlarged storage and operating capabilities that would result. One advantage of such an arrangement is that it provides backup for processing essential information in case of a breakdown in one computer. And, since there are substantial economies of scale to be realized with larger computers, distributing the workload among various computers makes the total operation more efficient.

Within this so-called *multiprocessing* environment, the interconnection permits integrating the use of smaller computers at outlying locations with a large-scale computer at a central location within the network. The smaller, front-end computers, when not engaged in local processing of small jobs, serve as input and output terminals for the large centralized computer, which is used for jobs requiring the larger main memory, corporate data bases, and faster capabilities. The data flow in these applications is in both directions, and the volume of data to be transmitted depends mainly on how the workload is apportioned among the interconnected computers. The computer utility concept encompasses the load-sharing idea, which is really the basis for it.

Computer facility time-sharing. The purpose of a time-sharing system is to make the services of a powerful computer available to a number of remote users concurrently. Such services may be provided by an outside time-sharing firm or, in large companies, by the company's internal computer department. There are two types of time-sharing: (1) interactive and (2) remote job entry.

In interactive systems, each user has a typewriter terminal which is used to transmit programs and data to the computer. Output resulting from computer processing is printed by the terminal, usually while the user waits. Such systems typically make available to users standard programs to solve routine problems, such as those found in statistical analysis.

Since these systems provide each user with limited direct access storage and since input is usually entered manually (or via punched paper tape), interactive time-sharing is intended for solving quantitative problems of modest size. For business management information systems, there are practical limitations as to the application of time-sharing.

Where voluminous output makes typewriter output too time-consuming, arrangements may be made to have it produced on a high-speed printer at the computer location and delivered to the user.

Remote job entry (RJE) is almost always an in-house capability where remotely located small computers are the terminals which are tied into a large computer. The small computers are equipped with high-speed printers, card readers and punches, and possibly tape and direct-access storage devices. RJE, which is often used by programmers for compiling and testing programs, has some similarities with computer load-sharing. But, unlike interactive time-sharing, the RJE user does not carry on a "dialogue" with the central computer. In most time-sharing systems, data flow is in both directions, with the remote terminal sending and receiving information.

Inquiry processing. Credit data systems and bank applications of audio-response systems (the "talking" computer) are examples of inquiry-processing systems (also known as query-and-response systems). An on-line inquiry system might be used in any business where it is essential for management to have immediate access to centrally filed data and where a prompt, simple response is required. As in the Sabre system, the inquiry-processing function is combined with real-time updating of the information in the central data files. Such real-time systems are more costly to operate than systems in which file updating can be delayed and scheduled for the most efficient use of the computer. Inquiry systems will often be used in this manner—that is, with on-line inquiry but batch-mode updating.

Collection of data. This functional classification is applied to systems designed to transmit data, collected at outlying locations, into a central point for further processing. These might be progress reports from manufacturing facilities, receiving and shipping notices from warehouses, or sales reports and orders from remote sales offices. Data flow is primarily one way, from each of the outlying locations into the processing center. In this type of system, it is usual to accumulate the information at each of the reporting stations and transmit the batched data on a fixed schedule. Depending on the volume, data may be transmitted one or more times during the day, or it may all be done during the night when common-carrier tariffs (to be explained) are lower.

Distribution of data. The purpose of applications in this class is the reverse of the data-collection application. That is, the data again flow in one direction, but now from a central point to outlying stations. Such a system may be used to broadcast the same information, perhaps price bulletins or inventory-status reports, to all stations. Or the distribution could be selective, such as the forwarding of shipping orders to a particular plant or warehouse.

Message concentration. In large and complex data-communication systems with many widely scattered input stations, it may be uneconomical for all terminals to have direct access to the central computer. Where the volume of data at certain stations in the network is relatively small and the distance to the central computer is great, savings can be realized in some cases by providing way stations—regional centers where relatively small computers effectively batch, or concentrate, the messages from several sources.

Low-speed, low-cost equipment and communication channels are employed to bring the messages from the many input terminals to the regional centers. Here they are strung together and concentrated into series of long messages by the regional computer. At this point, the messages may be recoded for more efficient transmission and better error-control on the next part of their trip. High-speed, high-cost equipment and communication facilities (private high-speed leased telephone lines) are then used to forward the concentrated messages from the regional centers to the large-scale computer at the central data center, at the lowest overall cost. The flow of data for this function could be in one direction, toward the regional centers or toward the central data center. Where traffic going the other way must also be accommodated, a message-switching concept is often used.

Message switching. Given the problem of a large number of widely separated locations where the volume of traffic is high in both directions, a computer-controlled message-switching system is likely to be the most practical solution. Each outlying terminal sends messages to a switching center where they are stored temporarily and then retransmitted to their intended destinations. Very large and complex networks may have two or more switching centers interconnected by high-speed communications facilities. In such a system, a message may be switched twice on its way. For example, a large organization with a nationwide network might have one switching center in San Francisco and another in New York City. Messages originating west of the Rockies designated for delivery in locations in the eastern part of the United States would first be sent to San Francisco, retransmitted to the New York switching center, and then retransmitted at the final destination. Concentrators are almost always found in these larger networks.

Functional Elements of a Data-Communication System

Figure 6-1 shows the components of a typical data-communication system arranged for one-way transmission. To conceive of a two-way application, one ned only visualize another such system, turned end-for-end and combined with the first so that each terminal can both transmit and receive.

While each of the functions is shown as a discrete unit in Figure 6-1, in actual systems several functions are combined in a single communications terminal or control device. They are often made part of the transmission-control units, the input–output devices, or the modulator–demodulator units. In systems where computers communicate directly with input–output devices or with each other, all the functions shown for each terminal, with the exception of those of the modulator and demodulator, would ordinarily be done by the computers at its end. In the following sections, where the components shown in Figure 6-1 are described, the reference numbers in parentheses are those used in the figure.

Data-communication terminal equipment. Data-communications terminal equipment provides the man-machine interfaces at the ends of a communications facility. These devices may be for input only or for output only, or they may be combination terminals.

Input devices (1). Examples of input devices include punched-card readers, magnetic-tape units, and keyboard devices for manually entering data into the system. Commonly used keyboard devices are the teletypewriters available from the Bell System and from Western Union. Similar devices are offered by computer manufacturers and companies specializing in input–output devices. They resemble an ordinary office electric typewriter. Indeed, some are arranged for dual use: off-line for ordinary typing and on-line for transmission of keyed information. The ordinary Touch-Tone telephone is finding increasing use as a keyboard device for putting information into a data-communications system where the volume of data to be input is low and where speeed of operation is not an important factor.

Output devices (11). Some examples of output devices are the receive-only teleprinter for producing printed copy from the transmitted data, paper-

FIGURE 6-1
Functional Elements of a Data-Communication System

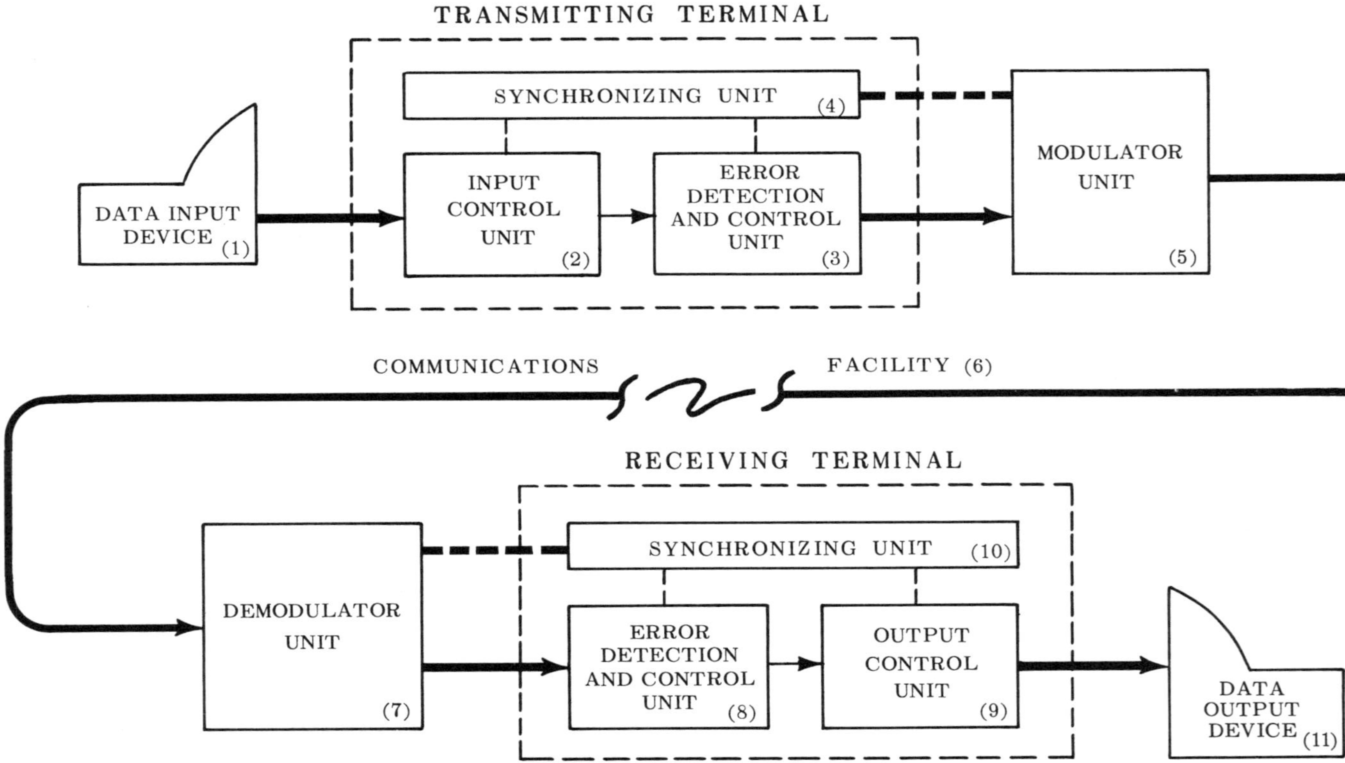

tape perforators, plotters (for graphs), card punches, and magnetic-tape recorders. Visual-display terminals (or CRTs) are gaining in popularity, especially for interfacing with computers in the conversational mode.

Input–output devices. Equipment with input–output capabilities may consist of various combinations of the separate input and separate output devices. For example, visual-display terminals will usually have a keyboard and may also be combined with a device that permits hard copy to be produced selectively.

Computer tie-ins with facsimile transmission systems are useful where signatures, sketches, photographs, or other graphic representations must be transmitted over communications channels. Closed-circuit television tie-ins were recently specified for the use of video tape in a military system, and they are likely to have future commercial application. New developments in the terminal area have been emerging rapidly. Terminals that combine computer-indexed microfilm retrieval with keyboard entry are now available. One manufacturer has even announced a color visual-display device.

Input and output control units (2, 9). The input control unit (2) accepts data from the input device (1) at a rate of speed usually dictated by the speed of the latter (which is, in turn, a function of the method—that is, keyed characters, magnetic tape, cards, and so forth). The input control unit stores (or buffers) the data temporarily and transmits it at a rate compatible with that of the communications facility (6).

At the receiving terminal, the process is reversed. The output control unit (9) accepts the transmitted data, stores it temporarily, and then feeds it to the output device (card punch, typewriter terminal, visual display, or whatever) at the speed required. In systems not employing speed-buffering, the transmission must proceed from end to end at the same speed.

In real-time data-communication systems, it is very important that the buffer storage provided in the input and output control units be of the right type and capacity. If not properly "matched" to the other components of the system (and to the intended application), terminal performance can be affected to the extent that real-time operation may not be attained.

Error detection and control units (3, 8). In transmitting data over a communications facility that may include wire lines, cables, microwave radio links, and, in the future, lasers, errors can be expected as a result of the nature of the communications facility (6) itself. This is due to "noise," fading, and phase delay, which distort the transmitted signals.

There are numerous techniques (mainly employing checkbits) for applying error-detection codes to the data at the sending end and for detecting errors introduced during transmission. Some error-control equipment merely detects and indicates errors. More sophisticated gear is available that also corrects certain types of errors or automatically requests retransmission.

Error-detection and error-correction capabilities add to the complexity and cost of data-communication systems. In determining whether or not to employ such features, the system designer must weigh the consequences of any error against the cost of installing error-detection and control equipment. For example, in teleprinter messages or in other output that is in word form, the scrambling of a few letters would not ordinarily prevent the human reader from understanding what was intended. On the other hand, in a list of unrelated numbers, it may be impossible to tell whether one is incorrect.

Synchronizing units (4, 10). Synchronization circuitry provides additional signals that are transmitted with the data to indicate the start and end of each *character* (asynchronous transmission), or it provides timing pulses to hold the sending and receiving equipment in step for each *message* (synchronous transmission). In *synchronous transmission,* the beginning of a message to be transmitted contains a series of synchronizing characters that are detected and used to put the timing circuitry in step. After this handshake, as it is called, the actual message is transmitted in its original form.

Asynchronous transmission requires that each character, rather than each message, be put in step. This is accomplished by adding two noninformation bits (start-stop bits) to the beginning and end of the character.

Since synchronous transmission does not require the extra bits on each character, it can transmit information faster than asynchronous transmission can. (The handshake loss is usually negligible.) However, there is a cost tradeoff involved because, as we have said elsewhere, higher speed means higher cost. In this case, the equipment for synchronous transmission costs more.

Modulator and demodulator units (5, 7). The devices that form an interface between each end of the communication facilities and the rest of the terminal equipment are the modulator, at the sending end, and the demodulator, at the receiving end. Since these two devices are usually combined in a single unit, physically separate from the other terminal equipment, they are commonly referred to as *modems* (*mo*dulator-*dem*odulator). Units furnished by some common carriers and by private manufacturers are called *data sets.* The terms "line adapter" and "coupler" are also used. Many of the modems available from the Bell System include a telephone handset for dialing up the connection (when used on the public switched network) and for providing two-way voice communication with the called data station. Modems furnished by the Bell System bear the trademark, Data-Phone.

Not all data-communication systems require the use of modems. For data transmission at speeds up to 75 bits per second, telegraph transmission techniques are still employed, especially for teleprinter communications over telegraph-grade lines. In this type of transmission, direct-current (DC) voltage levels are used to represent a "1" bit (or "mark") condition. A zero or negative voltage would represent a "0" bit (or "space") condition.

For data transmission at speeds higher than 75 bits per second, the "carrier" technique is used, and this always involves the use of modems. In the carrier technique, the DC pulses generated by the various input devices are not transmitted directly through the communications line, as is done in the telegraph transmission technique. Instead, these data pulses, after processing by the input and error control units, (2, 3), are fed to the modulator circuits of the modem (data set) where they are caused to "modulate" a carrier-transmission frequency that has been generated in the modem.

Depending on the bandwidth of the communications facility (6), the modem may be one that generates a single transmission frequency for serial transmission, or it may be one that generates several transmission frequencies for parallel transmission. In serial transmission, the characters making up the data are re-sent on their way bit by bit, as indicated in Figure 6-2 (A) and (B). In parallel transmission, all the bits representing each character are sent simultaneously, as indicated in Figure 6-2(C). Parallel transmission is, of course, faster than serial transmission, and it requires a communications facility of correspondingly wider bandwidth. The parallel-transmission carrier technique is extensively used by the communications common carriers to make more efficient use of communications facilities by packing many voice or data channels or both into a single wide-band channel.

As shown in Figure 6-3, there are four principal modulation techniques used to modify each carrier-transmission frequency so as to convey the information represented by the DC pulses from the input device. The four modulation methods commonly used are:

1. *On-off signal.* A signal of constant amplitude and frequency is turned "on" for a certain time interval to signify a "1" bit, and is turned "off" to signify a "0" bit.
2. *Frequency shift keying (FSK).* Signals of two different frequencies are transmitted to represent the "0" and "1" bits.
3. *Amplitude modulation (AM).* The amplitude of a constant frequency signal is varied to different levels to indicate the "0" and "1" bits and, in some cases, "start" and "stop" signals.
4. *Phase modulation.* The phase relationship between parts (of a cycle) of a signal of constant frequency and amplitude is varied to indicate the different levels of encoding.

The function of the demodulator (7) is to reverse the modulator process. That is, the information content is "stripped" from modulated serial or

FIGURE 6-2
Serial vs. Parallel Transmission

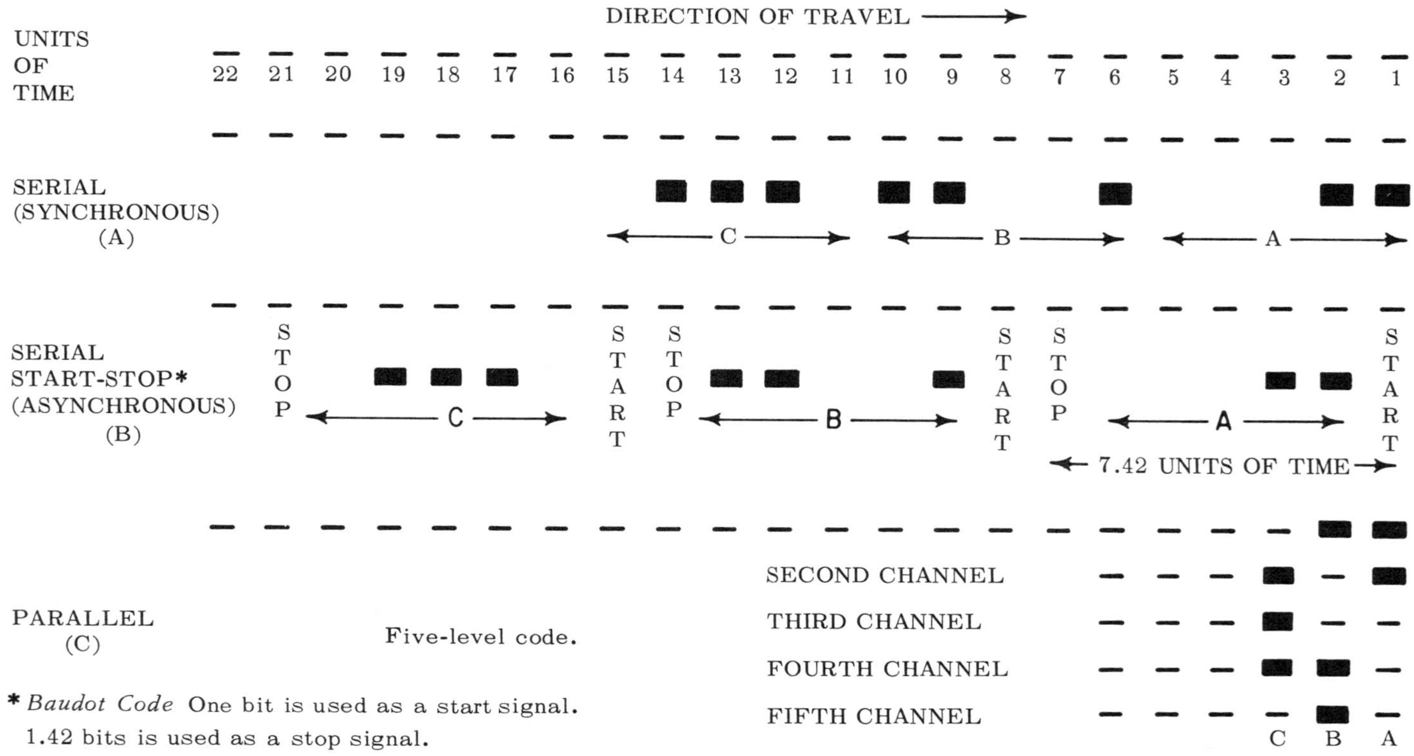

* *Baudot Code* One bit is used as a start signal. 1.42 bits is used as a stop signal.

FIGURE 6-3
Carrier Modulation Techniques

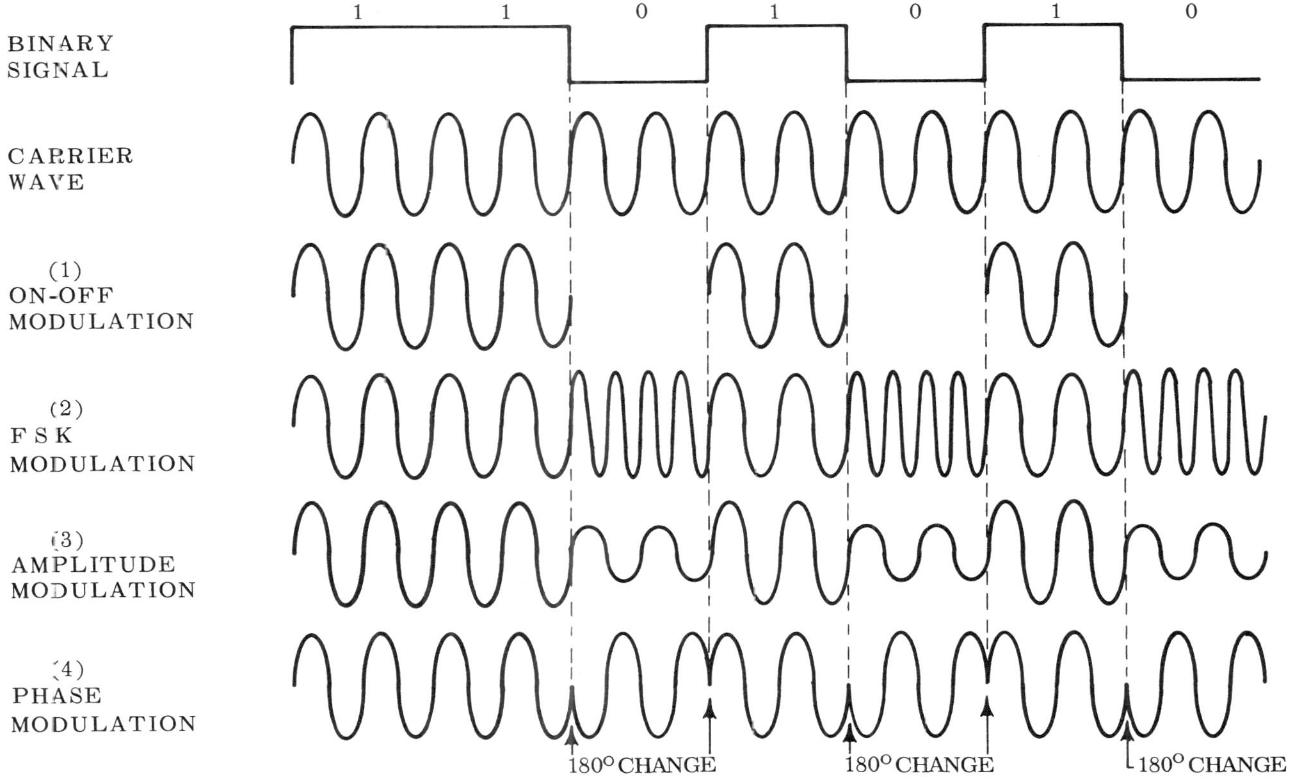

parallel signals received and is converted to a stream of bits, or coded into characters, as dictated by the design of the output control unit (9).

Communications facility (6). The communications facility is characterized by its channels, which may be a telephone or telegraph line, a radio link, a line-of-sight microwave link, or a combination of these and other facilities. Depending on the type of terminal equipment and the design of the system, the channels can be arranged for operation in one or more of the three basic modes:

1. *Simplex.* Transmission is made in one direction only.
2. *Half-duplex.* Provision is made for transmission in both directions, but not at the same time.
3. *Full-duplex.* Transmissions can be made in both directions simultaneously.

A practical data-communication system having several "legs" forming a network might require a combination of the three modes, depending on the type of terminal equipment used. In a half-duplex arrangement, reversing the flow of data requires a definite amount of time. This "turnaround time," which is mainly a function of the type of data set used, can seriously effect the volume of data that can be handled by the system. In planning a data-communication system, consideration must be given to the time required for "answer back" signals that control the flow of data.

Simplex, half-duplex, and full-duplex are types of circuits and are names used to describe the directional flow of data. Also important are the grades of lines ("line" being the common term to describe the communications channel). Lines are graded by "line speed," which is in direct proportion to the bandwidth.

Telegraph-grade lines are "narrow-band" and telephone lines "voice-band." "Broad-band" facilities are usually provided by special cables and line-of-sight microwave links.

Telegraph-grade lines. Telegraph-grade lines are narrow-band channels with line speeds in the range of approximately 45 to 75 bits per second. Information sent from one business machine to another in direct current pulses is transmitted serially bit by bit with the differentiation between the zeros and ones being accomplished through the presence or absence of a pulse of current. The differentiation may also be made by reversing the polarity of the current pulse. Over long distances, the signals become weak and distorted and must be regenerated. Regenerative repeaters sample the degenerated signal and generate a new undistorted signal to send forward on the line. Because such repeaters are code-sensitive, transmission by direct current may have to be restricted to the codes for which the repeaters have been designed.

Here, "code" refers to the representation and number of off-on bits having specific meanings. (Baudot, ASC11-8, and "4 out of 8" are code types.) Telegraph-grade lines are typically used for the transmission of manually keyed, punched paper tape, or punched-card data at 45, 56, and 75 bits per second.

Telephone lines. Because of their ready availability and relative economy, the standard telephone lines and the public switched network are the type most used for data transmission. Telephone-line facilities, although designed specifically for voice communication, are used for data transmission at higher speeds than are possible over telegraph-grade lines, with rates up to 2,400 bits per second not uncommon.

The Bell System, Western Union, and the independent telephone companies can also provide telephone-line (voice-band) facilities on a leased private line basis if desired by the customer. Broad-band communications facilities are also available from the common carriers, as described later.

A Couple of Notes on Rated Speed

The term *baud* or *baud rate* (named after the Frenchman J. M. E. Baudot, who in 1870 developed the 5-level baudot code) is sometimes used interchangeably with *bits per second* (bps). Actually, baud is defined differently, and, in asynchronous transmission, interchangeability may not hold exactly. Nor does it hold where bits are of different time duration: In different systems a stop bit may take 1.42 or 2 units of time, whereas all other bits take one unit of time.

Operating speeds in data-communications are also given in *words per minute* (wpm). A word consists of five characters plus a space, or six characters. If we know the bit encoding level and type of transmission, the bit rate can be calculated. For example, if there are seven information bits, a check bit, a start bit, and a stop bit, each character has ten bits. In this case, for 100 wpm the bit rate happens to be 100 bps, as shown by a simple calculation: 10 bits per character × 6 characters per word × 100 words per minute ÷ 60 seconds per minute = 100 bps.

Common-Carrier Services and Facilities

The agreement between the communications common carrier and the subscriber is basically an arrangement for the use of a certain type and grade of communication channel. The communications facility may be a telephone or telegraph line, a radio link, a line-of-sight microwave link, or a combination of these circuits. The particular combination depends on the physical facilities available in the geographical location for each leg of the system. The user is not ordinarily concerned with such details as the carrier frequencies used or the fact that a microwave link is utilized, but he does care whether the bandwidth of the channel is capable of carrying the required volume of data.

From a practical point of view, considering cost and performance, it has been found that the bandwidth of any communications facility should be about twice as wide—measured in Hertz (cycles per second)—as the number of bits to be transmitted per second. For instance, a channel with a bandwidth of 4,800 Hz. is required to transmit 2,400 bits per second.

There are three general classes of facilities that may be described as low-, medium-, and high-speed, for which tariffs have been filed with the Federal Communications Commission and the equivalent state and city regulatory agencies by the common carriers. Facilities for these three classes are narrow-band, voice-band, and broad-band channels.

Narrow-Band Service

The narrow-band, low-speed classification includes those facilities originally developed for use with teletypewriters and other channels for transmission ranging up to 300 bits per second. These include TWX, TELEX, and private-line teletypewriter exchange services.

TWX-teletypewriter exchange service. AT&T has sold TWX service, including the teletypewriters on the network that covers the United States and Canada, to Western Union. Present plans call for the continuation of the TWX service over the Bell System network for a period of five years after the date of the sale. Eventually, TWX service will be integrated with Western Union's TELEX service.

The Bell System TWX service provides two-way manually keyed or paper-tape communications via telephone-company switched networks between the approximately 50,000 TWX stations listed in a special TWX directory. Calls to other stations are made using the ordinary telephone dial or Touch-Tone pushbuttons provided as part of the station equipment. Card dialers, which employ prepunched cards for automatically dialing the numbers of the called stations, are also available. Teletypewriters can be equipped for "answering" and accepting messages when unattended. Stations so equipped are identified by a special symbol in the TWX directory.

TWX service is offered in two basic classes:

1. 60-speed, which can transmit and receive up to 60 words per minute, the equivalent of 45 bits per second. The teletypewriter, as furnished by the Bell System for this service, uses a 5-level code.

2. 100-speed, which can transmit and receive up to 100 words per minute, the equivalent of 110 bits per second. This machine uses the ASCII 8-level code. To take advantage of the maximum speed capabilities of these machines when transmitting typewritten material, it is the practice to use as input prepunched tapes, prepared from the keyboard when the machine is in an off-line mode.

The 60-speed and 100-speed stations can communicate with each other via speed and code-conversion equipment located in the telephone company switching office. The speeds of the two machines are coded in their directory numbers and the conversion equipment is switched in automatically. With this arrangement, however, the intercommunication is limited to 60 words per minute, and certain characters cannot be sent between the two.

Teletypewriters for receiving only are available and can be arranged to provide page copy and punched paper tape or both. When arrranged for page copy, single and multipart carbon interleaved forms can be used on the machine. The paper tape can be used for producing a printed page at a later time, or it can be used for resending the message to another station. In some applications, punched paper tape is used for input to a computer or some other business machine at the receiving location.

TWX CE. A TWX station equipped with customer-provided equipment is called TWX CPE station. The service is alternately known as TWX CE or TWX-Prime (TWX′). For TWX CE service, the Bell System can supply a data set to interface with the TWX network so that the customer's computer, or other business machine, can replace the teletypewriter. Arrangements can also be made for the alternate use of the teletypewriter at these stations.

With this arrangement, the TWX network can be used for two-way communication between the customer's own equipment. Subscribers to the 60-speed service with the CPE arrangement can receive and transmit in the half-duplex mode at a speed of 45 bits per second with no restrictions as to the codes used. The 100-speed TWX CPE stations can handle up to 150 bits per second with no code restrictions.

Cost of TWX and TWX CE service. The TWX network is available to subscribers on a full-time basis, 24 hours a day, 7 days a week. Usage charges are based on the airline distance for each connection dialed and the length of time the connection is held, on a per-minute basis with a minimum one-minute charge. Additional minutes or fractions of a minute are charged at the same rate as the initial minute.

The cost of TWX service includes a one-time installation charge for each subscriber loop and teletypewriter, a monthly service and equipment charge based on the speed and type of teletypewriter selected ($40 to $115), and a message or usage charge based on the distance between the two stations and the time the circuit is connected between the two stations. In general, the longer the distance, the lower the unit usage charge per mile per minute, as may be seen in the following table. Message charges are the same for both 60-speed and 100-speed machines, with a one-minute minimum period charge for both TWX and TWX CE.

TELEX. This is a worldwide, common-carrier, switched-network, teleprinter service offered by Western Union in major cities throughout the United States, Canada, and Mexico, and by other carriers. Messages can be transmitted at a maximum speed of 66 words per minute (50 bits per second). It should be noted that "teleprinter" is the Western Union term corresponding to "teletypewriter."

TELEX service operates in a manner similar to TWX in that keyboard or punched paper tape is used. But the subscriber dials the connection with no more than seven digits, while the TWX system usually requires that ten digits be dialed. Provisions can be made to connect a subscriber's business machines into the TELEX network with no restrictions on intercommunication. Unattended operation of the station equipment can also be provided for.

In some cities, TELEX subscribers may communicate directly with Western Union's local offices for the purpose of sending telegrams to non-TELEX subscribers in certain other cities, at a rate lower than regular telegram rates. This option is known as TELTEX service. Also, TELEX stations can

*TWX AND TWX CE INTERSTATE TWO-POINT CIRCUIT USAGE CHARGES**

Distance in Airline Miles	*Connect Time Each Minute or Fraction Thereof***
0 to 50	$0.20
51 to 110	0.25
111 to 185	0.30
186 to 280	0.35
281 to 450	0.40
451 to 800	0.45
801 to 1,300	0.50
1,301 to 2,000	0.55
2,000 and over	0.60

* Rates shown are approximate and are intended for illustration only. Federal taxes are not included.

** There is a one-minute minimum charge, and message charges apply to connect time only.

interconnect directly with over 100,000 other TELEX stations all over the world without speed or code conversion.

One main difference between TELEX and TWX services is that TWX maximum transmission speeds are either 45 bits per second or 110 bits per second. TELEX transmission speed is limited to a maximum of 50 bits per second.

A second principal difference involves usage rates. TWX usage rates are based on the airline distance between the two stations involved. There is a minimum one-minute period charge, and fractional minutes, after the first minute, are charged for as whole minutes. In TELEX, there are twelve rate areas bounded by state lines. One of eight rates determines the TELEX message charge. As shown in the accompanying table, the rates are applied as a function of the calling station's and called station's rate areas rather than the airline distance between the stations. Also, there is no minimum charge for TELEX messages, and fractions of minutes are charged to the nearest 2.5 cents. This is accomplished by dividing each of the eight rates into as many parts per minute as would represent the fraction of a minute allowed for the 2.5 cents at the basic rate. These fractional parts of a minute for each of the

*TELEX USAGE RATES**

Distance	*Pulse Rate in Pulses per Minute (PPM)*	*Equivalent Rate per Minute***	
		First 3,500 Pulses	*All Pulses Over 3,500*
The U.S. is divided into 12 rate areas and the pulse rate that applies is a function of the originating and terminating rate areas. It is not dependent on the mileage.	5	12.5¢	7.5¢
	7	17.5	10.5
	9	22.5	13.5
	12	30.0	18.0
	15	37.5	22.5
	18	45.0	27.0
	21	52.5	31.5
	24	60.0	36.0

* Rates shown do not include federal taxes and are intended for illustration only. Current rates can be obtained from Western Union.

** First 3,500 pulses in month are billed at 2.5 cents per pulse; all over 3,500 are billed at 1.5 cents per pulse.

eight area-to-area rates are called "pulse rates" and the number of parts for each rate are called "pulses per minute" (PPM). A 40 percent discount is applied for usage in excess of 3,500 PPM recorded in any monthly billing period. This amounts to a 40 percent discount on usage charges after the first $87.50 in any one month.

The TELEX rate structure offers at least three advantages. If most of the messages sent are very short, the lack of a minimum message charge is particularly attractive. In addition to paying only for the actual time used, the volume user has the advantage of the 40 percent discount, which applies to all "pulses" over the basic 3,500 in the billing month.

In addition to the TELEX message charges, three equipment charges apply. (Charges quoted are for illustration only; current rates should be obtained from Western Union.)

1. Teleprinter sending and receiving station—approximately $40 per month plus a one-time installation charge. (Actual charge will depend on type of teleprinter selected.)
2. Automatic punched paper-tape sending and receiving equipment—approximately $15 per month additional.
3. Adapter for interfacing with customer's business machine. Approximate range is $6 to $40 per month, depending on type of data set required, plus installation charges.

TELEX–TWX intercommunication. Arrangements can be made with Western Union to provide for the transferring of messages between TELEX stations and TWX stations. For this service, there is no physical connection made between the two networks. Instead, the "torn-tape" message-switching

*USAGE RATES FOR TELEX-TO-TWX MESSAGES**

Distance in Miles	*Charges per Minute or Fraction Thereof*	
0 to 100	$0.25	Plus $0.25 per Message (applies to all rates)
101 to 200	0.35	
201 to 400	0.45	
401 to 600	0.60	
601 to 900	0.75	
901 to 1,500	0.90	
1,501 to 2,100	1.05	
Over 2,100	1.20	

* Approximate Telex to TWX usage charges within the continental United States (except Alaska) are intended for illustration only. Federal taxes not included.

technique, described later, is used. Charges for this service are shown in the table of usage rates.

Private line teletypewriter systems. Various types of multistation narrow-band systems can be leased from the common carriers. While each installation is tailored for the particular application, these packaged systems are built around the use of teleprinters for printed or punched-tape transmission or both. Most of the variability from one system to the next is in the number of stations, the type of network, and the method of control or switching. Current availability and price information should be discussed with the common carriers' data-communications representatives or consultants.

Selective calling arrangement. A selective calling system is one of the least expensive methods for linking up a number of stations to form a network. In this system, all the teleprinters are connected on a single line very similar to a telephone party line. However, a message from any station on the line can direct a message to any other station, to be received only by that station. To accomplish this, each station is equipped with a special device, known as a *stunt-box*. This recognizes and responds to its own address code, which is included as part of the written message.

Since only one message can be sent over the common line at any one time, stations having messages to send must wait until the line is free. This is done by a series of timers that periodically test for a free line and are so arranged as to prevent any possibility of simultaneous transmission. This type of system is usually operated over half-duplex lines. The number of stations that can be properly served on a single line depends largely on the volume of traffic to be handled.

Polling systems. Another way of controlling traffic on single-circuit systems, and one that minimizes the waiting for a free line, is the polling system. Under this arrangement, one of the stations is equipped with additional control equipment. This control station periodically sends a signal to every other station. In turn, it requests the station to transmit its message. If the polled station has nothing to transmit, the query is sent to the next station, and so forth.

As explained in Chapter 5, polling can usually be made as sophisticated as desired. Traffic-load control and priority schemes, conference calling, multiple addressing, and "broadcast" of the same message to all stations can also be provided.

Polling systems can be designed to operate over half-duplex or full-duplex lines. Also, since polling time is negligible, these systems can accommodate many more stations than the selective calling system for the same volume of traffic. With teletypewriters, speeds are limited to a maximum of 75 bits per second; but, with special tape-to-tape equipment, transmission speeds of up to 1,200 bits per second can be realized on narrow-band private line systems.

Store-and-forward systems. In handling a large volume of message traffic, it is often more practical to have the individual outlying stations connected to a central control or switching center than to each other. Very complex networks might have two or more such "regional" switching centers connected by high-speed communication channels. In such a system, all messages are transmitted to the control center, stored there temporarily, and then retransmitted to the station addressed in the message.

Three types of systems for store-and-forward operation are available from the common carriers: automatic switching, semiautomatic switching, and torn-tape system.

In *automatic switching,* the receiving equipment at the switching center produces a punched tape having at its beginning, or "header," the address of its destination. This tape is automatically fed into a sending unit, where the header is interpreted by the equipment and switches the sender circuits to the correct outgoing line.

In *semiautomatic switching,* messages are received as in the automatic switching system. Here, the operator reads the message as it is fed into the sending unit and switches the sender circuits by operating push buttons. In some control centers, the punched tape is torn off at the receiver and manually fed to the sending unit.

The old-style *torn-tape system* requires that punched paper tape be torn from the receiver manually; the address is read and interpreted by the operator and the tape is carried across the room (or elsewhere) to the appropriate sending station. If the sending station is busy, the tape is held until the sender is free. Once the tape is inserted in the sender, the message is transmitted automatically when the line is free.

To insure that tapes are not discarded before being transmitted to all addresses, complex numbering plans are used for the tapes, and books are kept on all traffic handled.

The main advantage of a store-and-forward message system is that it provides *time-buffering,* which permits efficient utilization of the communications facilities. The sending station simply sends its message to the control center and then "hangs up." The stored message can be retransmitted at any time. It might be re-sent immediately or, if the receiving station is busy, held until the station is available to receive it. The disadvantages are that the delivery of an important message may be delayed and that the sending station has no way of knowing that the message has been delivered to its destination. To counter these disadvantages, some users include a priority-handling code in the heading of some important messages and ask for a retransmitted confirmation of receipt for other messages. These schemes, of course, add to the volume of traffic and to message-handling expense.

Charges for private-line systems. In addition to a one-time charge for the installation of the equipment at each terminal, there is a monthly charge for its use. Also, there is a fixed monthly charge for the local loop and a monthly charge, based on mileage, for each channel link between every two terminals. Each such link is priced separately, for mileage, at a regressive rate.

Subvoice facilities and service. Subvoice channels are usually subchannels of a voice-grade line. They have a lower speed than voice-grade lines, the limits ranging from 150 to about 600 bits per second.

Western Union and the telephone companies offer subvoice channels (lines only) on a lease basis or as a service with teletypewriter-equipped terminals. When teletypewriters are used, the speed of transmission is limited by that of the teletypewriter itself. The rate for leasing the lines from AT&T or Western Union is the same and is independent of whether or not the terminal equipment is leased from the carrier. The schedule of charges includes the various items listed for private line systems.

Voice-Band Services

The public switched-telephone network provided by the Bell System and the independent telephone companies can be used for the transmission of digital data at rates up to about 2,000 bits per second. In the Bell System, this type of service is called Data-Phone service, and the modems available from this common carrier are called Data-Phone data sets. Similar equipment and services are available from the independent telephone companies that also interconnect with the Bell System.

Computers or other business machines can also be connected to the public switched-telephone network through data sets other than those furnished by the common carriers. This is done via the Data Access Arrangement (DAA), introduced in 1969. DAA permits a customer to connect to the public switched-telephone network, data sets supplied by companies other than the Bell System.

Also available are acoustical coupling devices, which provide a nonphysical connection between a business machine and the telephone network. By merely placing the telephone handset on the coupling device, it is possible to create a truly portable computer terminal.

WATS (wide-area telephone service). WATS is a service provided by telephone companies for customers who make many long-distance telephone calls. This service can be used alternately for voice communication and data transmission, using Data-Phone service at the originating and called stations.

For a flat monthly charge, WATS permits a customer to make unlimited long-distance calls on a dial basis, by the use of an access line, to telephones in selected areas of the United States. The monthly charge is based on the size of the area in which the calls are placed, not on the number or length of individual calls.

Two classes of service are offered in WATS: full-time and measured-time. Under full-time service, the customer may use the access line every hour of the day, every day of the week, for making outgoing calls to telephones in the geographical service area for which he subscribes. He pays a flat monthly rate. Under measured-time service, the access line is continuously available, but the basic monthly rate covers the first ten hours of use per month for calls to telephones within the subscribed service area. Use beyond ten hours is charged by the hours and fractions of hours in increments of one-tenth. The monthly charge for WATS is determined by the calling area the customer desires. Calling areas and rates are determined by the total number of telephones the customer can reach and the distance to them from his home state.

For subscribers in any one state (or those at certain points in the larger states), the other states are assigned to one of six calling areas. Area 1 is a band of nearby states; area 6, a band that includes the most distant state or states. When a customer subscribes for WATS to a specific area, service to nearer areas is also included. Thus area 6 service includes all of the continental United States (except Alaska) except the subscriber's home state. Service within the home state may be subscribed for separately where intrastate WATS is offered.

WATS is an "originating service" requiring that the subscriber originate all calls. Once the call is established, however, the facility is the same as regular telephone service. Inward WATS, which allows incoming calls from the specified area to be charged to the subscriber at a flat rate, is available in some states.

WATS is well-suited to customers having a large volume of widespread one-way traffic or to those who can poll outlying locations for data input. Since one access line is limited to one call at a time, heavy traffic with simultaneous calling will require two or more access lines. The telephone company representative or a communications consultant can make an analysis of a customer's requirements, suggest the most economical arrangement, and furnish current rates for the service.

Data-Phone service. This service provides for the transmission of data among a variety of business machines over the regular telephone networks. Calls are dialed over the local or long-distance telephone networks or WATS lines in the same manner as ordinary telephone calls. This is accomplished by using a data set, which is connected to the business machine and electrically or acoustically coupled to the telephone network. The data set converts the electrical signals from the business machine into tones suitable for transmission over the telephone network and also provides the means for dialing the call.

Many types of data sets are available to provide compatibility with the various kinds of business machines designed for data transmission. Data-Phone data sets are available that operate at serial speeds of 300 bits per second, maximum, in the full-duplex mode; others operate in the half-duplex mode at serial speeds ranging up to 2,000 bits per second. Data sets for parallel transmission in the half-duplex mode at up to 75 characters per second, as well as analog units, can also be obtained from the Bell System.

There are also Data-Phone data sets that automatically establish calls for the transmission of data between business-machine terminals without the aid of operators. This is made possible by using a device called an automatic calling unit (ACU). When directed by the associated business machine, this device automatically dials the telephone call. These units can dial by using either the conventional rotary-dial technique or the Touch-Tone dialing system. Some Data-Phone data sets are also arranged to answer calls automatically. This unattended-answer feature permits an unattended location to have its machine turned on automatically by the calling set. The cost for Data-Phone service is the same as an ordinary telephone call (or WATS, if used), plus a monthly charge for the Data-Phone data set (if used).

Foreign exchange (FX) service. Practically all telephone companies can provide this service. A foreign exchange line is a combination of exchange and private-line services. For FX service, a customer's telephone is connected to a remote exchange ("foreign" in that it is distinct from his local exchange). This arrangement permits calls to or from points serviced by the foreign exchange to be made at the local message rate for that exchange. In addition, the customer pays a monthly charge for a business line in the foreign exchange plus the cost for a private voice-grade line between his location and it. This service is most economical for the customer having very heavy traffic between any two exchange areas.

Voice-grade leased lines. Voice-grade leased lines (channels) are available from Western Union and the telephone companies and may be used for data transmission. However, they are guaranteed by the common carrier only to the extent that they have the ability to carry voice signals. Experience has shown that these private channels are, on the average, better than the public switched-telephone network for long-distance data transmission.

Customer-furnished data sets may be used on these leased lines as well as on those available from the common carrier. Common-carrier data sets are available for various transmission speeds over private lines, ranging up to 2,000 bits per second in serial transmission and up to 75 characters per second in parallel transmission.

Rates for private voice-grade channels are based on the airline distance between the cities in which the terminals are located. For two-wire circuits (normally used in the half-duplex mode), the monthly rate is about $2 per mile for the first 250 miles. This rate decreases by about 15 percent for the next 250 miles and again by 15 percent for all distances over 500 miles. In addition, there are monthly charges for each channel terminal (about $15) and for each local loop ($10 to $15). Four-wire channels, required for full-duplex operation, are available, for about 10 percent higher cost, for each of the items mentioned.

Conditioned voice-grade channels. For an additional monthly charge for each voice-grade leased-channel terminal, the common carrier will "condition" the line to certain specifications. There are several specifications, or "classes," of conditioning, each imposing tighter limits (at increasing cost to the customer) on attenuation and frequency response of the line, and on minimization of delay and noise. Because such conditioning reduces noise on the line and distortion of the transmitted signals, greater speeds can be accommodated with fewer errors. Data sets that can be used with a maximum speed of 1,000 bits per second on an ordinary private voice-grade line can be used at 1,800 on a properly conditioned line. Speeds of up to 4,800 bits per second have been successfully demonstrated on these lines.

Since no definite standard relationships have been established relating the class of conditioning to the speed–error performance level, the trial-and-error method is usually employed by the common carrier when the equipment is installed and tested. The extra charges for channel conditioning range from about $10 to about $60 per terminal per month.

Broad-band exchange service (BEX). This service is offered by Western Union on a dial-up basis in and between certain U.S. cities. This is a four-wire full-duplex channel service for data transmission with alternate voice capabilities. The bandwidth the customer wishes to use (2kHz or 4kHz; greater bandwidths are to be announced) can be specified in the dialed number. Automatic calling units and automatic answering data sets are available for computer-to-computer transmission.

Each call is charged at toll rates according to the bandwidth used, with a one-minute minimum. There is also a monthly service charge and a monthly charge for a data set. However, a discount of 40 percent is given on the toll charges over a certain fixed amount in each monthly billing period.

Broad-Band Services

Where data are to be transmitted at speeds substantially higher than 2,400 bits per second, broad-band, or wide-band, facilities must be used.

These include communication channels having greater bandwidth capabilities than voice-band channels. Both the Bell System and Western Union, under the general name "Telpak Service," offer such facilities. AT&T and Western Union also offer certain switched services between a limited number of major cities.

Telpak service. This is a leased private-line service that provides communication-channel capacities suitably arranged for large-volume point-to-point transmission of voice, data, or other communication. Two classes of interstate services are offered under the Telpak name (also known as Series 5000 Channels):

- *Telpak C.* Service that has an equivalent base capacity of 60 voice channels and a maximum equivalent bandwidth of 240 kHz.
- *Telpak D.* Service that has an equivalent base capacity of 240 voice channels and a maximum equivalent bandwidth of 1,000 kHz.

The Telpak C service can be used as a single channel with a nominal transmission speed of 105,000 bps (15,000 characters per second). The Telpak D service has too wide a bandwidth (potential 500,000 bps) to be used as a single channel and must be subdivided into lower-speed channels.

All Telpak channels are full-duplex and can be arranged for digital data or analog signaling, or they can be subdivided into lower-speed channels. Each channel is provided with termination equipment by the common carrier. It is called a channel terminal, and includes a data set, a voice-coordinating channel, and the local loop. There is no provision for extensions. Charges for each class of Telpak service include the channel terminal plus line charges at a fixed rate per mile for the total distance.

In general, the full capacity of a Telpak channel must be leased, the common carrier arranging and equipping the subdivided channels as specified by the customer. The full capacity of the channel need not be equipped with a channel terminal (therefore not usable), but the full Telpak channel charge must, in any case, be paid.

A Telpak channel may be shared among several users if they are in the same business. Also, this business (for example, railroads or pipeline companies) must be one that is regulated by a federal, state, or local agency. Airlines pool their needs under this rule. Sharing is limited to dividing the base capacity (total number of equivalent voice channels) among the sharing users. Two different users may not share the same derived (subdivided) channel.

Non-Telpak broad-band services. These services have the equivalent capabilities of 6, 12, and 60 voice channels. Data transmission rates range from 18,750 to 230,400 bps. Certain of these services are available only to U.S. government agencies.

Series 8000 Channels, which are not restricted and which can be subdivided into voice channels, have speed capabilities ranging from 19,200 to 50,000 bps. Both AT&T and Western Union lease these services.

Switched broad-band services. These services are relatively new and are offered by AT&T and Western Union in selected U.S. cities at 50,000 and 40,800 bps, respectively.

AT&T's service, known as Data Phone 50, provides dial-up toll transmission between and within New York City, Chicago, Los Angeles, and Washington, D.C. The costs include a one-time terminal installation charge, a monthly terminal charge, and toll charges.

The scope of these services and the offering of similar services are expected to increase in the not too distant future as a result of increased demands by data transmission users.

Calculating Airline Distance

Airline mileage for leased-line data-communication network design is usually determined by using the *V-H coordinate* system, which covers rate and toll centers for most of North America. Each location in a network has unique V-H (vertical-horizontal) coordinates to within about a third of a mile. (The coordinates were developed by superimposing a grid on an elliptic map.) If the V-H coordinates of two locations are known, the airline distance (D) is determined by solving the trigonometric formula:

$$D = \sqrt{\frac{(V_1 - V_2)^2 + (H_1 - H_2)^2}{10}}$$

The network design programs mentioned in Chapter 5 carry out such calculations.

Communications Common Carriers

Communications common carriers are companies that offer communications facilities and services for hire to the public. Services include facilities for the transmission of voice, data, facsimile, telemetry, television, and printed messages. In addition to the communications channels, some of these companies also provide, on a rental or lease basis, part or all of the required data sets and terminal equipment. Users may also purchase or lease terminal equipment and data sets from independent manufacturers and may arrange for the use of the public switched-telephone networks or private communications channels leased from the common carrier.

The principal common carriers providing facilities for data transmission in the United States are the Bell System and Western Union. In some parts of the country, General Telephone and Electronics, while much smaller than the Bell System, offers practically all of the same services. There are also more than 2,500 independent telephone companies in the United States. While all have interconnection arrangements to the nationwide network for long-distance calling, their local facilities may be such that the end-to-end quality could not support some of the more sophisticated data-communication systems. No commitment should be made for the purchase or lease of data-communication equipment until the compatibility of available communications facilities is investigated and confirmed. Expert consultation is needed early in the planning of a system.

Telephone company representatives should be in a position to furnish current information as to facilities, services, rates, and billing arrangements. Independent telecommunications consultants, who are found in most larger cities, may also be called upon for help in determining system requirements and appropriate services.

Federal Communications Commission. The Federal Communications Commission has the responsibility for regulating interstate and international communications originating in the United States. Covered under the Act are telephone, telegraph, radio, television, telephoto, and facsimile transmission broadcasting, whether by wire, cable, or radio.

Common carriers must file with the FCC schedules of all charges, with descriptions of the services to be rendered to the public. Once approved by the FCC, these schedules, known as *tariffs,* become the basic contract between the carrier and the user who subscribes to the particular class of service, facility, or equipment described. Each common carrier does not have to submit a unique set of tariffs, but may concur in one or more of the schedules submitted by other common carriers. Thus many of the smaller carriers follow the lead of the major telephone and telegraph companies. Because of local conditions, however, some tariffs will vary from company to company.

The Bell System. This giant system includes 24 operating companies either wholly or partly owned and controlled by AT&T. With its approximately 67 million telephones in the continental United States, the Bell System offers a full array of communications facilities and services both in its public switched-telephone network and in leased equipment and channels. We explained earlier in this chapter the data-communication services it offers.

General Telephone and Electronics Corporation. GT&E is not only a communications common carrier but also a large and diversified manufacturing enterprise. Subsidiaries that manufacture equipment for communications are the Automatic Electric Company and the Lenkurt Electric Company, Incorporated. The products of both companies are, for the most part, compatible with the equipment made by Western Electric for the Bell System.

The General System's 5.5. million telephones, while only about a thirteenth the number in the Bell System, make it Bell's nearest competitor. GT&E can offer practically the same range of services available from Bell and can provide for interconnection with other common carriers to meet any customer requirements. General has more than 30 telephone operating subsidiaries in the United States, and others in Haiti, in the Dominican Republic and in British Columbia.

Independent Telephone Operating Companies

In many areas, the only telephone service available is from an independent operating company, of which there are over 2,500 in the United States. These range from small companies, some with fewer than 50 subscribers, to the larger independents, with 10,000 and more subscribers. Practically all these systems interconnect with one another and with the General and Bell Systems.

While many independents offer the same facilities and services as the Bell System's, local conditions must be investigated thoroughly. They may be such that the overall design of a planned data-communication system will have to be restructured to fit the transmission facilities available, as was indicated earlier.

Western Union Telegraph Company. While best known for its nationwide telegraph service, Western Union also furnishes communication services over wire lines and microwave radio links all over the country, as well as to foreign countries via submarine cable. Western Union offers TELEX direct-dial teleprinter services and also leases wire facilities for private voice, data, and facsimile transmission systems.

Western Union's nationwide microwave network is capable of handling all forms of communications at high speeds. Also, it can design special facilities to meet a particular user's requirements.

RCA Communications, Incorporated. RCA Communications, Incorporated, a subsidiary of the Radio Corporation of America, provides international telegraph-message TELEX service to practically every country in the world. Its facilities include radio, coaxial cable, and satellite channels.

RCA Communications also provides private leased-channel communications services to all parts of the world. For users requiring international data transmission, RCA provides DATEL and DATATELEX services.

ITT World Communications System. The ITT Worldcom System comprises 12 telecommunications operating subsidiaries of ITT. These companies form a worldwide network of circuits linking 20 countries with each other and with every important communications hub in the world.

Services offered by the ITT Worldcom System include international TELEX, DATEL, DATATELEX, and telegram services. They also provide private leased channels and international data transmission with associated voice channels.

Users in cities not having ITT terminals have access to the Worldcom System via the Bell System in this country of through domestic or international carriers overseas. ITT Worldcom System will undertake the design of special facilities to meet intercontinental data processing system requirements.

Microwave Communications, Incorporated. MCI, one of the newer and smaller communication common carriers, was approved by FCC to offer microwave channels for nontelephone interoffice and interplant communications between Chicago and St. Louis. MCI was granted a license to rent microwave channels to organizations for their own internal use. Unlike the telephone and other systems, this service is available only for sending communications from one office or plant of a company to another. It will provide channels for subscribers who will arrange their own terminal connections. It is anticipated that most users will use local telephone-company service to connect up with the microwave transmission system.

The completely new MCI service will supply its subscribers with channels of any bandwidth, to carry data, facsimile, teletype, and any other type of transmission except voice. Channels will not be routed through a switching office but will link subscriber plants, offices, and other facilities directly.

MCI and an affiliated Washington, D.C., organization, Microwave Communications of America, Incorporated, are working with other groups to seek out interested parties for participation in a variety of new routes in other parts of the country.

FCC approval of the MCI proposal is important to data-communications users. Not that many will be in a position to use the Chicago to St. Louis routes, but the door is perhaps now open for large users to have microwave routes tailor-made to particular geographical requirements.

Other companies, such as University Computing, are seeking FCC approval to set up extensive microwave data-transmission networks for public use. Such networks would of course compete with existing common-carrier services. Space satellites should also grow in their importance to worldwide data communications.

A number of companies have their own private microwave systems for voice and data transmission. Southern Railway Company, for one, has an extensive private system.

7

Hardware and Software Considerations

AT one time or another, everyone tries to find problems that fit the solutions that happen to be on hand. This also happens with MIS hardware and software, particularly where management has become preoccupied with these matters too early in the life of the project. Companies will order computers before they know what problems they will be trying to solve, and software decisions will be made before management's gaining a real understanding of application needs. Although they were regarded as tentative decisions at the time they were made, it becomes convenient to stabilize them and to proceed to design the system to fit the prejudged hardware and software.

As time goes on, it is more and more difficult to see that the hardware and software have become a focal point. And it also becomes increasingly impractical to revise these approaches, so deeply embedded are they in the structure of the application.

This is not to say that you can forget about hardware and software until the eleventh hour. On the contrary, it is important to grasp early the key technological implications.

Hardware and Software Technology

Today, we can get a lot more computing per dollar than ever before and have open to us many more choices. In the old days, we used to worry first about hardware capabilities, including maximum memory, number of allowable tape drives, upward compatibility, and the like. The range of practical possibilities was so limited that there was a sort of built-in protection to keep us from going too far astray. For example, the most popular computer of the second generation, the IBM 1401, allowed up to six tape drives, a limited number of disk drives, and 16,000 characters of main memory. IBM's comparable version in the third generation was the System/360 Model 30, which had over four times the memory of its predecessor and more tape and disk drives than anyone with a Model 30 was likely to want. The same is true of IBM's newer System/370 series.

Until about 1966, when third-generation computing power began its surge, the powerful computer capabilities needed to tackle MIS-type systems were found almost exclusively in defense-related applications. Even though these were advanced compared to what was going on in other fields, military management still could not, in many cases, buy the needed hardware capability off the shelf. Much of it was custom-built at great expense, and it represented pioneering efforts. This was also the case with the handful of advanced nondefense systems in existence at the time.

The third generation also ushered in the era of operating systems, monitors, executive programs, control programs, and the like. While these had formerly been used on large-scale equipment, the third generation's least elaborate operating system tended to make its large-scale predecessors look like child's play. Today, these programs, which mastermind the operation of the hardware resources, are used on almost all modern computers (except very small ones).

Random- or direct-access input–output devices that could store billions of pieces of data and retrieve a given piece in less than half a second also became popular in the third generation.

Data-communication terminals of all kinds and the computer hardware and software to go with them came out strong in the third generation. They showed the practical possibilities of the computer as a central processing point, accepting requests for information and processing data coming from remote terminals, perhaps thousands of miles away.

MIS was given a tremendous boost by all this newfound potential. It made the grand integrated-systems schemes of the past seem very close at hand, and at a price that was beginning to sound reasonable.

Today, we have much more than we had when the third generation was originally announced, and we even have packaged MIS applications of sorts, available for a price. Yet why is it that most of us do not yet have MIS? The answers can be found throughout this book. For the moment let us look mainly at the part that hardware and software have played.

Technology-Driven MIS

Technology and information demands are both vital in finding a practical MIS solution. If we look at a *need-driven* MIS, we can sometimes see where the need has not been properly met because the technology could not support it. Other problems are experienced in *technology-driven* systems. In some cases, we have seen the latest technological advances[1] in use, but having no practical value because they have not met management's information needs.

Today, there is considerable evidence that too many MIS efforts have not achieved the right kind of blending. In some companies, nearly every new development is implemented whether or not it has any immediate or even long-term use. Evidently, such companies are hoping that one of these developments will by chance pay off. But, in the meantime, a great deal of time and money is being spent with very little direction from the top. More than one executive has expressed his bitter frustration at having to put up with medieval information systems while a lot of his company's resources were tied up in MIS work that seemed to be helter-skelter.

One senior systems analyst was dissatisfied with his well-paying position on the corporate staff of a major petroleum company. Asked to explain his responsibilities, he reported that he was in charge of a computer graphics project, which had no special objective other than to find out how to use the ten cathode-ray-tube data-communication terminals his company had just installed. He explained that his company would often install various kinds of computing equipment and later determine what use, if any, could be made of it. He had been assigned the chore of soliciting takers for some of these "white elephants," and he found it so distressing that he decided to leave the company.

Almost every company is susceptible to situations where the MIS program fails to receive guidance and direction from upper management. In one

[1] For some insights into what the future holds in store for hardware and software, see George B. Bernstein, *A Fifteen-Year Forecast of Information-Processing Technology* (Springfield, Va.: Clearinghouse for Federal Scientific and Technical Information, Document No. AD681752, 1969).

well-known New Jersey manufacturing company, costs for the computing function had grown to nearly 2 percent of sales before management began to ask what it was getting for all that money. As it turned out, the company was buying up computer power, which it was hard put to use for applications having real value. Apparently, someone reasoned that the capability should be used for some purpose, whether or not the company could substantiate its value.

Technology's Impact on Computing Costs

In previous chapters, we have referred to development costs somewhat independently of implementation hardware (computers and peripheral gear) costs. We can easily fall prey to thinking that the relationship of MIS hardware dollars to company size (particularly similar businesses) tends to be proportionate. But it may not be, because the "laws" concerning economies of scale can come into play. There are limits beyond which we get into diminishing-return situations, but short of these limits the economies of scale can be dramatic. A rule of thumb (Grosch's Law) is that a computer's power increases in proportion to the square of its cost. Hence, a large company with a big computer gets more computing per dollar spent on computer hardware than does a smaller company. The hardware in question here is central processing units, not peripheral devices such as communication terminals.

As the central processor becomes less dominant in the total hardware cost, as will happen with MIS systems, the economies of scale become less evident. And this is happening more and more. For this reason, hardware may tend to be more in proportion to company size than development costs. This has special significance in a case where, for example, two competing companies require the same type of central processing unit. The difference in cost of peripheral gear for the same application tends to be strictly proportionate to company size, and the economies of scale can be considered negligible for peripherals. Because the central processor is the same, the marginal increase in cost is due to number of users, terminals, storage devices, and other peripherals that depend on company size.

There are other factors that tend to favor the smaller firm. Growth often means increasing bureacracy, hence MIS effort in a big company tends to cost more because the intracompany relationships are more complex. Also, the smaller company has fewer communication problems in MIS development, and costs grow in proportion to these problems. The impact of communication problems also tends to be greater in a bigger organization. In other words, severity is not necessarily a function of the number of problems.

We can conclude that MIS operating costs are likely to bear a much closer relationship to company size than MIS development costs. Our ensuing discussion will try to put in perspective some of the key concepts and management considerations in hardware and software for MIS. We shall begin with applications software.

MIS Applications Software: Three Dimensions

MIS programming projects usually mean excursions into three types of developmental categories: custom-tailored, generalized, and experimental. In order to visualize these three properties, it might be helpful to establish a reference point in three-dimensional space. We illustrate graphically in Figure 7-1, using the values along each of the three axes to represent the degree to which each variable is involved in the MIS project.

FIGURE 7-1
Three Dimensions of Software Development

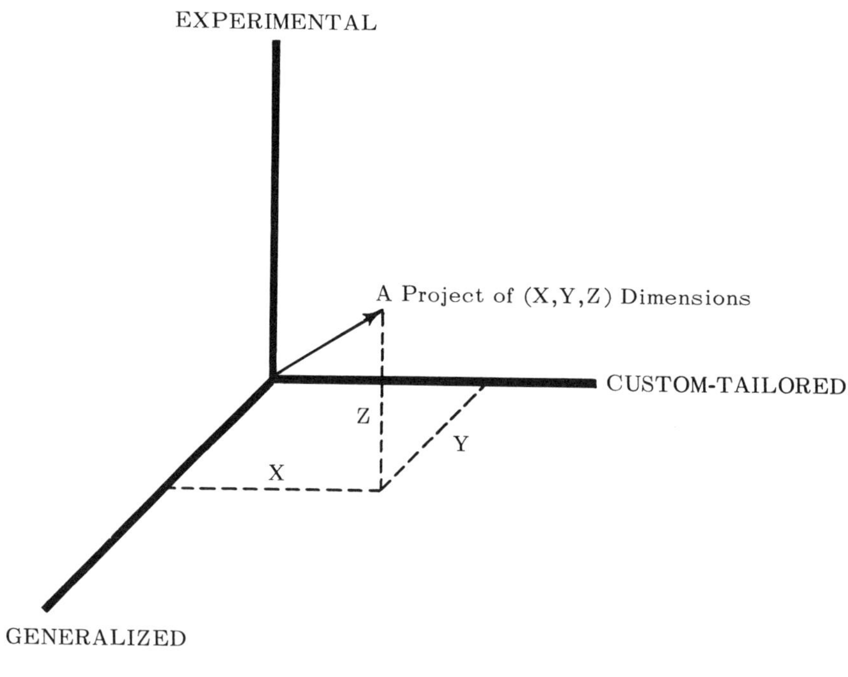

Accordingly, the farther from the origin the project reference point lies, the more expensive and complex the project becomes. However, each of the three variables has different weights that must be applied. For example, if we assign a weight of one to the degree of custom-tailoring, we might assign weights of five and ten to generalized and experimental, respectively. Thus the expense and complexity of a project that was completely experimental would have a relative value of ten, while the same project, if classified as completely generalized, would have a relative value of five. The same project on a custom-tailored basis would have a relative value of one. Let us now consider these three dimensions in terms of systems implications.

Custom-tailored systems. When we say "custom-tailored," we mean that the MIS is designed to perform a specific set of tasks and functions. The form and substance of what the system produces can be changed only by additional special programming or by reprogramming. In a sense, then, we might say that the custom-tailored system is nonanticipatory—at best, it can accommodate the known requirements. Unknown requirements are not programmed, so the MIS cannot be expected to handle conditions that *might* arise.

Forward-looking executives might ask, "Why build such a limited system, when business dynamics seem to dictate otherwise?" First, the custom-tailored MIS can be built relatively fast and at relatively low cost. Most of the speculation about what might be is eliminated, since the orientation is to what is. The real issues are pinpointed faster, and the MIS design and logic specifications tend to emerge rather quickly. And because highly tangible problems are involved, movement toward their solution is inclined to be straightforward: Alternatives from which a selection can be made are usually few.

Second, the programming of the computerized MIS is generally easier from the standpoint of logic. Besides, there is less of it—that is, fewer lines of coded instructions. Since such a project has a strong tendency to contain itself, administration and control are less burdensome. Opportunities to go off on a tangent are drastically reduced. Assuming project management knows what the system is to do, control and measurement of the work toward those ends are enhanced. And time and cost required to develop the MIS can be more closely estimated.

Whether to take a heavily custom-tailored approach to MIS depends on both the company's short-range objectives and its commitment to long-range MIS plans. It also depends on the particular applications that the system is to address. Clearly, the custom-tailored system is better suited to more stable business functions. As a rule, these are found buried deep in the organization and are separated from dynamics external to the business. For example, a personnel information system is impacted to a far smaller degree by environmental dynamics than is a marketing information system. Time is certainly a major consideration, too. Market changes often occur very rapidly, and information is critical to readjusting to them.

Generalized systems. These systems are the trickiest of the three we are discussing. Management and systems people often mistakenly perceive generalized systems to be just a bit more elaborate than custom-tailored systems. In practice, they are a *great deal* more elaborate. Companies that have developed them, or have tried to, have learned some harsh lessons. One company had estimated it would cost $150,000 to develop a generalized inquiry module for its MIS, which was scheduled to be operational after a year's work. At last report, the company had shelved the module uncompleted after two and a half years of work and an expenditure of $400,000. Similar stories have not been uncommon. In fact, we have only to look at the track record of software houses and computer manufacturers, which, in the aggregate, have shown time and cost overruns of sizable proportions.

Part of the difficulty with generalized systems stems from management's neglecting to account for the diminishing returns associated with expanded features. Systems capability is often added on during analysis and design, with unsuitable criteria used to justify it. The arguments sometimes go like this: "Now that we've come this far we may as well include the X capability too." In other words, the decision is based on what was done last and not on the objective being sought. This sort of justification can lead to more and more trivial system facilities, with time and cost escalation that is by no means trivial. Somewhere between the extremes, management must draw the line, making the necessary value judgments. A distinction between a generalized capability and a *general-purpose* capability also needs to be drawn. However, this is usually not a simple matter.

In developing a general-purpose system, or one tending in that direction, it happens that the resultant capabilities apply less and less to the particular business and its particular problems. A manufacturer developing an MIS tending toward general-purpose use would find system functions generalized well beyond the class of problems usually associated with manufacturing. At the extreme, a bank or retailer could theoretically use the manufacturer's general-purpose system by invoking the powers built into it.

Companies in the business of developing systems and programs either for outright sale or to be provided in conjunction with the sale of computer hardware have a clear justification for pursuing general-purpose systems. However, for other companies to spend time and money to build even a moderately general-purpose MIS may be questionable. (Some companies will deliberately generalize an application, hoping to sell the software or processing or both to other companies—for example, stockholder information systems, payroll, and so forth.)

At least two important considerations are involved when an MIS is tending toward general-purpose capability. First, there is the initial development cost and time, which exceed (often substantially) that otherwise needed to obtain a properly generalized MIS. Second, the general-purpose system almost always has significantly higher overhead once it goes into full production. How much higher it goes depends on the design approach taken. For example, some general-purpose systems are modularized in such a way that the user extracts and implements only those modules he intends to use. Hence, modules not of interest are not present in the production version of the MIS, although it is usually possible to add them (or remove existing ones) by regenerating a production system. Nevertheless, a module, used for whatever purpose, must be taken in its entirety. If there is unused capability in the module, that is overhead.

Costs arising from this overhead can be incurred in several places. Computer time used for regular running of the system is likely to be greater than otherwise. As a rule, general-purpose programs take longer to run, which certain cases have shown dramatically. In some especially bad cases, running times were two and more times higher. Small systems that run ten minutes instead of five per day are not of concern. What *is* serious is the eight-hour-per-day job that takes sixteen. So is the increase of service times in real-time systems.

Another kind of overhead cost results from the fact that many general-purpose systems require a bigger hardware configuration than would ordinarily be needed. Memory size and the number of input–output devices required can usually be expected to be greater.

Experimental systems. The word "experimental" is more likely to conjure up someone in a laboratory coat handling test tubes than a systems analyst in a gray flannel suit. Yet the experimental nature of at least some parts of the systems analyst's role in MIS is very real.

Identifying an experimental effort is anything but simple most of the time. One tip-off is what we call the trial-and-error solution. This is where the proposed systems approach has certain important functions to accomplish, which "we'll learn how to do when we get there." It may also exist where several alternatives are left standing just prior to going into full development, but a selection cannot be made because none really looks good now.

One systems director had some other ways of finding out what sort of work was being contemplated. First, he insisted on detailed presentations of systems plans, half of which he probably did not understand. But he would ask just enough questions to assure himself that his systems developers understood what they themselves were talking about. As a grand finale, he would ask each key man in the development team whether he would bet his job against the performance that was proposed. When any member was reluctant to do so, that individual would be asked to state his reasons. From these, the systems director plucked out and categorized experiments and other kinds of contingent factors in the proposal.

Having a "handle" on these items enabled the director to coordinate resources to minimize contingencies and clear roadblocks. He was also in a position to know what the experiments were and could monitor progress on them more closely and bring extra resources to bear on their outcome.

Note well: The systems director was not discouraging experiments. He just wanted to know what they were. And when he O.K.'d the project, he knew much more about the risks he was committing the company to. Everyone else, perhaps for the first time, also understood the project.

MIS projects will always have some element of experimentation. In general, management's posture should be such that projects can be considered successful even if the experimental parts fail to produce what is desired in the time period allotted. On a major MIS undertaking, management should have firm assurances of success in enough areas to at least break even. As we suggested earlier, the step-by-step developmental approach will enable the company to have a pay-as-you-go MIS. Here, management can evaluate success at preestablished milestones.

Nothing we have said should be interpreted so as to preclude projects that are entirely experimental; however, they should not encompass the functions of an entire MIS. Yet more and more experimental systems projects are having happy endings these days. One company in a process industry, for example, took on a sophisticated system employing operations research techniques. The project was not recognized as an experiment when it was begun. Funded at about $100,000, the system was to be operational within 12 months from its inception. The expected annual return on the investment was stated as 60 percent. As it happened, none of these estimates was even in the ballpark.

Three and a half years and $950,000 later, the company had operational a cutdown version of the originally conceived system. In this case, management's faith and incredible patience paid off to the tune of $2.2 million a year, which is what the system now saves the company.

Should You Pioneer?

The question of whether or not to pioneer is based on several major considerations. First and foremost is the potential return (in benefits as well as money) expected if you should be successful. Second is the question of whether you have the talent and background and skills necessary to tackle a pioneering effort. Third is the question of whether there are substitute means of solving the problem that may be better to use for the time being.

When you are pioneering, it is a good idea to be pioneering in a systems area with a direct relationship to company performance. Pioneering not deliberately aimed at business problems, such as developing a new programming language or something technically impressive, is usually not a good idea for MIS projects.

Original applied systems and hardware, which are unique in the computer field, understandably possess a number of unique attributes. They cost more to develop, of course, but what is bothersome in most pioneering efforts is that no one can say how much more. Even the most pessimistic time and cost maximums are often exceeded, if indeed these estimates were not sufficiently high as to discourage the project altogether. Still, this alone should not stop pioneering systems work. Risk, potential payoff, and the economics of alternative investments must be analyzed carefully, however, before deciding.

In the area of large-scale commercial systems, a classic example of a pioneering effort is American Airlines' Sabre System, a real-time system connecting reservation terminals all over the United States to a central computer complex in Briarcliff Manor, New York. Sabre was originally known as *Saber* (semiautomatic business environment research). From this title alone, we can infer that, at its inception, the project was viewed as a research undertaking. The shape of things changes over the years, however, and so it was with Sabre.

Developed as a joint effort of American Airlines and IBM, the system was for the most part designed from the ground up. The developers viewed each facet in terms of the real requirements, rather than trying to adapt reality to the then current technology. American Airlines first defined its needs, then issued the specifications for what was required to do the job. This involved sophisticated engineering on the part of the computer manufacturer and the common carrier providing data-communications facilities. Saber evolved in three carefully planned phases, the final one of which advanced the state of the art in commercial real-time systems.

To be sure, there are risks in systems pioneering work, but there should also be at least a fair degree of confidence that the mission will be a success. It is essential to see just where your pioneering work fits into state-of-the-art progress. While this judgment is essentially technical, it takes capable business judgment to interpret its meaning and read between the lines.

Let us say you are thinking about an application that would require the highly reliable identification and computer translation of signatures (handwritten, naturally), whereas the state of the art provides optical character recognition equipment that will read typewriter and computer-printed data and hand-printed numerals. The next step in the progression would seem to be the recognition of hand-printed letters, and a giant step it would be. Handwriting recognition is a much longer way off in the future, and an identification capability may be even more remote. Hence, the progression does not lead you to believe that your requirements will be satisfied in the next step or even the next two steps in the progression. Precedent simply does not point to this as coming any time soon, and therefore the system should not be made dependent upon it.

On the other hand, we may be considering a system requiring voice recognition. Since there have been a number of successful tests of this capability in the research laboratory, it would be reasonable to expect that something simple could be developed for your application in a few years.

Summing up on the matter of pioneering, these points should receive management's concentrated attention.

1. Be sure your pioneering aims for basic benefits to the company. Anticipated returns should be great.
2. Understand as fully as possible where your effort stands relative to the state of the art. One step in the progression is usually the practical limit.
3. Assess what skills and talents you can bring to bear, remembering that experts who understand the business as well as the technology will be needed in house.
4. Look diligently for substitute approaches that give the same result with less risk, but try not to give up important needs in the process.
5. Organize the program by steps, so that phases or plateaus of accomplishment can be realized in going the whole route.

Hardware and Software Compatibility

The issues directly concerned with compatibility of hardware and software have spurred much controversy in the latter half of the past decade. Some computer users felt all along that their hardware and software would be usable as they progressed to larger equipment. Some must have also assumed that changes in equipment suppliers could readily be accomplished. Most such hopes were dashed when users discovered that compatibility, if it could be accomplished at all, was attained only after great expenditures of money and time and at considerable sacrifice in operating efficiency.

Considering the size and scope of MIS as implemented by many companies today, the importance of compatibility or transferability cannot be minimized. Given the magnitude of MIS development expenditures and the growing importance of MIS to the effective management of company operations, it seems clear that the computer users cannot continue running off in completely new directions that require old systems to be abandoned. Further, because an MIS may be viewed as a continuing effort lasting many years, hardware and software must provide more continuity than had been customarily expected.

Classifying Software

There are three fundamental classifications of software that need to be defined briefly, since each has somewhat different compatibility aspects. A fourth classification, *system test software,* will be described later.

Applications software comprises programs that perform MIS functions directly related to the business-oriented objectives of MIS. Production, inventory, demand deposit, airline reservations, stock transfer, and accounts-payable systems are examples of applications software.

Systems software is another classification. These programs facilitate the use of computer hardware and, except for a few special cases, are application-independent. Operating systems, program compilers such as COBOL, and report-generator languages are in this classification.

The operating system for an MIS would control and supervise various functions, including:

- Allocation of main memory and mass storage.
- Queuing and priority of processing.
- Scheduling of input and output.
- Error checking.
- System measurement and performance logging.
- Program libraries' services.
- Message control.

General-purpose and utility software, the third classification, performs specific functions, such as sorting data, but is independent of particular applications. It differs from systems software in that it does not relate specifically to hardware and facilitating its use. Such software is usually describable in hardware-independent terms—that is, the concept and techniques used may be generally applied.

Software Compatibility

Systems software, except in mammoth systems, is out of the hands of the computer user. (Big real-time systems *often* have custom-designed operating systems to permit speedier and more versatile processing geared, in part, to the data-communication "front end.") Systems software must be closely meshed with the specific hardware features. Having accomplished this, there may be a bonus if such software turns out to be transferable. The incidence of true transferability, in practice, has been quite low to date. This has been a sore point with many computer users, who have been led to believe that transferability exists when in fact it does not.

Programming languages are not the worst offenders, but they are the most important. Touted as being compatible, languages, in general, have been disappointing. Even a language like COBOL, which was conceived with the specific intention of compatibility—it is an acronym for common business-oriented language—has missed its mark. Although COBOL accounts for most of whatever success there has been in language transferability, a number of practitioners consider it lucky if COBOL proves compatible within a single manufacturer's hardware line.

The standardization concepts found in COBOL are, nevertheless, workable. For example, it requires explicit environment specifications, which describe the computing hardware to be used. In addition, the data specifications in COBOL explicitly describe data elements as to their attributes. Attributes of data in many other languages are woven inextricably into the problem program itself, and the machine dependencies that are often involved make transferability impossible.

When hardware of a different computer-manufacturer or a different line of a single manufacturer's equipment is under consideration, the incompatibilities have been very significant, sometimes making it unfeasible to even attempt modifications. Operating systems, control programs, and the like, while in the category of systems software, are not expected to be transferable across manufacturer's lines. This is understandable, since they are so intimately related to the specific design features of the hardware. Within a line of compatible computers, however, it is rare to find that upward compatibility is a problem. In moving to a bigger system, however, this type of software may be found lacking in the capabilities needed to fully exploit the power of the hardware. Here, a company may have to move to a more powerful operating system, which entails applications program changes to adjust for compiler differences. It may also have to set up an entirely new series of job-control statements to activate the new operating system.

General-purpose and utility software, while its conceptual design is compatible as a rule, is transferable only when the programming language and operating system it uses are compatible. Often, the transferability of such software is not crucial, since many of the same general-purpose utility functions will be provided for a particular system. One exception is general-purpose data base or information management systems, which typically have unique features within a particular hardware line. Proprietary software offered by independent software houses, rather than hardware manufacturers, may be available in identical form for more than one manufacturer's line. The trend toward offering identical package programs that will operate on more than one manufacturer's equipment seems to be growing.

Applications software compatibility is the most problematical of the three classifications. It is in this area that the bulk of programming expense has been incurred. The seriousness of this was emphasized in strong terms at the Spring Joint Computer Conference of 1969 where, in one session, conferees concluded that the lack of transferability was a drag on the use of computers and slowed hardware advances.

In an *Electronic News* article (May 19, 1969), James A. Ward of the Department of Defense was quoted as saying:

> We do not have program transferability, and millions of dollars are spent each year on the uninspiring task of reprogramming. Not only are the programs nontransferable from one manufacturer's computer to that of another, but in some instances they cannot be run on two computers of the same make and model with memories of different sizes.

In the same article, Robert W. Bemer of General Electric pointed out that the worst problems arise when a processor accepts a program that it "thinks it can do and really can't and therefore doesn't say anything."

Managers responsible for MIS development must ascertain the extent to which the system will be compatible. In this connection, the evaluation and choice of programming languages and other systems software are an important function. Standards and the commonality of the proposed languages are critical in the sense that their presence tends to justify the hope for compatibility. The supplier of the language compiler should be pressed for a representation of compatibility, defining exactly what is and what is not compatible.

Hardware Compatibility

Where hardware is concerned, compatibility has two aspects. One is the ability to upgrade the central processing configuration within a single hardware manufacturer's line. The other is the ability to make changes across manufacturers' lines. Both aspects concern the degree to which established application systems have to be altered to work properly on the new computer system under consideration.

If a given hardware manufacturer has carefully planned his product line, there is very likely to be upward compatibility. This means that bigger, more powerful computers can run jobs that are running on smaller computers using the identical programs. Under circumstances to be described shortly, there may also be downward compatibility.

Not too long ago, few if any manufacturers attempted to provide for orderly growth through compatible equipment within their own lines. True compatibility across different manufacturers' lines was unheard of. Today, both of these situations have changed somewhat.

Within a manufacturer's hardware line, compatibility relates to several things. *Instruction repertoire* is one of the most important. And in this connection, we are looking for identical hardware-instruction-sets up and down the line. Having upward compatibility implies that the bigger central processing units will at least have all the instructions provided in all of their smaller units. The bigger hardware may have more instructions, but not fewer. Where more instructions are provided, downward compatibility, in a formal sense, is precluded. In a less formal sense, downward compatibility may be realized if the additional instructions are not used.

Memory-size limitations for particular computer models are important for downward compatibility, but are not a problem for upward compatibility since every bigger computer can be ordered with larger memory.

Memory-addressing schemes and the internal data representation (such as character, byte, binary words, floating point words) can be important, depending on whether the program has been written to relate to these features. This is often a consideration where low-level languages, such as Assembler, are used.

Bit encoding can sometimes be important, again especially where low-level programming languages are involved. By bit encoding, we mean the specific combinations of off-on bits that represent the various letters, numbers, and special characters in memory. Examples of two encoding schemes are EBCDIC (Extended Binary Coded Decimal Interchange Code) and ASCII (American Standard Code for Information Interchange). Both are eight-level codes, which means that one character is represented in an eight-bit configuration.

Time dependency is a consideration related almost entirely to downward compatibility. It refers to the need to have sufficient internal processing speeds (mostly a function of a computer's basic cycle time) to control certain devices (such as an MICR or OCR device) or meet real-time response or turnaround time requirements.

Channel speeds are another consideration in downward compatibility. Certain high-speed input–output devices, such as drum storage, transmit data at a rate of speed that may exceed a central processing unit's ability to accept it. Therefore, the device cannot be used.

Types and numbers of particular input–output devices are always a consideration in determining compatibility. If, for example, a program requires six tape drives and three disk drives, an otherwise compatible system must also satisfy this requirement. So, too, must requirements for special hardware features be satisfied for compatible operation.

Achieving Compatibility

Compatibility between two incompatible central processing units may be achieved through conversion, emulation, or simulation, or a combination of the latter two.

Emulation is accomplished exclusively by hardware features that permit programs written for one computer to be run on another. Most modern computers have designed into them what is called programmable micrologic, sometimes referred to as read-only storage, or "firmware." Micrologic specifies the configuration of the most elemental electrical circuits in the central processor and can be changed by special procedures. For example, the internal representation of an add instruction is recognized as such by the micrologic program. By changing the micrologic, it is possible, for example, to make the central processor recognize the identical instruction as a subtract, multiply, compare, or other instruction. Special instructions have been created, using read-only storage, for list-processing functions discussed in Chapter 5. Conceivably, an infinite variety of instructions could be created, such as one that multiplies and divides, giving both answers. As a result, it is possible to arrange the micrologic program to interpret instructions foreign to its native mode—that is, those of another computer processing unit.

Simulation accomplishes the same thing as emulation except that the means is an ordinary stored program and not a micrologic program—software instead of hardware. Formally, the simulation is done by an interpretive program, which traps and decodes the instructions of a foreign machine as they are presented for execution. In so doing, it determines what the foreign instructions are supposed to do. It then causes the same result to be obtained by composing and executing the necessary instructions from its own hardware instruction set.

The practice of using hardware and software together is sometimes called *hardware-assisted compatibility*. Some instructions are understood directly and emulated under this scheme, especially the common ones. Others are simulated. The computer "traps" and passes over to the interpretive program those instructions it does not understand, whereupon they are deciphered and executed.

Language conversion is just what its name implies—that is, a program written in one language is converted to another. Examples are Assembler to

COBOL and COBOL for one machine to COBOL for another. A program is especially written to accomplish a language conversion, but may also be done partly or completely "by hand." Depending on the kind of conversion being attempted and the competence of the programmer who developed the conversion program, the effort can range from success to failure. Problems with the program's incorrectly converting instructions have not generally been serious. The problem is more critical where instructions cannot be interpreted by the conversion program, whereupon a programmer has to attempt to do it. This hand-tailoring is more error-prone, not to mention time-consuming and relatively expensive. The low efficiency of such work is often sufficient to justify designing a completely new system that, unlike the converted one, will take advantage of the more powerful capabilities of the new hardware.

Operational efficiency is an important consideration where the programs to be converted account for substantial running time. Relative to the performance that could be realized from the new hardware, the efficiency losses can be significant.

Simulation is the least efficient means of achieving compatibility, since it involves a special program that analyzes each incoming instruction. The extra time this takes accounts for some of the loss in efficiency. Hardware-assisted compatibility with partial simulation is probably the next least efficient.

Emulation can be fairly efficient because the kind of interpretation required with simulation is not needed. However, the losses in efficiency resulting from suboptimum design may be significant.

Language conversion can provide good efficiency, since the final, executable program will run in native mode. With some hand-tailoring, some programs can be made to run near optimum. That language conversion promises greater benefits to the computer users is consistent with its being more difficult, time-consuming, and expensive. Remember: You are taking a program that has already been tested and debugged and creating a new program that has to be retested and re-debugged.

Evaluating MIS Programming Languages

Criteria that can be applied to language selection are weighted differently according to the situation faced by a particular company. Additionally, individual program characteristics and program types have an important influence on the decisions to be made. For example, the data-communications control program and real-time application programs used in an on-line MIS are more likely to be coded in a powerful and efficient low-level language, whereas off-line report programs are likely to be coded in a less efficient, high-level language (COBOL, for example).

A low-level language is one that closely parallels the one the computer understands directly, which is called machine language. Assembler is one such low-level language. It is one step removed from machine language, and the programmer must be intimately acquainted with the hardware to use it effectively. A mnemonic language, Assembler bears a one-for-one relationship to the machine instructions, meaning that one programmer coded instruction generates one machine language instruction. High-level languages, on the other hand, can yield many machine instructions for a single programmer instruction.

Anything that the computer is capable of doing can be made to happen using a low-level language. Providing the ultimate in flexibility, programming in a low-level language also permits highly efficient programs to be written. Compared to high-level languages, this means they will run faster, or take less memory, or both. Benefits can be realized through lower computer costs as well as the faster response times that are required in an on-line system.

Obviously, there are tradeoffs between the use of a high-level and a low-level language. Otherwise, the latter would seem to be the way to go on everything. And there are quite a number of major considerations.

To begin, let us list some of the considerations relative to a high-level language such as COBOL, FORTRAN, or PL/1 as compared with a low-level language like Assembler:

Training. It takes much longer to train a programmer for Assembler—perhaps three or four times longer.

Proficiency. It takes much longer for the Assembler programmer to become proficient—more than four times longer.

Aptitude and intellect. An average high-level-language programmer may not be able to cope effectively with Assembler, whereas the reverse is seldom if ever the case.

Availability of talent. There are far fewer truly competent Assembler programmers.

Programmer pay. The scarcity of competent Assembler programmers has created a salary differential—perhaps 20 to 50 percent. (This also results from the greater complexity of typical programming jobs.)

Program development time. It generally takes longer to produce an identical program in Assembler—perhaps three to four times longer.

Program development cost. For the reasons already mentioned, it costs more to develop an Assembler language program—perhaps three times as much.

Program maintenance time and cost. The intricacies of an Assembler program, as well as its difficulty, make it more costly and time-consuming to change.

For these reasons and others, companies are making every effort to get around the need to use low-level languages. This holds even for such time-critical programs as would be found in on-line applications. The extent to which low-level languages can or should be avoided hinges on a couple of determinations.

First, you have to ascertain what the theoretical loss in efficiency would be as a result of using a higher-level language. The range of losses is quite wide, depending on how good the compiler is and how well the programmer understands the high-level language from an efficiency standpoint. In the case of compilers, evaluations have pointed up significant differences. The identical program compiled by two different compilers can have vastly different running times, sometimes a difference of 100 percent. Programmer familiarity with the language-usage techniques to keep down running time makes a big difference too. Dramatic differences have been experienced by programming a desired program function using different approaches to accomplish the same end result.

Second, efforts are being made to render high-level languages as efficient as low-level ones. This can never be fully achieved, but the gap has become so narrow in many cases that a number of relative considerations are much less pronounced. Today, for example, it takes an exceptionally able Assembler programmer to "beat" running times achieved by an average COBOL or PL/1 programmer. And even the difference in memory requirements is not as significant as it used to be, due in part to the lower cost of memory and the trend toward buying bigger memory. So, in short, it is quite possible to incur the added expense and time of using a low-level language and get nothing in return.

On the other hand, there will continue to be uses for Assembler language programs. System software such as real-time control programs, and some data-management programs, will likely be coded in low-level languages in the foreseeable future. The powerful instructions available and the fast-response requirements are expected to justify its use in special cases. Key programmers working on such software must be top-notch professionals. Since such individuals are rare, not to mention the fact that many companies would find their cost too great, it is becoming more common to use the services of a software house, which can attract them, pay them, and keep them interested.

General-Purpose and Special-Purpose Hardware

Most MIS will be implemented using general-purpose hardware. This means that the computer and devices attached to it will be standard equipment chosen from a manufacturer's catalog. If a single manufacturer happens to sell what is needed at the price we are willing to pay, chances are that the hardware configuration will be made up entirely of its equipment. On the other hand, we can often mix various manufacturers' equipment in order to obtain the desired configuration and performance at the price we want to pay. Delivery schedules can also become an important factor in selecting one manufacturer's equipment instead of another's.

Some years ago, it was rare to see a mixed-vendor configuration. Today, it is becoming more and more common. This is especially true of data-communications hardware. Terminal equipment of all kinds is available from more than a score of manufacturers tending to specialize in this area. They, as well as computer manufacturers, will also specially engineer equipment in cases where it is not reasonable to force the MIS to fit preestablished hardware features and capabilities.

Perhaps the area of greatest importance in this connection is custom engineering done on terminal design. Communications line adapters, modems, concentrators, remote multiplexers, and related gear may also be specially designed or modified to achieve greater efficiency, improved reliability, and lower cost.

Central processing units and peripheral devices may be equipped with both special features and custom-engineered features. Special features are optional and may be specified as part of the computer configuration when it is bought, or they can be added later. As an analogy, the typical automobile comes with standard equipment, but there is a long list of optional equipment that can be had for a price.

Custom-engineered equipment is of two types: "second time," when someone else has had custom engineering work done and that becomes available to a subsequent buyer; and the "first time" custom-engineered feature or device. Here, the buyer will typically *request a price quotation* (RPQ) from the hardware manufacturer, whereupon engineering and manufacturing people decide (1) whether the RPQ is for something that can work in the environment of the main system; (2) whether, as a matter of policy, the custom feature should be made available; and (3) price and time to develop.

In one case, a user wanted a set of locks installed on terminals so that the computer would be able to determine when a particular lock had a key in it. This feature was desired because of special security requirements. To design it, engineers had to concern themselves with changes to the terminal, the type of switch lock to be used, the special identification signal each lock would emit, and the modifications to the computer to enable it to recognize the signal.

Another custom-engineering job was undertaken in order to provide visual and audio alarms when a real-time system was failing or when checks and balances provided by the application program were out of line. Flashing red lights on a wall-mounted panel and a gong were hooked into the computer at points where special commands triggered their activation. The audio-alarm feature later became a standard option on this particular manufacturer's equipment.

Specially engineered terminals are found in banking, brokerage, airline reservation, and other systems where certain unique requirements are best met through hardware design.

Backup Considerations

Where the MIS has been accepted by management as an essential component in business planning, administration, and control, the question of what needs to be done in case of a breakdown becomes quite important. By that time, however, it can be too late to answer the question. Consequences of this delayed action can pose a grave threat to company operations. Backup is a matter that must, therefore, be initially incorporated into the overall MIS planning and development effort. When operational status is then achieved, the system will offer the wherewithal to provide continuity of service under adverse conditions.

Among the adversities that have to be accounted for in considering MIS backup are:

1. Loss or erroneous alteration of data bases.
2. Problems created by software bugs.
3. Computer-system hardware failure.
4. Data-communications system breakdown.
5. Power failures and air conditioner breakdown.
6. Destruction (partial or complete) of computing center and operational data bases from fire, flood, or other disaster.

Needless to say, the efforts relating to the foregoing must be two-sided, one directed toward prevention and the other toward recovery.

Before discussing these points we would like to make a few observations on the issue of reliability, which looms large as a limiting factor in what can and cannot be done. This is a technology problem involving improved design and better components, and in many cases it relates to the mechanical rather than electronic aspects of hardware. Malfunctions and failures are becoming less and less tolerable as a result of the sharp increase in the number of on-line and real-time MIS applications. Technology limits what can be done at a practical cost to significantly improve the hardware's ability to fail soft, fail and automatically recover, and reduce the level of service gracefully.

Also, it is becoming more and more difficult to find maintenance and repair technicians who have the aptitude and desire to wrestle with some of the complex components found in today's systems. Nowadays the top-notch maintenance engineer has to be well trained and highly knowledgeable in the area of systems software, especially in operating systems and monitors that control or supervise the hardware functioning. The shortage of competent technicians has been at crisis proportions since the mid-1960s. Consequently, there is a tendency to skimp on preventive maintenance so that performance on emergency service will be bearable. Hence, as less thorough preventive maintenance work is done, more emergency-service requirements are generated, resulting in even less thorough preventive maintenance and longer waits for fixes. Thus the whole basis of service is sent into a tailspin.

To the computer user who is considering critical applications like MIS, the reliability and service considerations certainly must be viewed in the light of what others have been experiencing. The unfortunate part about this is that potential users sometimes fail to investigate reliability by contacting other users. And, since it is not usually possible to get reliability information from hardware manufacturers, potential users make decisions on the basis of sales pitches rather than more concrete information. Users should press hard for guarantees of minimum performance.

Loss and Erroneous Alteration of Data Bases

If for any reason part or all of a data base is lost, backup data must exist to re-create it. While data losses from nonphysical causes should be rare, they are far more frequent than losses from physical damage.

Prevention of data loss begins with sound procedures at the working level for handling the physical data media. Probably the single biggest problem area, this has to do with check-out and check-in activities governing access to the data library. Where operating procedures at the computing facility are sloppily administered, it is not rare to find in-use data files and backup data files inadvertently released for other uses. When the mistake is discovered, file re-creation must be effected. If the backup data media have also been given out, you may be out of business. With luck, you may be able to go back to printouts and other scraps of information to reconstruct. A very expensive and time-consuming activity—it may take months—reconstruction is sometimes not even possible.

An installation does not have to be large to have thousands of reels of magnetic tape and perhaps hundreds of disk packs. A carefully planned and executed inventory system to control access to them is obviously vital. Further, all programs should include standard data-file label-checking logic. This will read and analyze the magnetically recorded identifying information at the start of a set of data, called *header label,* in order to determine whether it is permissible to reuse the medium. The header label would contain the date the file was created and say how many days it is to be retained. Knowing today's date, the system can determine whether it is appropriate to release the file.

Trailer labels, which are usually recorded at the end of a set of data, contain control totals checked by the system against running counts, accumulated during processing, in order to determine whether records have been lost. In a tape system these counts are always checked, since all records are passed. Hence, in the case of a record count, the number of records read in should equal the number originally recorded.

In real-time processing, or wherever records are directly accessed, counts are also kept. But these are dynamic: They are added to and subtracted from as transactions occur. At any instant in time, however, they should reflect the current situation, unless something has gone wrong. The only way to find this out is by having the system periodically read all records on file, keeping a running count as would be done in a tape system and making the appropriate comparisons.

Often, losses or erroneous alterations of data records occur when program modifications, additions, or deletions are made to an operational application and systems software. Because of the complex and numerous interrelationships that can exist in a system, the art of making changes without disturbing the integrity of existing processing functions is indeed delicate.

In addition to thorough testing and validation when changes are made, spot-checking methods to detect erroneous changes in processing programs (or even willful changes, as in spying or fraud) and data losses are also recommended. The system may be designed to regularly produce special reports for auditors. Special audit and checking transactions and the capability to set up dummy records or test master records may also be provided. In addition, auditors will often develop their own verification programs to check processing in the course of surprise audits.

Auditors sometimes maintain duplicate application programs, which they keep current with all authorized changes. Periodically, they will bring such programs to the data center and run a matching program to learn whether the operational program matches theirs. Should it not, an investigation will be undertaken immediately.

Discrepancies in processing functions may also be turned up through the running of a program or the entire system with standard test data. These data exercise all the functions, the expected results being known. Deviations from those expected results will signal the launching of an investigation.

In general, control and verification functions should be split away from operations and development functions for maximum effectiveness. This is important from the standpoint of more thorough and comprehensive check-ups on operations and systems-development functions.

Problems Created by Software "Bugs"

Software does not break down like hardware. Instead, there are inherent "bugs," which, under conditions neither tested nor anticipated, introduce data errors. They may also cause other problems.

It is of prime importance that software be developed under stringent quality control and that it be tested thoroughly prior to its live use. Even when all this has been done, there are still potential problems because of residual bugs in any complex system. The protection that can be provided against problems brought about by bugs in the software can take the form of a hardware control feature, as well as the fundamental means discussed in the previous section. Certain controls, as was pointed out, may have to be checked by the verification and control staff, while others depend on programmed methods to determine whether a malfunction has occurred.

One common hardware feature is memory protection. This inhibits a program from inadvertently destroying or altering another program sharing the computer's memory. There is also data-storage protection, which may involve both hardware and software checking. In the case of both types of protection, the program wishing to access or alter data from the allocated memory or storage device must have an acceptable passkey to do so.

A big factor in software reliability has to do with software changes made after the original development effort. This is likely to have been carried out professionally, making for a software product that was thoroughly tested and found to work properly under any of the test conditions. However, once it goes into actual use, certain changes are likely to be necessary. And sometimes these changes will not be tested as thoroughly as was the original system. Management attention and controls, as previously mentioned, must be applied.

Real-time systems are especially difficult to debug thoroughly. They require dynamic testing procedures, which cannot possibly provide for every condition that will be met under live operating circumstances. Overload conditions, in particular, can cause tricky problems, and must be simulated to provide adequate verification as to the system's workability.

Computer Hardware Breakdown

The more critical MIS becomes to the operation of the organization on a day-to-day basis, the more you have to study what to do in case it breaks down. More often than not, there is a direct correlation between the amount of additional money spent and the degree of backup protection. Providing close to 100 percent backup can double the hardware cost. Always present is the question of the various degrees or kinds of hardware backup that are appropriate for the organization. In other words, you have to try to balance the risk of losses that would be incurred as a result of system failures with the cost of insuring against those losses. Expected loss is mainly a function of mean time between failures and mean time to repair. Failures come in three main varieties: hard, soft, and intermittent.

In computer parlance, a *hard failure* means that the entire hardware complex is inoperative. This may be because one or more components of the system is down. When this happens, a company may or may not have alternatives to reinitiate operations while waiting for repairs. One of the first determinations to be made is how long it will take to fix the system. If the manufacturer's engineer responds promptly or is on-site to handle a trouble call, he can often give an estimate within a half-hour or so after initiating diagnosis. The built-in diagnostic programs of the better operating systems and the complete problem reports given by alert computer operators can cut significantly the time required for diagnosis.

On the basis of the diagnosis and repair estimate, a decision as to course of action can be made. As indicated, there may be no choice but to wait until the hardware is repaired. On the other hand, if an installation has multiple computer configurations that can be substituted for the system that is down, work on one of the other systems can be considered. Real-time MIS would be switched to a secondary system immediately. For batch jobs, depending on the time estimate for repairing the primary system, installation management may decide to run the data files and programs elsewhere. This could be at a computer service bureau or at another company's installation.

The possibility of using other off-premises equipment becomes more and more unlikely as the hardware configuration becomes more sophisticated. Such is frequently the case where MIS is involved. It is quite rare that another installation would be able to accommodate a real-time system with perhaps 100 remote terminals on-line, simply because the hardware configurations do not match. But this, of course, is not the only problem. There may be no computer time available at the other installation, and always, the transition will take some time and may not ultimately be worth the effort.

Soft failures are those that partly rather than completely incapacitate the system. In such cases, depending on which component fails, it may be possible to run the MIS in a degraded mode of operation and, in addition, to run jobs that do not require the components that are down.

There are also *intermittent failures,* which occur periodically, incapacitating the system only briefly. These are the most annoying of all failures because of the difficulty in diagnosing their cause. There are also transient failures, which have no pattern and which may be impossible to diagnose.

One saving grace in nearly all types of computer hardware failures is the computer-checking logic, which is able to determine that a device or system component is malfunctioning. When such detection occurs, the system "locks up" in such a way that errors cannot be introduced into the applications processing.

Because failures do occur, modern installations operating in a critical-response environment will often have provisions for backing up the system in some way. Dual systems or redundant (duplicate) pieces of hardware may be employed. The practice, called *duplexing,* may enable the system to accomplish some or even all of the functions of the primary system. When partial service is available, the system is said to be operating in a *degraded mode.*

Every device on the system may be duplexed, but this is often too costly. Quite frequently, the data-base storage devices are duplexed in some way. The obvious question is: How much should we spend on duplexed hardware? In one case it may be 10 percent above the primary system's cost, and in another, 30 or 40 or even 100 percent higher. In a communications-based system handling important work, the entire central-processing configuration is usually duplexed.

Failures that can imperil human life are the most serious of all. The nation's defense systems, such as SAGE (Semi-Automatic Ground Environment) and the various early-warning systems are fully protected by extensive backup provisions. Aircraft-control systems, which should be fully computer-based by the end of the decade, require extensive backup. Federal Aviation Agency air traffic control systems are being designed to have considerable backup depth. NASA's manned space-flight program has four computers backing up each other, any one of which can provide full service, should the need ever arise.

There is a branch of industrial operations research associated with the statistical and probabilistic study of maintenance, repair, and the question of backup. Through the use of these techniques, the frequency and duration of down time can be predicted. Then, if the figure represents an unsatisfactory operating environment, certain backup provisions may be contemplated for the configuration and the estimated frequency and duration of down time recalculated. All the calculation and study in the world, however, cannot overcome the truth of the age-old maxim: The chain is no better than its weakest link.

For example, a rather big configuration ($100,000 a month rental) was completely knocked out of service a number of times because the typewriter console, used by the operator to direct the system, broke down. Because a $100-a-month typewriter broke down, a $100,000-a-month system went out of service along with its operating staff and all the users who depend on it. Yet other kinds of much less critical backup provisions are often provided in such big systems.

In one system, there were several magnetic-tape drives costing about $600 a month each that were mainly for standby. But some of the more failure-prone mechanical devices, like the card reader and typewriter console, were not backed up. Both of these were needed to run the system, and, as it turned out, both created more problems than the tape drives.

Preventive maintenance, naturally, is very important in keeping the equipment in good operating order. The reliability of certain kinds of devices is dramatically related to the quality and regularity of preventive maintenance. One of the difficulties with a real-time MIS is giving up the system for preventive maintenance. Using just part of the system for checkout, there is some question as to how thorough it is.

Data-Communications System Breakdown

Backing up data communications facilities directly is not usually within the power of MIS developers. Where data-transmission channels are provided by common carriers, we can only hope that a repair call will bring fast results. Depending upon the type of service and failure, it may be possible for the carrier to reroute communications so as to circumvent the problem. Realizing that the appropriate circuit alternatives may neither exist nor be available when needed, MIS management must give some thought to the matter of continuing systems services at least in a partial or degraded fashion. This may involve provisions for batch processing, alternative ways of reestablishing a connection (dial-up substituted for leased-line service), the use of the various telegram and message-switching services, and, conceivably, hand delivery. Network designers should look at the technical design considerations with an eye to alternative methods of backup. The justification for whatever levels of added expense would be involved may be decided by project management.

Terminals can be troublesome because electromechanical hardware is involved. Regularly scheduled preventive maintenance greatly diminishes the chance of failure, but of course cannot reduce it to zero. The crucial question with terminal breakdown is whether the user is completely cut off from any communication with the system while the terminal undergoes repair or is replaced. This is another way of asking whether there will be a terminal nearby that can be shared or used for higher priority transactions. How critical the application is will determine whether total silence can be tolerated and if so, for how long.

System communications software can help provide advance warning of some impending failure. By maintaining error and retransmit counts, which are automatically compared to such figures under normal conditions, trouble can be spotted and a rectifying investigation begun. Such controls would show suspected line noise or impairment and detect certain terminal and other communications-hardware malfunctions.

Power and Air Conditioner Failures

Backup to sustain operation of the system in the event of a power failure can be expensive. Costs to provide emergency power using various alternatives must be viewed with regard to the probability and duration of a failure.

The effects of the system's being down vary greatly depending on how critical the applications and, in the case of real-time systems, geographical coverage. If two different companies have identical systems, except that one is nationwide and the other is limited to a 50-mile radius from the processing center, the backup-power considerations are somewhat different. If power is out at the computing center, chances are that power is also out in most places within a 50-mile radius. Practically speaking, there will be so many other impediments to commerce under such circumstances that the absence of the MIS for the duration may not matter much. Conversely, if the regional blackout necessitates shutting down nationwide access to the system, a more compelling rationale for backup power to sustain operations would seem to exist.

Intracompany systems, as opposed to systems that directly serve the buying public, can usually stand a somewhat higher risk of power failure. The workforce can be doubled up and otherwise mobilized to catch up on the work. Making up for lost time in a customer-related situation, however, may be impossible. This is especially true where fast-response requirements characterize the relationship.

Strictly batch-processing management information systems rarely warrant backup power of any kind, whereas the more time-critical on-line or real-time systems may call for any of a combination of methods. Let us consider some of these.

Power failures are generally of short duration. Restoration of service is effected within an hour or two in most cases, although the power blackout experienced in the northeastern United States some years ago and other severe failures attest to the fact that longer power losses do occur.

To deal with the momentary losses, some installations employ a motor generator set with a heavy flywheel. Should power be lost for a brief period, the flywheel momentum continues to supply the energy needed to generate power for a little while. Motor generator sets are also used in numerous real-time and other operations to prevent brief surges and drops in line power from getting to the computer hardware. Certain types of computer hardware are quite sensitive to power variations and can give unpredictable or erroneous results when such variations occur.

Wet-cell batteries are also used to sustain power for a short period of time, at most a half-hour. Connected to a D.C. motor generator set, which provides A.C. power, a wet-cell system automatically cuts in when normal electric service cuts out.

The power produced when these short-service methods are activated will usually be designed to run the *life-support systems* (air conditioning, lighting, and so forth) as well as the computer. Since this cannot go on long, an alarm of some kind will sound after the loss has been sustained for more than a few minutes. Preparation is then made to shut down the system *gracefully*. Users working on remote terminals are signaled to wrap up what they are doing so that the system will not be in use when it is finally turned off perhaps ten minutes later. This kind of power-off procedure insures the integrity of the system and its data. Programmed actions are terminated normally and final updating takes place, as would be the usual practice at the end-of-day "going off the air" notice.

By way of contrast, an abrupt power cutoff would leave actions hanging suspended, transactions partly completed, and controls invalidated. Such abnormal conditions could cause erroneous processing or transient malfunctions, the results of which are unpredictable. Under such conditions, in the dynamic environment of real time, it is almost impossible to reconstruct the original circumstances when power comes on again.

Longer-term electrical backup may be provided through gasoline or diesel-powered electric generators. These are quite costly, even to sustain a modest installation, but may be justified in areas where power losses are relatively frequent and their duration sufficiently long to cause distressing processing interruptions. Since it takes time to start up such generating equipment, real-time systems will usually need some means of interim power if continuity is to be maintained. Generating equipment needs to be run and tested at least once a week to insure its effectiveness in an emergency. And, by all means, equip the system with a large fuel-storage tank. Remember that fuel suppliers will not have electricity to run their pumps and may therefore be unable to supply fuel in a blackout.

Air-conditioning breakdown is another peril that can knock out computing systems. Should the temperature in the computer room become too high, built-in thermal switches "unplug" the hardware. To guard against such a happening, two air-conditioning systems may be used, both being run under normal operating conditions. However, in the event that one breaks down, the other would have sufficient capacity to keep the temperature and humidity within operating range while the first is being repaired.

When a Computing Center Is Destroyed

Preventive action in connection with the physical destruction of the computing center is a many-sided affair. It begins well before any MIS becomes operational.

Selecting the site for the facility is one early activity that needs to be governed to some extent by backup and recovery considerations. Were there no other factors coming into play, an ideal site might be in some cave in Vermont or South Dakota. Some time in the future, corporate MIS facilities may be found in such locations. However, today you are likely to have gigantic problems finding enough professionals willing to man the technical and operations staff in such locations, and there may also be an insufficient clerical pool from which to draw.

On the opposite extreme, you could locate the center in a densely populated major metropolitan area where professional personnel, labor, and utilities are no problem but where space is scarce and very expensive. Additionally, salaries, the likelihood of fire or riot damage, and insurance rates will all be higher, and expansion may be difficult.

The selection of a computer-center site is also influenced by economics of the optimally designed data-communications network for real-time MIS. And some management consultants strongly urge that a centralized MIS function be headquartered apart from any divisions it serves.

There is no pat answer as to whether a remote or metropolitan location is the best choice. However, there is a trend toward selecting a site in a suburban location within 50 miles of a major city. Companies doing this buy acreage in or around industrial parks on which they can build and expand for many years without difficulty. Unless the selection is made carefully, however, a suburban location may be a very bad choice. Companies have made some unfortunate mistakes in selecting sites in relatively rich suburban areas, such as Westchester County in New York, Fairfield County in Connecticut, certain areas around San Francisco and Los Angeles, and others. One top computer executive exclaimed that he would have been better off in New York City paying $13 to $17 per square foot for space. Not only were personnel scarce but what few there were commanded very high salaries in these suburbs.

Once the site is selected, it is important to retain an architect and a contractor who know about the various preventive measures and devices that may be employed to guard the center against serious damage. In fact, there are some construction and architectural concerns that do nothing but computer facility work. They will be familiar with the air-conditioning, fire- and smoke-detection devices, and construction features required to provide optimum protection.

But suppose that, despite all the precautions, there is a disaster? This question must be answered, in part, by the designers of the system, since most of the company's vital operating records will be in this central location. Many companies would be in terrible straits if their computer centers went up in smoke. They would have no means of recovering vital records, some of which might be required to substantiate fire insurance claims. Ignorant of the seriousness of the potential problem, responsible individuals have never brought pressure to bear to have off-premises backup records and programs.

Recovery from a disaster may be facilitated if backup data files are retained in a safekeeping location far removed from the computer center. The usual practice is to keep backup files on magnetic tape, which is stored periodically. Daily or perhaps weekly cycles may be suitable, depending upon the degree of recovery you are willing to pay for. Consider a customer master file that is updated daily. If copy is stored once a week, at worst, should disaster come, you would be missing one week's updates; at best, one day's updates; and on the average, half a week's updates.

Basically, you have to decide what you can live with, remembering that 100 percent recovery will not be possible through the use of backup files, since new work for which there is no backup will almost always be in the center when disaster strikes.

A little over ten years ago a spectacular fire at the Pentagon's computer center in Washington demonstrated vividly the relationship between the value of the data media as compared with the cost to re-create the information contained thereon. Some $300,000 to $500,000 worth of data media were lost in the fire. Stories on the recovery cost varied widely, the estimate running from $6 million or $7 million up to $30 million. In any case, the difference was striking.

Besides backing up data files, it is also necessary to back up computer programs and operational documentation. Programs may be kept on magnetic tape, which serves as the library of programs. Periodically, perhaps every two weeks, the library may be copied and stored in a safekeeping location.

Documentation, which would include system flow charts, logic diagrams, design and program specifications, and operating instructions, can be protected by its being microfilmed and stored in a safekeeping location. Video tape has also been used for this purpose. The changes and new programs can be kept track of through periodically microfilming all changes and new program documentation completed during the period, which may be two weeks. Once a year, a completely new set of microfilmed documentation may be created to replace what would then be a starting series of film plus perhaps two dozen others containing the past year's changes and additions.

In the event of a disaster, the microfilmed documentation can be used to re-create hard copy, which would be edited for purposes of consolidation and updating. The degree to which recovery can be effected, remember, will be a little less than 100 percent for the reason just mentioned.

It should be noted that a tape-oriented MIS creates backup automatically each time the data base is updated. This is because updating a data file on tape necessitates the creation of a completely new data file, even though there may be only a relatively small number of updates. Disk file records except those used like tape—that is, straight sequential—may usually be updated in place, which obviates an automatic backup file. Hence, it will be necessary to copy the disk-stored records onto tape (the least expensive medium) for backup.

Recovery Provisions in Systems Design

Everything in the area of backup and recovery is the proper concern of those who plan and design an MIS. Incorporated into the design itself, a number of techniques permitting recovery may exist in both the applications and systems software.

Of major concern in the typical MIS operation is minimizing the time during which users are unable to gain access to the data bases and processing. This means minimizing the time needed to recover from failures, which may involve the computer hardware, data communications network, systems software, and applications programs.

Logging transactions as they occur in a real-time MIS environment is one common way to permit speedy restoration of operations. By recording on tape or disk the status of each transaction—say, for every terminal on the system—it will be possible to reconstruct the operational conditions that existed just before the system went down. Doing this will later allow users, in most cases, to pick up where they left off by rekeying the previous transaction. The degree to which this sort of recovery technique is justified depends partly on the nuisance cost of reinitiating contact if the user has to start over from the beginning. Further, such a procedure may be required in MIS applications where half of the transaction could have been completed and the data base incompletely updated when the failure occurred. Here, it would be quite important to notify users to finish their transactions when the system returned to operation status. The nature of some MIS applications makes it very difficult if not totally impractical to avoid partial updating. Therefore, the foregoing provisions are necessary. However, the skill and knowledge of a capable MIS designer can bear heavily on whether the actual updating in the course of transaction processing is needed. There are usually a number of alternatives for handling intermediate results.

Checkpoint and restart is another recovery technique that is usually found in batch-mode systems; it provides for "snapshots" of portions of main memory at logical control intervals. Such intervals are often associated with external control levels, as, say, customer-number groupings for ledger posting. Should something go wrong with the system, the last snapshot taken is used as the basis to restart operations. All tapes and other devices are repositioned as they were when the last snapshot was taken, and operations resume from this checkpoint. In the absence of a checkpoint and restart technique of some kind, it is frequently necessary to go back and start from the very beginning. This might mean, if the system went down in the last ten minutes of the initial run, that a five-hour processing run has to be done over. Conversely, checkpoint and restart might require only an additional 15 or 30 minutes to complete the job.

The longer the running time, the higher the probability that something will go wrong and the higher the average cost and inconvenience of starting the job from the beginning. Therefore, it is a good practice to incorporate a restart capability where program running time exceeds some cost and time value. An hour is a common rule of thumb for the latter. Control totals and certain other information may be logged in some way to provide a restart capability substantially the same as that offered by checkpoint and restart.

As we pointed out, planned recovery reduces the inconvenience as well as the cost of lost time. The objective is to provide ways to quickly reload the memory and position input-output devices to their prior state so that operations may continue. Device reassignment capabilities and alternatives are important in this regard and need to be reviewed in the context of system software. Checkpoint and restart may also be within the realm of system software if it is a generalized capability, one that can be used by any program by supplying the proper control parameters.

Systems designers also need to concern themselves with the opportunities for operating the system in a degraded mode. Where an application has been designed in such a way that it must be operated on a maximum configuration, degraded operations are rendered impossible. Here again, the alert and capable MIS designer will be in a good position to see how degraded-mode provisions can be worked into the overall design. Sometimes it is surprisingly simple to make such provisions.

Program and System Testing

Debugging programs and testing systems have always been two of the more troublesome activities in systems development. The eventually crippling side effects of a poorly managed testing phase can build to a point where the company's operations may be in jeopardy.

Adequate testing of any system is a painstaking effort to isolate and correct errors before the system becomes operational. Even with the best testing, however, residual bugs will remain. These can be agonizing when they crop up in live operations. Batch-mode systems present serious problems in this sense. But real-time MIS involve much more risk and therefore more comprehensive testing because of the time-dependent and concurrent processing of multiple transactions, the use of complex hardware configurations and systems software, and the user demands placed at random on such systems.

M. G. Ginzberg has described the nature of real-time system testing in "Notes on Testing Real-Time System Programs," which appeared in the *IBM Systems Journal* (Volume 4, No. 1, 1965; pp. 58–72). Most of the terms described in the following section are drawn from that source.

Test Phases

Seven major types of tests are mandatory for real-time MIS. They are:

1. *Unit testing* consists of debugging individual programs or, in the case of larger programs, program modules. This testing is not unique to real-time systems.
2. *Package testing* checks the operation of an integrated logical or functional subdivision of the system; it consists of the complete processing of a particular input message or group of inputs. All possible variations of the inputs, as well as intentionally created errors, are checked out. This type of testing is not unique to real-time systems.
3. *Single-thread testing* is unique to real-time system debugging. It consists of entering inputs one by one from a single terminal and fully checking the results as in package testing.
4. *Multithread testing* consists of entering multiple inputs concurrently in order to detect errors arising from a mix of inputs being processed concurrently. To give the effect of multiple-terminal interaction, an environment-simulator program is used.
5. *Volume testing* uses a simulator program to apply a heavy volume of representative transactions to the system. All the file processing and other functions of the system are checked to insure that the cumulative result is correct. These runs simulate closely the actual operation of the system over a compressed period of time.
6. *Field testing* is used to check out the data-communications network under live conditions. It also provides a check on the system's ability to cope with variations and errors introduced by human operators.
7. *Parallel testing* is the final check of the system before it is cut over to live operation. Typically, it begins with running a few terminals side by side with an existing operation (if one exists), comparing results,

then putting them in live operation. Successive cutovers then take place, usually increasing in size each time, over a period of months.

In general, with the exception of parallel testing, tests that immediately follow one another may be overlapped. For example, package testing for one part of the system could take place while single-thread testing is done for work completed earlier.

Test Tools

There are a number of important test tools (programs) that must be developed to test a real-time MIS. Three such key tools are vitally important and represent a significant investment of time and money.

A *test-file generator* is used to construct data records used in connection with checking out the system.

An *environment simulator* permits the testing of the system on a standard (non-real-time) computer. Used with records created by the test-file generator, it closely approximates real operating conditions for multithread and volume testing. It can be used to drive the system under many different circumstances, including peak and overload situations.

A *real-time tracer,* sometimes called a DDT (dynamic debugging tool), provides the programmer with "before" and "after" snapshots of records, main memory, status indications, and the like, wherever he specifies. In this way, the flow of processing may be tracked. Tracing may be started and stopped wherever specified and can be limited to certain program functions. Other capabilities found in real-time tracers enable the programmer to modify data and registers, perform memory searches, and enter temporary logic to control program execution. Tracing may be done while the system is being driven by the environment simulator.

There are a number of other less important testing aids, such as output-compare programs, which check for discrepancies after two runnings that are expected to be identical. New variations in testing techniques are emerging as more real-time systems come into being. One such technique generates input automatically, given the record formats and acceptable values and ranges of data elements. Literally millions of combinations of data-element values can be tested in this way. This is especially important for extreme end-range testing, which is often responsible for activating obscure bugs.

Software Development Estimates

In Chapter 1 we tried to highlight various MIS programs with respect to time and cost for development. Those figures were presented without detailed comment on the software-development time and cost. In this section, through the use of a sample case, we will try to provide some insights into the nature of these matters.

Consider a real-time MIS in use in a financial organization. This system provides on-line inquiry, data-base updating, and administrative message switching. Having about 300 terminals and operating on a 12-hour real-time day, this system processes an average of 6,000 transactions and messages an hour. Typically, 25 transactions will be in various stages of processing continuously. The data processing logic for this particular system is not too complex as management information systems go. Measured in lines of program code (computer instructions for the most part), the software developed was as follows:

Type of Software	*Lines of Code*
Real-time application programs	40,000
Batch application programs	60,000
Real-time control programs	30,000
System test and simulate programs	50,000
Utility and support programs	50,000

About 5,000 hours of computer test time were used to check out the code within the final 12 months of the project. Let us now make some computations to gauge the magnitude of the foregoing MIS development program.

A common way to estimate a project is to use program development rates expressed as lines of code per man-month. These rates have been ascertained through various studies done over the years. The rate represents the number of lines of working code produced divided by the time spent by programmer–analysts. This time includes all their work, commencing with general systems design and ending with final system test. Hence, the end-result program code is averaged over the job (excluding systems analysis). Typical rates used in estimating are shown below:

Software Type	*Lines per Man-Month*
Application (real-time)	170
Application (batch)	250
Control supervisor (real-time)	90
Miscellaneous (batch)	200

Under certain exceptional conditions, these rates have been known to as much as double. However, conservative planning would rule out estimating on the basis of exceptional performance.

Using the rates just given for our sample case, let us draw certain conclusions as to the man-months of effort represented.

Software Type	*Lines of Code*	*Rate*	*Total Man-Months*
Application (real-time)	40,000	170	235
Application (batch)	60,000	250	240
Control supervisor (real-time)	30,000	90	333
Miscellaneous (batch)	100,000	200	500
			1,308

Assuming a man-month costs the company, with overhead and fringe benefits, $1,500 on the average, it may be seen that this portion of the project will cost $1,500 × 1,308 or about $2 million. Systems analysis might run another $750,000, depending on how well the job had been previously defined. Computer test time, figuring an average rate of $200 per hour, would run $200 × 5,000 or $1 million. Management of the project and other related time might run another $250,000.

Adding up these figures ($2 million + $750,000 + $1 million + $250,000) we can see that this MIS is a $4 million development effort. This does not include such items as data conversion and operational hardware. Looking at the man-months for software (1,308) we may compute that a professional staff of 35 to 40 would be needed for a three-year development program.

The preceding system is certainly not small, but neither is it big, as systems go. With respect to lines of code relating to the application, it has 100,000 in all. Giant systems may have five to ten times that amount.

8

MIS Project Organization and Sponsorship

THIS chapter is about what to do to get things done. It tries to hit the major MIS management considerations and to highlight some of the more subtle weak points that have hampered MIS ventures. Most of what it has to say relates to people.

As is done in most management literature, we will be recommending useful concepts that have emerged over the years. Yet the intelligent application of these concepts must be related to MIS in some rather special ways. For one thing, MIS is an internally used product, different from those we make and sell to outsiders. The close interrelationship that a well-conceived MIS must have with its ultimate user is necessarily quite personal.

Little perception is needed for managers to understand that those in the company who have control of the MIS are destined to be the custodians of substantial power. Hence, it is not surprising to find behind-the-scenes maneuvering and even open debate as the prospects strive to achieve an advantageous juxtaposition—or to at least maintain the status quo.

Over the past few decades, American business has been going in the direction of increased decentralization. The accompanying specialization of business has become a rationale for erecting barriers that have hampered progress toward common objectives. Although there are many indications that business has begun to change to different and more workable organization forms, MIS proponents today must cut across organizational boundaries—within divisions of the company, at the corporate level, in line functions, in staff functions.

MIS gets at the heart of business activity. Unlike a companywide payroll system, which is of little consequence so long as it works properly, MIS is woven into the very fabric of the business. Much more than a conventional systems-engineering job is needed, for MIS represents an unparalleled opportunity to put the pieces of the business back together in such a way that they function in a truly synchronized manner. The project to bring an MIS into being therefore has to be given serious attention at the very highest level.

Making a Preparedness Evaluation

Sober appraisals need to be made regularly throughout the life of an MIS project. One key to success is a correct first appraisal. As in putting together a model airplane, you should check to see that all the pieces are there and in good order.

There are three fronts that need close attention in determining whether a company is equipped to undertake MIS development: (1) top management backing, (2) rank and file management support, and (3) systems staff competence.

Should these three ingredients all rate "excellent," the MIS project has a very good chance to be an outstanding success. There is also a very good chance that the company can take on a more sophisticated variety of MIS and be successful. Many good things can happen if two out of three are excellent, but excellence will not be one of them. Preparedness must of course relate to the question of what you propose to do and the level of success you require.

Suppose we have a top management that exhibits moderate support, a middle management that does the same, and a systems staff that is better than average. If these conditions are to prevail for the duration of the MIS project, we should define a set of moderate objectives.

Let us consider another set of conditions. Suppose top and middle management are eager but the systems staff is just average. For some reason or other (pay, working conditions, whatever), highly competent systems people cannot be attracted. Unless this can be changed—and there should be concrete evidence to that effect—you would be well-advised to aim for a moderate MIS.

On the other hand, if any of the three factors is judged to be below average, MIS *should not be attempted.* The odds of success in such a case are not promising, and the project is not likely to go at all with a substandard systems staff. However, some companies get lucky and succeed with one or the other user management group not fully committed. But it has never worked out, nor will it ever, if *both* management groups are dragging their feet.

Elaborating further on preparedness is difficult, because only a detailed examination of your particular situation can provide the measure of relativity needed, as there are personalities to contend with. As for the external factors, such as the systems staff's competence, you have to go to other companies (especially in your industry) and learn what kind of talent they have and relate their performance (based on what they are accomplishing) to what your own staff is accomplishing. Here, you also need to look for reasons. A qualified computer management consultant can help you do some of this, but you also have to make a personal visual inspection.

Top Management's Role

Exactly where upper management will come into the picture and exactly what it will do needs to be worked out on an individual company basis. Special emphasis, however, ought to be placed on participation early in the life of the MIS effort. The judgments made in this period will affect the direction and parameters governing the end product. In addition, this is the appropriate time to begin forming an opinion as to the chances for success. Under scrutiny will be the people, what they are trying to do, what they know, and what they do not know. There must also be an intelligible working plan that clearly conveys an in-depth comprehension of the areas of MIS activity.

Now we can ask ourselves whether it makes sense to continue with the project, with some reasonable hope of being right because the "homework" has been taken seriously. But does top management really need to get involved at this level? Emphatically yes. Nevertheless, if after participating for some time, an executive fails to contribute further to the proceedings he can simply excuse himself and perhaps send an alternate.

Middle Management Support

The impact of middle management on MIS success varies greatly with company size, organization style, and industry. Its relative importance to the MIS project is about the same as its relative importance in the company.

Industrial giants often have a strong and stylized middle management. This seems especially true with companies engaged in diverse fields or in businesses where there are many products requiring different marketing approaches. By the same token, there are large companies whose middle management performs essentially a shepherding operation. And of course some companies contain both. It goes without saying that support from a strong middle management is vital to MIS success.

MIS practitioners need to find out who runs the company—who decides what the company does and who sets policy. Interestingly, these functions are not always where the classical organization chart would show them to be.

Divisional executives and the managers reporting to them in some companies, for all practical purposes, run their divisions as independent organizations. This independence can include such matters as vital policy decisions, long-range capital commitments, and decisions on new business directions.

Where such situations exist, it must be recognized that the ordinary conception of middle management must be thrown out. Here, for all practical purposes, divisional management is top management. And here an MIS may focus exclusively on the activities of a division, with little or no direct connection with corporate-level systems or officers.

If corporate management is happy with the performance of a division that has been operating autonomously, then there may be little motivation to interfere with it. On the other hand, corporate management may not be satisfied with divisional performance and may view an MIS as an effective way to apply controls or, perhaps, inhibit divisional management. Using MIS in this connection will not produce the desired results. It bears repeating that basic management problems will not evaporate as a result of introducing an MIS. Indeed, they will probably get worse—if the system continues to function at all. Systematizing chaos or poor management only intensifies problems because it will typically permit more bad decisions to be made faster and more easily.

However, MIS *can* help in conjunction with sound management reforms. MIS can be valuable, even essential, to the successful implementation of revised business approaches and realignments. But because it is ultimately people who really count, the answer is the intelligent application of managerial principles, not computers.

Avoiding the Common Mistakes

Ordinary MIS projects can have extraordinary problems in getting off the ground because of flaws in the organizational scheme set up for them. Conquering such problems is often not simply a matter of reorganization. For one thing, personalities do not as a rule change, and they may be the crux of the problem. Nor is drawing new organization charts going to help—unless a serious appraisal of root causes has been made. But common mistakes in organizing the project can sometimes be avoided through an awareness of the experience of others.

MIS developers who privately (and sometimes publicly) state their case seem to be convinced about what not to do, since factors contributing directly to success are often more subtle. The following areas are examined in this light, although they are not hard scientific facts or incontrovertible guidelines:

1. Don't take on an MIS project in the absence of a partnership type of arrangement between operating management (MIS users) and the computer systems development function.
2. Don't approve plans and expenditures for MIS projects at a level of management lower than that required for other expenditures of a similar magnitude.
3. Don't assume the project's division of responsibility will automatically become clear with the passage of time.
4. Don't fragment ultimate project responsibility by having two or more managers in charge, unless your company has successfully executed shared managerships in other functions.

Who Is Responsible?

Leaving the question of MIS responsibility and leadership open until the last minute has been a monumental error of judgment in a number of companies. Top executives in these and other companies are inclined to let this issue take care of itself, either because they consider themselves incapable of making an informed decision in this area or because they are faced with a politically hot situation.

Responsibility for the MIS development program can be vested in either the systems department or the operating division, or it can be shared by them. A five-year special effort to learn which approach is most likely to be successful leads to the conclusion that no one approach has significant advantages over any other. However, if you pick the wrong one (in the light of local conditions) you will have very serious problems.

The best approach for a company might well be one patterned after the organization of its other business affairs. For instance, suppose the company has done well with shared-responsibility projects, wherein a staff man and a line man are actually co-managers of a project. This approach, then, should be given top consideration. Conversely, there are numerous top executives and managers who have had bad experiences with dual managerships and three-way managerships and who simply will not sponsor such arrangements.

Deciding who should be responsible for the MIS project is not an easy task in those companies where there are at least two organizations involved and where the system will cut across a number of lines of functional responsibility. Depending on the power structure in the organization and the political climate at the time, the task of deciding who should be in charge and what department he should come from may be subject to numerous external factors. So much depends on the origin of top management support that generalizations are difficult to apply. There is one generalization that does hold, however, and that is that the project management must be definitely decided before getting into too much work.

Who Makes Decisions?

Few things are as great an impediment to MIS success as confusion or uncertainty about who makes project decisions. All kinds of decisions need to be made, of course—both day-to-day decisions and high-level policy statements.

Without exception, the most successful MIS programs have been those where the men with the last word were available to make decisions on short notice. Project organizers in these cases have made it their business to see that decision makers would be available through the life of the project. In virtually every area, they established with top management a definite plan for cutting through red tape. Understanding the need for and importance of these measures, top management stood behind its proclamations as to who would have the last word on what.

The talented individuals who join together to pull off a successful MIS represent a bright and a necessarily critical audience. They will be interested in decisions, but more than that they will want to know who made them and why.

So what can MIS project management and the company do to answer the decision-making problem? First, push decisions down in the organization, to the very lowest level where they can reasonably be made. This will force the man with the problem to solve it and to be responsible for his decision. It will also create a sense of urgency that may not otherwise be felt.

Second, carefully plan and designate decision responsibility. Business decisions should ultimately remain in the hands of user management; technical decisions, in the hands of competent technical personnel. Top management should provide leadership and direction.

Third, to the extent possible, organize team and individual functions so that the assignment of tasks is definite. Then, make your performance expectations known and take a fair but tough-minded attitude about the importance of meeting them and the consequences of failing to meet them. Concentrate special attention on understanding what factors bear on the success of the tasks, particularly those not within the control of the team or individual. For these areas, either put the needed resource at the command of the responsible group or establish a coordination function to see that the resource gets to it in order to satisfy its needs.

Who Pays for MIS?

One way to answer the question of who pays is to say "the company" and let it go at that. However, this fails to answer the question behind the question, which concerns the allocation of costs. Distributing costs for MIS, in turn, raises the question of whether a division or function of the company has the right to refuse the system and therefore to refuse the associated costs.

Before we go on, let us define the two costs we are referring to. Research and development cost, which takes in all expenditures to bring MIS from an idea to an operational system, is one; operating and maintenance cost is the other. A number of companies treat these two costs differently for purposes of distribution. Deciding on a formula to govern the question of how the distribution takes effect is not as clear-cut as it may appear at first glance. And, rather than be arbitrary, most companies seek to find an equitable formula with which everyone is reasonably well satisfied.

Let us consider R&D cost first. One method of charging out this cost is to start with the assumption that the MIS project is sponsored at the corporate level. Under this arrangement, costs are distributed by the fixed formula regularly used to allocate corporate overhead. If corporate overhead is not ordinarily allocated, costs either may be fully absorbed as undistributed cost or may be partly absorbed. In the latter instance, we might want to have absorbed items include project management, hardware evaluations, software analysis, and communications studies. To a large extent, these activities do not pertain exclusively to any one special MIS function, but cut across the whole system and all its functions. And, it can take as much software analysis to specify a data-management system for a $10 million company division as for a $100 million division.

Outside of the cost that is fully absorbed, the remaining R&D items would be distributed among the participating organizations according to some preestablished criterion. As was just pointed out, one way to distribute this cost is by the usual ratios used to charge corporate overhead. Another way is to charge actual costs incurred in R&D efforts being directed to the MIS wants and needs peculiar to each participating organization.

Operating and maintenance cost for MIS includes elements such as computer, data-communications, and related hardware; systems programming support for system software fixes, changes, and operating improvements; and applications programmers and analysts for fixes, minor changes, and operating improvements. Not included are costs incurred as a result of adding new or improved functional extensions to the MIS. Such costs would follow whatever plan has been adopted for R&D.

On the other hand, the bulk of operating and maintenance costs would be allocated on a usage basis—that is, each user group would pay only for the MIS services it actually used. However, these variable charges could conceivably be added to a base or fixed charge (a standby cost for making the service available, even if it is not used).

As mentioned earlier, some companies have highly independent, almost autonomous divisions, which are handled gently by corporate top management as long as performance is up to expectations. If top management wants a companywide MIS, it may have trouble convincing some divisions that having an MIS is in their best interests. One way out is clear: Do not force the issue and drop plans to proceed with companywide MIS.

On the other hand, management may want to sweeten the proposition to make it more palatable to the resisters and others as well. Exactly what needs to be done along these lines depends upon the motives for resistance. If divisions accept the concept but are not ready to pay for all or some part of it right away, that is one problem. Another arises where the proposed MIS concept is not viewed favorably and where the refusal to pay is not yet at issue.

Assuming that the concept has been bought and has, in some way, been endorsed, there are sometimes other problems. Reaction could go like this: "It's a great idea but . . . I'm not ready . . . I don't want to spend the money . . . funding should come out of corporate coffers."

One easy way out is to take on MIS as a corporate project, especially if it has multidivisional application. Life being what it is, however, this may not prove to be the best possible answer. This is because people who get something for nothing may not have strong interests in fostering the project.

Top management has to spend the time and energy to insure strong divisional participation to start with and has to continue its involvement throughout the MIS project to sustain such participation. This is as close as we can get to a guarantee of success.

Who Does the Work?

There are two types of people who will enter some sort of partnership as MIS developers: those representing management and those representing the computer system function. Top management faces the problem of seeing that the right quantities and qualities of both types are blended into a unified working force for the project.

The availability of computer people is one major problem that has to be faced. High-level computer types can be attracted if management is willing to ante up the big money they now command. But this is becoming more and more difficult, with the growing demand for skilled people outstripping supply and forcing up the ante.

A vice-president of data processing in a medium-size company gave a vivid interpretation of the seeming dilemma when he told of his attempt to find a senior analyst to tackle an MIS project. He put it this way: "After about ten weeks of interviewing, we finally hit upon a man who seemed to meet our requirements. This obviously capable young man had an exceptionally impressive record of accomplishment, and the three men on my staff who interviewed him also thought highly of him. But when we started talking money, the whole thing fell apart. He was already earning almost as much as I do, and I'm responsible for 225 people, of whom 30 are professionals. My company pays pretty well, so I just don't know how to reconcile the fact that I have 15 years more experience and am 16 years older than he is. Within the next three months following this, I had two more experiences that were essentially the same as the first. From what I can tell, the situation is going to get worse before it gets better."

Another top computer executive explained that his MIS plans were about to end up on the rocks as a result of his having lost four senior computer people. Each man had more than five years with the company (not too common in itself) and figured heavily in its long-range MIS plan. Part of the problem was line management's indecision on the direction of MIS in the company. But, said the executive: "We couldn't have come even close to matching three out of the four salary offers." He went on to say that the loss in experience and know-how would cost the company hundreds of thousands of dollars. It is not certain whether he was referring to replacing the total package of talent and experience or the lost opportunities in delaying MIS. Perhaps he meant both. In this particular company, management had diligently made attempts to keep up with compensation trends, and until recent times, as is true of many companies, they had been successful.

Let us now look at the other side of the staffing problem. MIS user representatives are a bit more plentiful and certainly more stable than systems personnel, but the difference between the two groups ends there. Both sides need to have the best obtainable for MIS work. While the computer function will no doubt put its best into action, the line organization often holds back because its superstars are occupied with other things. Not infrequently, MIS is left with second- or third-string participants who are mysteriously available at just the right moment.

Top management should know that it will have to supply some valuable talent from the line organization when it approves the MIS proposal. In fact, some of them should be directly involved long before the proposal for the project comes into being.

Selecting line men for the MIS staff can be done on the basis of major MIS functions and the organization to which they pertain. For any major function, three levels of personnel need to be on the MIS team to keep it supplied with (1) top management perspectives, (2) middle management operations knowledge and experience, (3) knowledge of and experience with existing systems and procedures.

Several companies with very successful MIS have taken what should be the obvious approach to solving these staffing requirements. They have brought in:

- At least one top executive.
- A number of middle management people.
- A number of systems and procedures people.
- A number of industrial engineers.
- Some up-and-coming young executives.

Exceptionally able people found the potential challenges and rewards of the MIS project very much to their liking. For the younger men, it was an opportunity to gain exposure to company people and problems on a broader scale, while at the same time contributing special knowledge in narrower areas.

More senior men and the executives seemed to feel that this was an important opportunity to shape the destiny of company operations in the future—something that had always been needed and that merited more personal attention than they had been able to give it in the past.

Everyone, in varying degrees, was thinking that this was an ideal way to gain a lot of knowledge about the company and its problems. Hence, they would be in an enviable position for promotion earlier than they otherwise might have been.

It was this kind of intracompany public relations work that sold the project to would-be participants. Many, of course, could have simply been assigned or transferred into it. However, had there been reluctance, these individuals might have contributed much less to the MIS. The positive feeling at the outset had a lot to do with the success of the entire project. And, periodically, the "sales pitch" was repeated in an attempt to insure that the momentum would continue.

Underlying a sound organizational and philosophical framework for a successful project are competent personnel. Assuming that most other recommended management practices and policies have been "written into law," it is finally and chiefly people who will make or break the project. If you are earnestly concerned about the challenges, opportunities, and environment you will be creating for MIS staff members, then serious problems will be minimal. If, on the other hand, you fail to create an atmosphere to the liking of highly competent computer professionals, you can expect to attract and retain very few. The company embarking on an MIS must create an image as an outstanding place to work, a place that pays top dollar and otherwise appreciates and recognizes excellence.

Computer Staffing Problems Can Get Sticky

Numerous companies have become so fed up with the excessive turnover of computer experts that they have gone the "homegrown" route to combat it —training employees with aptitude in the hope that they will become computer experts constituting the bulk of the systems workforce. But does the homegrown approach work any better? Not generally. This is a qualified no, because in many cases the homegrown method is undertaken for the wrong reasons.

Some companies consider it a cheap labor supply. As has been demonstrated time after time, once the employee has been trained and gains computer experience, he expects to be paid and treated accordingly. Unless his remuneration is close to his value in the open market, he tends to view his company loyalty as foolish and leaves. Then not only has the company lost a computer expert whom it has paid dearly to train, but it has also lost the skills and experience the man had acquired before joining the computer staff. Discontent has about the same effect, except that the man's lessened productivity may make it economically worse than if he had left the company. On the other hand, companies that use the homegrown method more successfully have taken appropriate steps to combat such problems. However, even here there are some very real and significant pitfalls. Consider the pay and treatment of computer people compared with the rest of the company. This creates an incentive for many people to "get into the computer department" whether they belong there or not. Some may figure that the pay is worth doing a job they do not really like.

These are just a few of the problems management must face. Relying heavily or exclusively on the existing systems staff and even on the existing user representatives has its drawbacks. We find, for example, that mental inbreeding is a common ailment in closed environments. Bad habits flourish under such circumstances, and the approaches taken to solve problems requiring imagination eventually will have a sameness about them. The ingredients to produce creative solutions may no longer be present or, more commonly, will lack a suitable catalyst.

Qualified personnel brought in from outside the company can frequently either bring in or stimulate fresh approaches and improved methods. Several companies have sought new blood with the specific intention of rejuvenating their staff. Results have been gratifying in most cases. The stultification that had existed was overcome and a new rapport emerged. Project management should watch for and curtail stereotyped thinking among users and systems staff members.

MIS Project Steering Committee

"Steering committee," as a term and as a concept, creates a sour impression with some executives. Part of this may be due to their dislike of committees of almost any type, and part of it to their direct experience with steering committees. Though both reasons are understandable, a properly constituted advisory body is necessary to insure the success of an MIS project.

Some companies are able to utilize committees in many different activities, with gratifying results. Others, for reasons that may never be clear, find it just about impossible to employ committees effectively.

In the following sections, we will use the term "committee," understanding that there may be more suitable nomenclature (advisory board, planning council, review board, planning and review group, coordination team, steering board, system directorate, project liaison group, and others). The committee stigma may be lessened if we pick another term, but we must go much further.

Committee Activities and Responsibilities

Introducing recommendations that keep narrow personal or departmental interests and broad corporate interests in proper balance is perhaps the most important committee task. Interestingly, such groups are often effective in this role. Temporary impasses resulting from organizational entanglements can often be overcome quickly, with the influence of committee VIPs. Energies can be set in motion to solve problems, quash delaying tactics, and clear roadblocks hampering the MIS-related activities of both users and systems personnel.

For example, one MIS team presented systems concepts to user management, expecting a prompt decision as to their applicability. Feedback from the users was vital to the project's direction. Project management, however, found it awkward to insist on a response, and as things continued to drag on, it became apparent that the matter had a low priority. Fortunately, the committee members soon moved to rectify the situation.

Chartering the Committee

In organizing the committee, top management should seek to have the appropriate mix of interests represented by line and staff management people. Project management can then obtain the full measure of the combined influence and expertise. And it is essential that members be able to devote the time and energy necessary to review, evaluate, and make recommendations.

If it is to create an effective committee, top management must begin by setting forth what it expects of committee members. As a sounding board for new approaches, systems development proposals, intentions, and ideas, the committee is an important part of the decision-making process. And as a project planning and review body, its members are advised of and give advice on both progress and problems. In this way, the committee constitutes a vital communication link, carrying information to project management and at the same time facilitating the flow of information from the project team to operating groups.

Committee Members

Members of the committee should include key executives from the divisional and functional organizations the system is being designed to serve. In this sense, these members represent their own interests. In a larger sense, however, they represent the company's best interests.

Corporate-level executives responsible for organizations and activities to which the MIS relates would always be members of the committee. Their counterparts in operating divisions, subsidiaries, and affiliates would be members, provided that the MIS project related to their operations. For example, if a large division was doing an MIS with manufacturing and personnel applications, the division heads as well as the corporate vice-presidents for manufacturing and personnel would be members of the committee.

In very large decentralized companies, steering-committee size can become a problem in companywide MIS efforts. If a personnel and manufacturing MIS is to affect 20 divisions, a committee of, say, 42 is impractical. One way around this is to appoint a smaller standing committee that represents a core group. Perhaps this would have 12 members. The remaining 30, who would be ad hoc committee members, would receive memorandums for comment, but would sit only for meetings of major importance.

Project Manager–Committee Relationship

Not a few project managers who have been responsible to committees rather than to one individual (as is customarily considered good practice) have had some grim tales to tell. One common one is that the committee will make important decisions for which the burden of responsibility will fall not on it but on the project manager. As a rule, projects operating under this arrangement tend to be sluggish because of the inertia of the decision-making process and the splintered decision responsibility. Despite these seemingly natural tendencies in management-by-committee situations, some companies are able to do an effective job. In general, unless there has been favorable experience to the contrary, this approach should be avoided. But, whatever you do, before you hire or appoint the project manager find out whether he can work for a committee—if that is to be the arrangement.

Better odds for success prevail where the committee acts in a staff capacity to the project manager. Under this arrangement, the project manager, at least in theory, makes the final decisions in project matters and is responsible to the company's top computer executive or to the president. The committee brings its wisdom and advice to bear and may recommend certain courses of action, but the prerogatives and authority rest with the project manager. Clearly, the influential character of the committee is such that the project manager and committee members cannot be at odds too often or too long.

Project Management

Only within the past five years or so has systems management received critical and thoughtful review. Much had gone by unnoticed in the 20 or so years in which computerized data processing experienced its rapid growth. Now, with the cost so much higher, it is vitally important that the matter of managing systems development be guided by the lessons of hindsight as well as the lessons of today. Compared to the types of automated accounting systems that companies were putting in ten years ago, MIS is in a vastly different, more exciting realm.

Some systems management people like to perpetuate the idea that they can still refer to MIS projects as experiments and get away with it. In defense of such a position, it has been pointed out that an MIS is one of a kind and that there are no performance standards by which the effort can be controlled and its product measured. As a matter of fact, such arguments are invalid. If they were valid, we could use them to escape accountability in hundreds of other kinds of commercial projects.

Despite the irrational character of these arguments, they have been accepted in a great many organizations. And the bigger the projects undertaken by those organizations, the greater the problem becomes. They have become too big to hide and too substantial for top management to continue avoiding.

Face-to-face confrontations have already taken place in a number of companies and more are due. Consequently, both sides are trying to devise effective remedies for problems that often have grown to crisis proportions. Areas that have to be studied in depth include project planning, reporting and management controls, personnel and organizations, and scheduling and estimating.

While these are classic management functions, remedies to their problems have some new twists in the world of computer-based systems. Most, however, are not new and will be recognized as simply good management practice. It is important to discuss both, in order to represent certain critical management points.

Project management problems do not seem to affect one stage of the project more than any others. You may find predicaments in one or more of the aforementioned management areas. Their intensity and the remedies brought to bear can be equally severe, regardless of whether we are talking about MIS analysis, design, programming, testing, or implementation.

Project management becomes meaningful only after the goals, priorities, and policies for the system have been established. These items need to be decided at the very highest echelon of the company and must be stated in a conceptual plan. Such a plan describes the organizational arrangement, the placement of responsibility and authority, and the controls to insure that (1) the guidelines are followed, (2) authority is brought to bear, and (3) progress toward predetermined objectives is made as planned. Failing to meet the above criteria, which constitute a framework for success, it makes little difference what project management does. More than one company's MIS program has fallen into disarray because the top MIS executive failed to exercise the great authority he had been given. Accordingly, he had few excuses when the chief executive officer sought an accounting for responsibility.

Project Planning

All too often, project planning is relegated to the same period of time when the financial side of the project is planned or up for review. Some systems managers have fallen into this pattern because it has proved convenient, while others have had to exert energy because the budgeting cycle and planning cycle of the organization are one and the same. Unhappily, the planning activity is limited exclusively to these times. It is this that creates difficulties for many well-intentioned MIS managers.

Since the financial-planning time lapse is usually a long one, tying the much more dynamic MIS-planning activity to it is bound to bring about work based on an obsolete plan. The usual outcome is that people work along, partly or completely disregarding any plan because they know it is obsolete. For this reason, between project review points the project effort is a headless task.

To make a planning function meaningful, you must see a plan as something drawn up to be used throughout the development process. Assuming this is the prevailing point of view, the advantage lies in replanning, as needed, without regard to the budgeting cycle. This is of tremendous importance and requires the close scrutiny of management.

In the absence of this dynamic approach to project planning, incompatibilities in the systems design invariably emerge. Unless the planning cycle is short enough, the relationships between MIS subsystems, and even within a subsystem, will no longer be valid because the development work can no longer be controlled. Objectives become clouded when planning is felt to be an exercise rather than a necessary activity of project management. Included within the scope of plan dynamics are task redefinition, updating progress controls and schedules, revising estimates, and updating organization and personnel assignments.

Procedures for making changes in the plan need to be set forth at the outset, so that the systems development management team directs its information through the proper communication channels. If the methods for altering the plan are appropriately devised, those who are expected to use them will do so. However, if project management makes a mockery of such methods, they will be ignored or, at the least, made much less effective.

Encouraging a Cohesive Effort

We mentioned earlier the need to develop a basis of communication between users and systems development personnel. In order to overcome the language barriers and related difficulties, project management must bring to bear various educational programs: classroom learning, seminars, programmed instruction, movies, and specially prepared training aids. To have real value, the lessons learned must be applied in a live environment. Systems personnel and users must be encouraged, if not compelled, to maintain a continuing dialogue, one that must produce meaningful critiques of the work done on both sides.

Another side of the cohesiveness that project management must encourage is between subsystems. If the people on either end of the connection fail to "talk" with one another, there is a very good possibility that the connection required will someday be impossible. Here, again, those charged with the leadership of the project must encourage frequent contact among personnel working on the appropriate subsystems.

Communication

As previously indicated, a strong communication program is vital to the success of MIS. It must emerge as such at the time the project is initiated and must continue to be effective throughout the life of the project.

Maintaining an understanding of systems considerations among the development personnel is one side of the communication problem. The other is building an understanding between users and systems development personnel.

Throughout the project, everyone has to be kept up to date on system objectives and goals. Various subsystems and the contributions they make have to be explained regularly, with their relationship to the overall objectives and other subsystems carefully noted.

Schedules and assignments should be incorporated into MIS project communications so that everyone involved can know where his work and the work of others fit into the scheme of things. The major points should be emphasized in a newsletter or periodic memorandum, which at the same time refers to whatever more elaborate documentation may be required. On larger projects, this activity is so important that it may require the full-time efforts of more than one person. More modest MIS programs can get along with less, but the responsibilities for formal programs must be fixed and should be at a high level in the project organization.

One of the most critical components of an MIS communication program concerns the coordination, control, and dissemination of information relating to changes in the system. Changes are inevitable in functional features of the MIS and are inevitable also if the system is to be refined. But beyond a point, they cause serious difficulties. What often happens is that a plan is drawn up reflecting a great deal of careful thought, but the procedures for making changes to the plan are not defined. Consequently, it is surprisingly easy for changes to be introduced without notifying all parties who should be made aware of the changes. When this is permitted, incompatibilities between subsystems will exist—that is, a number of different designs that do not mesh will have been developed. Introducing nonessential changes after the system design is approved and frozen is also one of the primary causes for MIS project time and cost overruns.

For these reasons and others, it is imperative to establish a *change order procedure* that calls for the review and approval of changes by project and user management. Some changes, it may be decided, can wait to be implemented after the system is operational. Some others will have to be introduced during development. Their approval goes hand in hand with an authorization to spend the estimated additional money and time they require.

Another important facet of the communication program should be *clarification procedures,* whereby anyone concerned with the project can enter a clarification request on a docket containing other such requests. Items appearing on the docket are assigned, by the project manager, to appropriate individuals charged with answering the requests. Each week, a new list is issued on which answers appear along with all open requests. After several issues, the answered items no longer appear.

Another effort to keep project activities on the right track is the preparation of a *glossary of terms* used in connection with the MIS. Ambiguous terminology is a potential trouble spot in even small MIS projects, but in bigger projects it can be disastrous.

Design review meetings are another important component of project communication. These meetings may involve representatives from two interfacing subsystems or may involve the user who interacts directly with one subsystem. The common understanding sought from these reviews has to grow over a period of time, during which progressively more detail is introduced as the shape of the system emerges. Such reviews should start very early in the game and should continue through design, programming, and system testing.

Special forms of project reviews have proved successful in bringing into focus everyone's work on the system. Exposing everyone to work plans, budgetary considerations, and important problems encourages suggestions from the group at large. Project personnel want to feel their work is important and want to be consulted on decisions affecting the destiny of the entire project.

Project Management Controls

The monitoring of achievement relative to planned performance is a common means for controlling performance. The monitoring of expenditures, actual versus planned (or budgeted), is another management control function. Used by itself, money control leaves a great deal to be desired. For one thing, it does not tell us what we bought for the money. Conversely, achievement control supposedly tells us what we bought, but does not tell us how much it cost.

These two types of controls are always used together by management with a consistent success record. Discussions on such controls systems appear in most literature on the subject of controls and are related directly to computer application projects and project management books. Such controls, while they are musts, may fall short in a couple of areas of crucial importance to MIS. Let us call them value controls and target controls.

Value controls provide management with information and insight on the question of whether the consumption of monetary and other resources relates favorably to (1) the value of the service or product purchased—in an absolute as well as comparative sense—and (2) the value realized on the alternative uses of similar monetary and other resources.

It is important to remember that effective value control revolves around marginal analysis. This means that managers must look at the bidirectional attributes of both value received and resource consumption. Should value and resources be related to one another in a linearly proportionate way, marginal differences are strictly proportionate. Hence, the conclusions that can be drawn from marginal analysis are easy to deal with.

However, it is not infrequent to find that strictly linear relationships do not exist. Consider, for example, the many cases where the laws of diminishing return apply. In an MIS where an inventory management subsystem is being developed, it is possible to spend a long time and a lot of money refining the inventory model. Forecasting could become quite sophisticated in the refining process. So could the customer service, production, and distribution considerations represented in the system.

Increased value growing out of this extra "polishing" effort can fall off rapidly, even in modest attempts to improve the system. In some cases, the added improvements put the MIS in the position of dignifying bad data. This means that, as a result of inherent inaccuracies in the data, the answers are no more meaningful than they had been previously. To illustrate this point, let us say that our key input data are accurate within plus or minus 10 percent. This being the case, it is not useful to refine the processing to output answers that are more accurate, say plus or minus 5 percent. In fact, the accuracy tolerance of the result cannot be smaller than the overall accuracy of the data—that is, where each input data element is accurate to within plus or minus 10 percent, it would not be realistic to claim the answer is more accurate.

To put this in a different light, by way of analogy: Consider whether it is sensible to manufacture a saw that has settings to 1/1000th of an inch when it is impossible for carpenters to be more accurate than 1/64th of an inch.

Not to mention that it is impossible for wood to hold a tolerance of anything approaching 1/1000th of an inch because of its expansion, contraction, and warping properties.

MIS developers also need to consider how time affects the value and usefulness of management information, as well as the uses to which information is put. In many cases, being accurate and timely, beyond a certain point, does not pay.

Information used for longer-range planning purposes and strategic decision making rarely needs to be even close to 100 percent accurate in order to provide acceptable usefulness. Making such information available in a fast-response system is not usually essential. Yet companies spend inordinate sums of money to satisfy nonexistent or unjustifiable requirements for accuracy and timeliness.

In general, information pertaining to events planned for the more distant future can be less accurate than information for more imminent events. Estimated production volumes a year from now can have more tolerance than those for next week. Response requirements generally also follow the same sort of rule.

Target controls relate to the project's end product, the operational MIS. At each major milestone, it is usually easy to see how the accomplishment relates to the end product. However, the tasks and activities that take place between milestones also need to be viewed and controlled by management, as they relate to the end product.

To administer target controls, having a set of objectives for an MIS is absolutely essential. Such objectives should have been formulated as a result of a considerable amount of contemplation by top management and discussion with operating management.

In the course of carrying out a task in the MIS project, questions concerning direction of the project inevitably arise. Often, such questions are in the form of one or more alternatives. Management's role is to see that the alternative selected or the answer to the question is in line with the MIS project objectives. Every participant in the project also needs to keep before him a well-stated set of objectives to permit target control to be exercised on a more personal basis. Considerations that come up in the course of day-to-day MIS development can then be answered in the light of what the company is trying to accomplish.

A Systems Management Case History

It is always interesting and beneficial to learn what a project manager considers to be the reasons for his own success. Our case concerns the man in charge of a large real-time MIS project, which took about three years to complete and involved the installation of nearly 300 on-line terminals. This manager's experience consisted of eight years of systems work ranging from small batch-mode systems to a modest MIS type of system. The real-time system was the first he had been involved with, and he gave every indication that he knew in advance what he was about to tackle.

Development and implementation were to proceed under a very tight schedule. The justification for the system dictated that this schedule be met if the project was to avoid being cancelled. Any slippage in the schedule would rapidly push up costs to the point where the original economic gains would be erased.

The philosophy of project management encompassed key points relating to personnel, system testing, project management reviews, standards, and user training. The points described in this connection follow closely those offered by a number of other systems managers responsible for important MIS efforts.

In the area of personnel there is one very simple concept that most systems managers espouse—all key project personnel should be the best obtainable in their area of competence. Appropriate systems experience, high intelligence, and the ability to express ideas conversationally and in writing were among the selection criteria. Individuals selected for the project had records of solid accomplishment and were reported to persevere in order to meet deadlines. As it turned out, nearly every professional staff member had a bachelor's degree; almost a third, advanced degrees. In all, the staff was highly experienced and had gone through systems development efforts in the past. Only a few, however, had real-time systems development experience.

Because it was approached in this way, recruiting resulted in a minimum-size MIS staff, which reduced the communications, interfacing, and management reviews ordinarily required. Besides being smaller, the staff was organized in such a way that each man was responsible for tasks that he carried out from beginning to end. Programmer–analysts were assigned one or more modules of the system, for which they carried out the design, programming, testing, and documentation.

For each module of work, the man responsible committed himself to meet a deadline that he agreed to as being reasonable. By the same token, project management represented certain guarantees of computer test time and related services such as keypunching and secretarial functions. Interestingly, each side in this deal viewed the agreement as binding. As a result, indications of work slippage were accompanied not by schedule changes but rather by hustling to meet the commitment. Management's position was to maintain the schedule, and its method of doing so encouraged the extra expenditures of energy needed to meet commitments.

In addition to the applications groups, the organization of the project included what was called a technical services group, which included systems software specialists, systems programmers, communications consultants, and some broad-gauge applications consultants. The hardware manufacturer's systems specialists worked closely with this group on a full-time basis.

Among other things, this group was responsible for providing all data management modules needed by the applications groups—the data-management functions were application-independent. Information storage and retrieval functions, under this plan, were not of concern to the applications programmer. A standard means of making data requests was provided to all applications programmers, but the actual access and storing commands were issued only by data-management software. This protected data and indexes from inadvertent destruction since all data storage was managed by centralized software. It checked the security passwords and other identification and also validated control counts and identification records.

The applications programmer had the advantage of being able to call on the powerful features of a data-management system (through the use of specially tailored macro-instructions), having only to concern himself with the application and not with systems software. There was more confidence in the data as a result of this kind of hands-off policy, which prevented programs from being able to directly access information. Additionally, changes to improve data-management software did not require applications program changes—the interface remained the same.

Another feature of the project team was a test and training group, whose job it was to provide programmers with all necessary data to check out their programs and the system as a whole. Test data-base software was designed and implemented by the technical-services group, with contents being provided by the test and training group. Verification and approval of system-test results and consultation on program-test results were also a function of the test and training group, which consisted mainly of user staff members whose business experience uniquely qualified them to prepare comprehensive test situations. Part of their job included user information surveys and methods studies at terminal locations in the field.

Finally, this group was fully responsible for user orientation and training for the new system. They developed a series of teaching aids, including a programmed instruction manual, and specified the form and content of computer-assisted instruction programs.

As we said earlier, this MIS project was a resounding success.

9

MIS Impact on the Organization

THE advanced capabilities that MIS seem to possess has captivated the imagination of many students of management. Some see vast change resulting from MIS, while others argue that less dramatic reorientation is more realistic. Few believe that no changes will result with the advent of MIS.

In a great many companies, the mighty sums of money and other resources being consumed in MIS work are a solid indication of their management's belief in the promises of MIS. The emphasis on putting MIS to work is underscored by such statements as this: "The day may not be far distant when those who analyze annual business failures can add another category to their list of causes—failure to exploit the computer."[1]

[1] Neal J. Dean, "The Computer Comes of Age," *Harvard Business Review,* January–February 1968, p. 91.

Change Factors in Organization Design

The impact that MIS can have on organizational change rests on the answers to some rather basic questions. The two questions at the root of this issue are: (1) What causes organizations to look the way they do? (2) What are the major reasons for dissatisfaction with organization structures as they now stand? Both questions relate to business problems of some kind—past and present. Most such problems can be described under four general headings: time, location, ability, size.

The shape an organization takes reflects decisions made to resolve problems, actual or potential, in one or more of these four matters. Accordingly, the so-called span of control, or span of management, is solidified until the next organization recasting takes place.

From time to time, new organizational concepts and managerial tools will emerge that affect the four variables. Time may be compressed by some technique. Location may become less of a problem as communication is made more effective or distance is shrunk by transportation innovations. Ability may be extended through new management techniques and tools (PERT, computers, and so on), and it may be diminished by business diversification. Size of a particular group to be managed may be collapsed by innovations in automation, improved controls, or other advances.

Changes in the organization often result from the appearance of new problems or the disappearance of conditions that created old problems. They also result from the revelation of a better way. In either case, the selection of a solution often is based on remedies known at the time, so that the decision to pursue one alternative rather than another is made on relative merit.

Today, there is a new mechanism afoot for changing the balance of relative merit: computer-based MIS. As to the current organization structure and its problems, MIS offers some new approaches. As to where the organization is headed, MIS can play an important part in defining its shape. For it does affect time, location, ability, and size—the key agents of change.

Changes in Delegation of Responsibility

A classic management topic, delegation certainly has an overt impact on the organization structure. How can MIS affect this and what result could be anticipated if it did? Perhaps it would be well to take a harder look at delegation before we try to answer the question.

Delegation is not a benevolent act with the objective of keeping more people employed. Instead, it may be said to serve a real or apparent need. If the company president wants to spend more time on the golf course, he may delegate. Or he may be working 15 hours a day and find not only that he is not as effective as he would like to be, but that he does not want to work such long hours. Time, then, is an obvious factor in deciding to delegate. Ability is another. Here it becomes increasingly important to utilize specialists as the business grows. Size is a third, but overlaps the time variable to a great extent. It is common for business growth to necessitate delegation. Then there is location. Since no manager can be in two places at the same time, it generally takes more managers to run a company scattered all over the world than to run a one-location company.

The effectiveness of company communication also relates to time, ability, size, and location. Being a key variable in management's decisions to delegate, communication has received attention over the years in a number of ways. For example, communications-based MIS and many other kinds of communication improvements have helped management to get more done in the same amount of time; they have also lessened the problem of distance, helped improve control, and made possible better utilization of ability. In a sense, pure communication connects the parts of the system but adds nothing new to it.

MIS also connects the parts of the system, but goes much further because it also contributes something new in the way of integration. Moreover, it is a member of the system, not just a conduit for information. The computer permits automatic reasoning and arithmetic computations to be done quickly and with consistent precision.

Gilbert Burck, the author of many articles relating to computer technology, sees MIS leading management to new conclusions about delegation. He writes:

> The machine's [the computer's] power to help U.S. managers control their operations has generated what appears to be nothing less than a pervasive recentralization or reintegration movement. For 25 years or so, decentralization has been the word for corporations all over the world and the reason seemed obvious enough. As companies grew larger and more complex or more diversified, one man or a small group was no longer able to run them directly. So top managers broke down their organization functionally, and delegated authority to divisional managers who were often assigned divisional profit goals, and often spurred by profit sharing.[2]

Numerous companies have decentralized to such an extent that management control of delegated responsibilities has become impossible. This problem predates MIS, of course, and is not necessarily a candidate for remedy by MIS. In the oft-quoted words of Richard F. Neuschel: "If decentralization is

[2] "Management Will Never Be the Same Again," *Fortune*, August 1964, p. 125.

to mean delegation rather than abdication, then the executive who used to run the whole show himself must learn instead how to evaluate the way someone else is running it."[3]

Computer-based MIS may even help executives accomplish decentralization once they have learned to evaluate how someone else is running the show. In the words of L. C. Guest, Jr., discussing the computing function at Sylvania Electric Products in the mid 1950s: "Sylvania's firm belief is that *centralized data processing will make decentralization even more effective.* The decentralizated organization will be able to act more rapidly and with more flexibility."[4]

Changes in Light of a New Technological Base

Perry E. Rosove, in his book *Developing Computer-Based Information Systems,* discusses MIS impact on organization design and personnel. In fact, he points out that a key step in successfully implementing MIS calls for efforts to make MIS and the organization compatible. He emphasizes: "The developer cannot accept the existing personnel system or organization of the enterprise as fixed; he must examine it in the light of a new technological base." Rosove advises:

> With respect to the personnel of the new system, the developer must resolve these types of questions:
>
> - What new tasks must be performed to carry out new system functions?
> - What behavioral problems are associated with the conduct of the new tasks?
> - What kinds of skills, intelligence, and knowledge must the system personnel possess if they are to perform the tasks efficiently?
> - What kinds of people possess the required skills, intelligence, and knowledge or could acquire them with the least effort if necessary?
> - What is the impact of a computer-based technology upon the job classification system in use in the enterprise?
> - To what extent will the content of existing jobs be changed by the introduction of a new, computer-based information system?
> - What will be the effect of the new system upon existing career ladders?
>
> Insofar as the organizational characteristics of the new system are concerned, the developer is faced with the following types of questions:

[3] *Management by System* (New York: McGraw-Hill Book Company, 1960), p. 205.
[4] "Administrative Automation at Sylvania: Centralized Data Processing–Decentralized Management," *Office Management Series 144* (AMA, 1956), p. 33.

- How shall tasks be grouped into jobs or positions?
- What combination of positions shall comprise work units, groups, or crews?
- What is the most efficient spatial and temporal arrangement of work units for the conduct of system functions?
- How does the introduction of a computer-based information system affect the centralization/decentralization ratio in the enterprise? Does it necessarily imply "recentralization"?
- Will the use of a computer for routine types of decisions eliminate jobs at the level of middle management?
- What effect will the automation of information processing have upon the chain of command in the enterprise?
- Does the use of a computer-based information system imply changes in the relationships between top management and staff personnel? Between staff and line personnel? Between management and line personnel?[5]

Changes Reflecting New Abilities and Attitudes

MIS should permit skills to be used more effectively. It should grow to a point where more jobs are custom-fitted to a man's interests and skills. Today, it is rare to find a company that comes even close to having its employees contribute optimally. A man working as a competent engineer who may also be a whiz at advertising is never consulted concerning the latter. MIS could very well provide the mechanism for helping indentify and more fully utilizing a man's talents. If our prediction is accurate, the organization under MIS, such as it may be, will probably not have traditional lines, or at least there will be differences in the conduct of activity as we now know it.

Changes in personal attitudes that occur somewhat independent of MIS influences are becoming increasingly relevant to its functioning, especially among younger business managers. There is a fervent campaign to eliminate drudgery and routine from their sphere of activity. This attitude is also very much alive among younger nonmanagement personnel of all types, from the factory laborer to the Ph.D. researcher.

People seem to have a growing desire to exercise their specialized creative ability and individual skills. Young businessmen are refusing to serve 20- or 30-year apprenticeships to do big things—that is, to join top management. They want to avoid, at almost any cost, the corporate paperwork jungle with its mountains of memorandums and periodic budget-juggling acts. In short, they want to contribute in important business affairs and work with and through other people.

[5] New York: John Wiley & Sons, Inc., pp. 170–171.

Some companies, acknowledging these trends, have taken steps to create a suitable environment for today's young manager. As a result, highly capable men are attracted to such companies. Since they have a burning desire to run the company, in many cases top management has been glad to get out from under heavy pressures by placing important responsibilities in the hands of these younger men. Of course, management still keeps an eye on things and occasionally tugs on the reins. But by developing new managers for the big jobs, top managers are now finding the time for the contemplative analysis of long-range policy considerations that they have long wanted to get at.

The Changing Problem-Solving Environment: "War Rooms"

The topic of "war rooms" is becoming fashionable and relates to augmenting some of the more futuristic applications of MIS. Two schools of thought exist about the relationship of war rooms to computer-based MIS: (1) that an MIS tie-in is logical and necessary, and (2) that it is not. The first of these points of view seems valid—understanding, however, that the sophisticated and massive data bases ordinarily envisioned for such applications are nonexistent in the vast majority of MIS development programs being undertaken today.

War rooms go by perhaps a dozen different (and probably better) names, including management information center, management briefing center, situation room, executive chart room, operations briefing center, command control room, operations briefing room, chart room, management communications center, decision center, management information and control center.

Some or all of the following audiovisual aids may be found in war rooms: chart easels, wall-hung chart-display panels, chalkboard, slide projectors, bulletin board, overhead transparency and opaque projectors, motion picture projectors, television, radio, audio tape recorders, video tape recorders, and transparency and paper copiers.

More advanced rooms may include closed circuit television, Picturephones, facsimile transmission equipment, visual display terminals, teletypes and typewriter terminals (in soundproof enclosures), large-image wall displays, microfilm retrieval and printout unit, multiple projection (two, three, four slides) systems, and rear-image projection equipment.

Organizations have begun efforts to bring the computer closer to the activities of the war room, but, apart from military users, few have actually done so. This is the direction many see war rooms taking—that is, on-line hookup to MIS.

Certain companies have gone for plush, sophisticated war rooms while others are rather austere. Some have comfortable armchairs with push-button controls for the visual displays and no conference table of any kind. Other rooms look very much like ordinary conference rooms.

War rooms of one sort or another are to be found in many companies. Most, however, are better described as chart rooms because that is what they contain. The military, understandably, has by far the most advanced war rooms. Many are manned 24 hours a day by specially trained personnel who handle emergency or alert situations.

Charts found in war rooms will show as many as several hundred company indicators including ratios. Economic, industry, and other external indicators may also number in the hundreds. It is typical that no more than 50 indicators in each group are considered key items. Smaller companies may find that 50 indicators all told will adequately serve their needs. The number and variety of key items are dependent on the business line and complexity of the particular company's organization.

More obscure economic indicators will be of value when periodically interpreted by corporate or independent consulting economists. Market and financial analysts would "work the charts" that contain the not-so-obvious interpretations impinging on these particular areas.

E. I. du Pont de Nemours & Company is often credited with having developed one of the earliest corporate chart rooms in 1919. The Irving Trust Company, a large New York City bank, reportedly has an elaborate chart room pretty much in a class by itself insofar as banking goes. Begun in 1920, the chart system includes almost 700 regularly updated charts relating to the economy, the stock market, interest rates, financing trends, prices, and industrial production. In addition to these charts, which contain data available from published sources, Irving Trust maintains a set of charts with data relevant to the bank's own operation.

The American Machine & Foundry Company's chart room provides more than 200 charts, in addition to which there is an assortment of semipermanent charts relating to special studies.

Sperry & Hutchinson was one of the earliest experimenters with modern day war rooms and reportedly has several such facilities.

The Department of the Navy established its Management Information Center in 1964 for top-level reviews and problem evaluation.

United Air Lines and Eastern Airlines use their briefing centers daily to review events of the previous 24 hours. Additionally, Eastern uses its center as a situation room. It is staffed with specialists around the clock who work out logistics problems in flight operations as they arise—for example, when a sudden weather change necessitates diverting aircraft to another airport. American Airlines has a situation center in Tulsa, Oklahoma, designed specifically to handle such problems for its fleet 24 hours a day, 7 days a week.

Other companies whose war rooms have been mentioned in the trade press include AT&T, IBM, Pillsbury, First National Bank of Chicago, International Paper, NCR, General Motors, Kodak, and National Gypsum.

At this writing there are known to be a half dozen companies specializing in the specification and design of war rooms.

Predictions About Management Systems

"Computers and Management" was the topic of the 1967 Leatherbee Lecture Series at the Harvard Business School. One speaker was Hershner Cross, vice-president and group executive of General Electric's Industrial and Information Group, who contended that progress in MIS was not as fast as many had predicted. In explaining some of the reasons in his paper "A Generalized Management View of Computers," he said: "The management process, as we perform it today, is certainly heavily entrenched in the precomputer era, and I think we'll require very heavy readjustments in modes of thinking, organization, and methods."[6]

Robert N. Anthony, then Assistant Secretary of Defense (Comptroller), another lecturer in the 1967 Leatherbee Series, saw the need for an entirely new approach to designing MIS. In his paper "Future Uses of Computers in Large and Complex Organizations," Mr. Anthony focused sharply on the concept of a data library, emphasizing the need for data bases from which a user could rapidly access facts and relationships of interest to him, without knowing in advance what information was available. The benefits of such a system according to Anthony, would be these:

> 1. We will no longer need to design systems by first answering the question, "What does management need to know?" The plain fact is that the system designer cannot find out what management needs to know. We discovered long ago that it is futile to *ask* managers what data they need; they simply cannot foresee the uses that might be made of new information that can be made available to them. We are now learning that the alternative of analyzing information needs in terms of job content or organizational relationships does not provide the answer either. No matter how much care and thought are given to the design of a report structure, the experience of everyone seems to be that the available data are seldom exactly what he would want to have for a particular problem when it comes along. Reports typed on pieces of paper are necessarily highly structured, whereas the data library I am trying to describe would be relatively unstructured—analogous, in a crude way, to the manner in which data are stored in the human brain.

[6] *Computers and Management: The 1967 Leatherbee Lectures* (Boston: Harvard University Graduate School of Business Administration, 1967), p. 14.

2. There will be a single, unambiguous source of data. In a large organization, the presence of conflicting "facts" about a single phenomenon causes more waste of time and more bickering than anyone who has never worked in such an organization can possibly imagine. These conflicting facts arise when two reports have slightly different definitions for what purports to be the same item, when simple arithmetic errors occur, or when one person uses a report with a different date from that used by another. In a data library there would be, hopefully, one description for each phenomenon: one fact. If the library said that 367 units of Item X were in inventory in usable condition, everyone interested would use the number 367, and not the number that was on hand last week, or the number that was in inventory but not usable, or the number that is due in for Item X, or the number for Item X^1, which is almost, but not quite, like Item X.

3. There should be a drastic decrease in the number of reports that are prepared. I do not refer to management control reports; these would be unaffected. But most reports are prepared just in case the information may be useful to some person at some time, and such reports can be done away with. At first the reduction in report output will be slight. The pace will accelerate as managers learn to rely increasingly on asking the computer what they would like to know, but this evolution requires a change in the report-reading habits to which managers have become accustomed.

4. Cross-functional integration of data should be easier. With data stored in more elemental or fundamental forms in relatively unstructured files, it should be much easier to relate data from different systems. For example, we should not tolerate much longer a system containing information on inventory quantities that is completely independent from another system containing information on inventory dollar values.

5. The user will be able to employ available data to test different proposals quickly. His approach will be more heuristic, less structured. It will be of his own choosing, not subject to the interpretation of a programmer.[7]

Professor Adrian M. McDonough offers five predictions about what will be accomplished in management systems in his book *Information Economics and Management Systems*. He believes business has barely scratched the surface in advanced management uses of systems. In the following excerpts from his predictions, note the heavy emphasis on developments directly related to the company systems function itself.

Prediction 1: Development of Systems Theory. To date our systems knowledge has been achieved by experience—by trial and error. The time is ripe for the development of a theoretical framework as the guide for larger systems analysis. . . . My prediction is that we can expect increased attempts to explain systems from a theoretical viewpoint.

[7] Ibid., pp. 117–118.

Prediction 2: Development of Techniques to Aid Abstraction and Symbolism. . . . The very essence of analysis is the ability to select from, or abstract the significant factors from, a complicated situation.

Reality is too complicated. Analysis through critical abstraction is necessary to bring problems down to manageable size. To date, such abstracting has been intuitive. Now we expect to see the development of techniques that will help us to support intuition as we seek to isolate the important elements in a systems problem. . . .

Prediction 3: Telescopes and Microscopes. . . . If one accepts the goal or ideal of total integrated systems, he should expect that analysis must get to such a detailed level that common characteristics can be found which allow meshing of now separated systems. The dramatic analogy is the development of atomic energy. Success was achieved only after theories showed how to identify subdivisions of matter. At some critical subdivision it becomes possible to connect the apparently quite separate elements into a really continuous system of energy. . . . It is especially because of the challenge to handle problems with more rigorous analysis that we shall see mathematics grow in business applications.

Prediction 4: The Business Simulation Laboratory. . . . The use of the computer for business simulation requires explicit description of business functions well beyond the traditional intuitive approaches now used. The development of business simulation, for other than case-study training, will not take place overnight, and it will be expensive. The point to remember is that the opportunities in business simulation appear to be great, and it can be expected that efforts will increase to take advantage of these opportunities.

Prediction 5: Organization of the Systems Function. I have suggested that increased attention will be paid to:

1. Systems theory.
2. Techniques of abstraction and symbolism.
3. Enlarge problem scope and detail.
4. Business simulation.

If these predictions hold, we can anticipate changes in the organization of the systems function.

1. As with other advancing fields of knowledge, greater degrees of specialization can be expected.

2. These degrees of specialization will require that greater attention be paid to coordination of systems work.

3. As a result of coordination efforts, management research, operations research, and systems research will be shown to have apparent rather than

real differences, and less effort will be wasted in polarizing professional achievements.

4. As a result of the maturing of the systems function, it can be expected that the highest level of systems work will have the opportunity to achieve the professional authority and status of business, legal, and medical advisers.[8]

In the closing remarks of the book from which the foregoing predictions are quoted, Professor McDonough cites three specific changes he expects in systems-department orientation: (1) Information systems will admittedly be used to formulate company policy. With complete information available, the facts will make many decisions self-evident. (2) Job responsibilities, organizational patterns, and information systems will develop in a unified way, so that emphasis will be on job content and related information needs. (3) The rate at which new management problems emerge relative to the speed at which current problems are being solved by systems will determine centralization and decentralization movements within the organization.

Considerations in Shaping the New Organization

Company presidents and upper-rung management teams should be aware of the organizational problems that can crop up in trying to apply MIS that cuts across functional organizational lines. Such systems will need to be accompanied by a revised management policy having common guidelines that will cause functional management to focus on optimum company performance as opposed to functional achievement. The relationships between inventory policy, production planning, marketing strategy, purchasing practices, capital investment criteria, and so forth need to be rethought and spelled out so that functional managers will appreciate the corporate effects of their decisions. Too often, MIS developers forget to plan for this type of indoctrination and later realize that, to everyone's dismay, the organization is not working effectively through MIS. Furthermore, management will sometimes attempt to reverse this situation very quickly after it has been discovered. Such action precipitates resentment and misunderstanding. Ample time must be allowed for organizational change and for personnel to make necessary adjustments. You cannot expect a complete reversal overnight.

Decentralized organizations will typically have some major problems to overcome before MIS can be made to function at a level approaching full effectiveness. Meaningful management information will require unified standards for data. Input-data standards, for example, will have to be devised

[8] New York: © McGraw-Hill Book Company, 1963, pp. 285–288.

and promulgated throughout the affected organization. Management control and follow-up in this connection is quite important. Cost information, for example, will have to relate to the same cost categories and be defined in uniform ways in order for centralized financial controls to be meaningful. Executives in decentralized organizations, in addition to their responsibility for a decentralized operation of some kind, will have to be charged with responsibility for the impact their decisions have on the corporation.

Several Views on the New Organization

Some of the earliest insights concerning the long-range impact of computer-based systems were those of Harold J. Leavitt and Thomas L. Whisler. These are some of the things they said in their widely quoted article:

> We believe that information technology will spread rapidly. One important reason for expecting fast changes in current practices is that information technology will make centralization much easier. By permitting more information to be organized more simply and processed more rapidly it will, in effect, extend the thinking range of individuals. It will allow the top level of management intelligently to categorize, digest, and act on a wider range of problems. Moreover, by quantifying more information it will extend top management's control over the decision processes of subordinates.
>
> If centralization becomes easier to implement, managers will probably revert to it. Decentralization has, after all, been largely negatively motivated. Top managers have backed into it because they have been unable to keep up with size and technology. They could not design and maintain the huge and complex communication systems that their large, centralized organizations needed. Information technology should make recentralization possible. It may also obviate other major reasons for decentralization. For example, speed and flexibility will be possible despite large size, and top executives will be less dependent on subordinates because there will be fewer "experience" and "judgment" areas in which the junior men have more working knowledge. In addition, more efficient information-processing techniques can be expected to shorten radically the feedback loop that tests the accuracy of original observations and decisions.[9]

Another facet of the recentralization question was expressed by Professor Donald C. Carroll of M.I.T.'s Sloan School of Management. In his paper "Implications of On-Line, Real-Time Systems for Managerial Decision-Making," he stated:

[9] "Management in the 1980's," *Harvard Business Review,* November–December 1958, p. 43.

The capabilities inherent in the generalized computer systems do raise some intriguing questions on one issue, this being the tendency towards "recentralization" of decisions. In the type of management systems described here, the centralized data base and decision programs certainly imply the *feasibility* of centralized decision making; but the important points are (1) they do not *require* it, and (2) they may alleviate one major reason for it. The first follows directly from the fact that the human decision maker may be located "out in the field." The second is a more complex argument. One of the major pressures to centralize decision making stems from locally suboptimal decisions. That is, one organizational subunit cannot consider the status of other remote but interdependent subunits and, as a consequence, may, if allowed decision autonomy, make decisions inconsistent with overall corporate welfare. But, if the subunit can be given access to the corporate data base, then its decisions can be reconciled with full corporate status and, in theory, be made consistent with corporate status and objectives.[10]

In concluding his book *The Shape of Automation for Men and Management,* Herbert A. Simon sketches a picture of the new organization that he believes will emerge with more advanced systems. Although he looks toward significant improvements resulting from the application of the new decision-making techniques, the new organizations he sees will resemble, to a large extent, those now in existence.

1. Organizations will still be constructed in three layers: an underlying system of physical production and distribution processes, a layer of programmed (and probably largely automated) decision processes for governing the routine day-to-day operation of the physical system, and a layer of non-programmed decision processes (carried out in a man-machine system) for monitoring the first-level processes, redesigning them, and changing parameter values.

2. Organizations will still be hierarchical in form. The organization will be divided into major subparts, each of these into parts, and so on, in familiar forms of departmentalization. The exact bases for drawing departmental lines may change somewhat. Product divisions may become even more important than they are today, while the sharp lines of demarcation among purchasing, manufacturing, engineering, and sales are likely to fade.

But there is a more fundamental way in which the organizations of the future will appear to those in them very much like the organizations of today. Man is a problem-solving, skill-using, social animal. Once he has satisfied his hunger, two main kinds of experiences are significant to him. One of his deepest needs is to apply his skills, whatever they be, to challenging tasks to feel the exhilaration of the well-struck ball or the

[10] Charles A. Myers (ed.), *The Impact of Computers on Management* (Cambridge, Mass.: The M.I.T. Press, 1967), p. 162.

> well-solved problem. The other need is to find meaningful and warm relations with a few other human beings—to love and be loved, to share experience, to respect and be respected, to work in common tasks.
>
> Particular characteristics of the physical environment and the task environment are significant to man only as they affect these needs. The scientist satisfies them in one environment, the artist in another; but they are the same needs. A good business novel or business biography is not about business. It is about love, hate, pride, craftsmanship, jealousy, comradeship, ambition, pleasure. These have been, and will continue to be man's central concerns.
>
> The automation and rationalization of decision making will, to be sure, alter the climate of organizations in ways important to these human concerns. I have indicated what some of the changes may be. On balance, they seem to me changes that will make it easier rather than harder for the executive's daily work to be a significant and satisfying part of his life.[11]

Professor John Dearden, who has over the years made a number of thoughtful observations concerning computers and management, has concluded that the computer will have no impact on the organization of top and divisional management and only a very limited impact on the management organization below these levels. Dearden's view is quite the opposite of that of Leavitt and Whisler and numerous others who hint strongly at sweeping changes, particularly with regard to recentralization.

Dearden does conclude, however, that certain other changes may be expected. In his paper "Computers and Profit Centers," he says:

> Within the division, the main changes that will occur from the automation and centralization of logistics and data processing will be at the plant or warehouse level. As I see it, the following four changes can be expected:
>
> 1. The divisional manager will tend to spend less time coordinating and solving logistics problems because these will be handled automatically at a lower level.
>
> 2. Anyone at a plant, warehouse, or geographically decentralized office who is principally concerned with the supervision of data processing personnel may have his job either changed or eliminated. For example, the plant controller who is now concerned mostly with maintaining accounting records will have to become more of an interpreter of data and a financial adviser to the divisional manager.
>
> 3. Anyone at the plant or warehouse who is largely engaged in making logistics decisions (that is, ordering parts or scheduling production) may have his job downgraded or eliminated. For example, the manager of a parts warehouse may well become merely a supervisor of stock handlers, receiving

[11] New York: © Harper & Row, Publishers, 1965, pp. 110–111.

and shipping parts in accordance with a schedule received from the divisional office.

4. Anyone who is concerned with making logistics decisions may have that part of his job eliminated. (Because most jobs are becoming more complex, I do not think that generally the elimination of logistics decisions will affect the job status.)

Notice that these changes will have a limited impact on most managers at any level. They will be confined to relatively two types—managers engaged primarily in supervising decentralized data processing or logistics activities. Further, not all of these managers will be affected. With respect to logistics, they must be engaged in the type of activity that can be logically centralized. In some situations, local conditions are so important that a centralization of these decisions is not practical. With respect to data processing, the type and extent of this activity must be such that centralization is economic.[12]

A View Concerning Operations Management

John A. Beckett, who has studied the impact of systems on management under the auspices of the American Foundation for Management Research and the Ford Foundation, has made a number of interesting observations as a result of his in-depth research.

Discussing management systems for the operations end of the business, Beckett sees "a great many repetitive actions which, when studied carefully, can be 'managed' readily by the routine application of rules and procedures which may be applied either by men or machines—depending on which is more economical."[13]

As operating systems are perfected, myriad programmed decisions will be built in, which, according to Beckett, will tend to remove the need as well as the practicability of any manager's making interim operating decisions. "To the extent that this occurs, *systems manage systems* and in this sense *men manage less and less.*"

He continues:

> . . . as improved operations systems are implemented, *information about the condition of the operating system itself is becoming more important, and information about how to run it is becoming less important.* There are really just three purposes for information systems to serve, in this environment:
>
> - Triggering those human decisions about the "management" of planned operations that have not yet been built into the system itself.

[12] Myers, op. cit., pp. 188–189.

[13] "Management, Motivation, and Management Information Systems," *Advanced Management Journal,* January 1965, p. 67.

- Measuring the effectiveness with which the operating system and its parts are accomplishing what it is presently designed to do.
- Exposing additional opportunities for improving the operations systems.

The first of these decreases in importance as the second and third increase.[14]

Some Final Thoughts and Predictions

Evolution and not revolution as a systems development philosophy is taking on a new relevance and meaning in MIS. Those who have not already done so will learn that MIS is a commitment to constant change, an ever growing and expanding capability.

The initial impact of MIS will be in the area of improved reporting on a companywide basis. It will be used to overcome abysmal communications as well as to provide timely management information. Both will be needed to support more advanced MIS development.

There will be competitive uses of MIS in nearly all business functions. Growth in MIS applications will be experienced in stages, starting with extensive batch-processed management information and moving rapidly into on-line and real-time MIS, which will be heavily involved with operational aspects. After mammoth efforts to achieve systems to provide timely, comprehensive information, management's hopes will remain unfulfilled. True success will be elusive because the existence of the working system will prove concretely, over and over again, that the knowledge required to give the information value has yet to be acquired.

Poorly defined decision rules will continue to plague MIS expansion efforts in most companies. Much effort will be expended toward developing management standards to go with the decision rules, which will be developed only after painstaking analysis. Operations research will play an important part in this work.

Decision information systems will enter the scene next, but at a more moderate pace. These systems will depart from their predecessors in that information which had been used in the past by management to make decisions will be handled automatically. Between the on-line systems and decision system stages, management will virtually "play" with computer-based MIS in a conversational mode. Simulations of all kinds will be carried out to enable management to learn what goes into effective decision making.

Exceptional systems will be found in those companies where top management has actually participated in systems analysis and design. In some cases, this will mean company presidents and other high-level officers thrusting

[14] Ibid., pp. 68–69.

themselves into the mainstream of the work, acting as systems planners to shape the architecture of MIS functions and capabilities. Improbable though it may seem, since it would be a shattering blow to tradition, we predict it will happen. In fact, it has already begun in a very few companies whose fate will, in the judgment of their key executives, depend on their leaping ahead in advanced computer uses.

One company president has been staying late and coming to the office on Saturdays to run a mathematical model that simulates his business operations for three years in the future. Marketing, production, personnel, capital expenditure, cash flow, and other factors are built into the model. The president, as well as other key executives, has been having an exciting experience interacting with the model through a time-sharing communications terminal. Reports by these men express considerable praise for the system; it has given them an infinitely more effective way to plan and to see vividly the effects of many decisions and conditions before they are undertaken.

The president has had a number of questions about the factors in the model because certain decisions that should alter outcomes do not. Perhaps for the first time, he is really seeing what happens to a decision once he makes it. Some of what he sees he does not like, and he has taken immediate action to have the condition changed and the model changed accordingly. Since the model is time-staged, he can see the effects of delays and speedups of various kinds. In this particular model, the advertising cycle represented a real bottleneck under many of the simulation studies. This was one area the president later ordered studied with an eye to cutting down delays. In three weeks he had a recommendation that he accepted and implemented. The business model was changed accordingly to reflect the new times.

The model was set up so that the president and other executives could change it without much trouble. If some change was improperly made, or caused program execution problems, diagnostic messages described the problem so the executive could correct it. Besides this, the company has available the telephone numbers of several systems analysts able to answer almost any problem on the phone. In one case, the analyst took a portable terminal home for emergency help. Had the president had trouble on Saturday, the analyst could have debugged the problem immediately by using his own portable terminal, which could be acoustically coupled to his home telephone.

Keeping an Eye on Practicality

It is common to find that 75 percent of a system's requirements are satisfied by a 50 percent time and cost expenditure. Therefore, 50 percent of the total expenditure can relate to accomplishing the final 25 percent. Management has to keep a sharp lookout for this phenomenon, for it is also common to find that payoff in terms of value does not justify the spending needed to go all the way.

The practicality dimension is seen in the cost analysis of wishes versus value or net worth. It is also important to understand that apparent management information problems may not be amenable to computer-based solutions.

It is also practical to recognize the limitations of the service MIS provides and to acknowledge that information for management decisions is subject to interpretation. For example, "profitability analysis" does not mean much in a systems sense unless it is specified what exactly is meant by it. The meaning and implications change from industry to industry and from company to company. Marginal costs, fixed costs, marginal profit, price breaks, taxes, and so forth, can all come into play. Usual accounting systems and procedures may not be suited to some of the analytical purposes of MIS. Additionally, there may be company or division optimization strategies to govern the "global" picture. Tampering with a subglobal set of variables by introducing new strategies may improve the profitability in a local function while reducing it by multiples on a global scale.

While celebrating the advent of computer-based MIS, companies need to take stock and make an earnest effort to grapple with these kinds of problems. We are not suggesting that a lot of what is uncovered will be insuperable. On the other hand, we do think that some of the factors, uncovered later rather than sooner, could sound the death knell for the MIS project. Management by surprise may not be effective where there is insufficient cushion to absorb the shock.

Sometimes the alarm is the result of implementing a problem solution that has been carefully conceived but that, if it solves any problem, solves the wrong one. Since we mentioned profitability analysis, let us now get down to cases and use examples to explain something of the nature of potential problems.

Many businesses have for a number of years thought that profitability analysis, done by computer for each customer, would help improve earnings. The idea is to have this part of MIS look at the total relationship of customer with company. A chemical or fertilizer company, for example, may find that certain customers always seem to need extra service or special favors. Some customers may agree to take a minimum monthly supply of a custom-blended product that is stocked especially for them. However, the company finds that the monthly minimum is not met half the time and that the customer usually calls around 5 P.M., requesting midnight delivery when the delivery lead time is supposed to be 24 hours and delivery time from 8 A.M. to 5 P.M. The overstocked product and extra charges for delivery during overtime periods make doing business with this customer less desirable or even unprofitable. In this case the company would do itself a service to drop the customer. Or, with facts in hand, it could request payment for extra service.

Often the situation is not as simple as the one just described. Perhaps the customer is a subsidiary of a large parent company that represents a good overall profit source. It is at this point that the supplier's management must decide what to do, if anything, with the unprofitable sales to a subsidiary. What might the parent company and its other subsidiaries do if one subsidiary were to go to the competition? Would management be giving the competition a chance to prove itself worthy to supply products other than the one that was given up as a loss? All this requires information.

If an MIS is going to report profitability, it will have to present accurate and complete information in those places where it has been designed to do so. If, in the case just cited, parent–subsidiary affiliations are not identified, those using the system must be aware of that fact and must know enough to make a further study. By the same token, where there is partial reporting of some information and disregarding of other data, this needs to be understood.

Management Involvement

Time after time, business literature has hammered away at top managers, exhorting them to get involved in the company's MIS effort. Indeed, the warnings have been so ominous that every top executive should make a point of finding out for himself what he should do about MIS.

As things stand now in the majority of companies, computer technicians are still setting goals and making decisions as to where computing power is used. This they have been doing for better than a decade, and some of the results are living testimonials to that fact—viewed regularly with anguish by many upper management men. Should the prognostications about the critical importance of MIS come true or even close to it, the computer man will soon be running the company (assuming it survives) unless top management gets into the act soon. How, then, does a senior executive do that?

Very simply, he does what he has done all through his career. First, he puts away any hope of finding some royal road to comprehension and success. Second, he gets involved. The top operating executive has to be able to maintain a dialogue with his senior computer systems man. Working through the chain of command will not do, because he will be shortchanged much of the time, too much being lost in translation. Actually, talking with the computer man should be rewarding. Often, he is knowledgeable, clever, and, most important, interested in and concerned about the business and his contribution to it.

If this sort of attitude does not exist in your company, you can be fairly sure that it has some big problems in the MIS area. Ask yourself whether things would be different if you gave more personal attention to them.

Let us suppose, though, that the senior systems analyst *is* interested and concerned. You might then want to find out what he thinks the company ought to be doing with MIS applications. Perhaps he will answer the question by asking what kind of problems you are trying to solve, or what your information wishes are, or how you are related to the bigger picture. Maybe the two of you will focus on something of special concern and discuss possible solutions, and perhaps another discussion with a couple of other key people will be arranged. In short, it is of the utmost importance for top executives to know the situation firsthand.

Some Things to Come

As author of one of AMA's research studies on MIS, James D. Gallagher offered the following observations. They are as valid now as they were when he made them.

> In order to give credence to the ideas expressed in these terms [automatic decision making, office revolution], three basic assumptions must be made: (1) that a great deal is known today about the process of decision making at the managerial level; (2) that a great deal is known about *how* to apply data processing and advanced business systems techniques to these processes and to solution of managerial problems; and (3) that the management processes and the rate of introduction of new problems remain static.
>
> There is little evidence that any one of these conditions is true. Much work, of course, is now in progress in the areas represented by the first two of these assumptions, but nothing will reduce the need for managerial skills. The growth of the demand for these skills is beyond all proportion to the supply and will continue so, even if sophisticated management information systems become more prevalent.[15]

We have said repeatedly that computer-based management information systems are not substitutes for sound management, but can enable management to do things not previously possible. And they can increase the effectiveness of an already effective management.

[15] *Management Information Systems and the Computer* (AMA, 1961), p. 56.

The MIS goals a company sets for itself must be achievable; more than that, they must be reasonable in terms of the present. A company that places a high premium on acquiring the skills and knowledge envisioned as a benefit of MIS must be prepared to do more than implement MIS. In one organization, the present state of affairs may be ripe for introducing MIS with only minor readjustments. Another may call for sweeping changes and a wholly new management outlook.

In years to come, MIS will be seen as the unifying thread that draws together the many staff functions of a business. Top management will be taking a hard look at existing staff functions in order to learn what roles they should play in running the business. Out of this examination, some important but hidden capabilities will become evident. Others will be found to be unnecessary as permanent functions. The decision then will be to keep outside consultants on retainer for use as the need arises.

Company operations will become more dependent on fewer people, proportionately, than previously. The programmable decisions that are made by hordes of people today will be made by systems. Feedback loops, providing full-circle automation, will evolve at a slower rate, making necessary a great deal of control activity that will have to be done by people.

Company organizations will change, with MIS helping to bring about the demise of the pyramidal form of organization as we know it today. In its place, a "flat" organization structure will come into being. Key executives will broaden their span of visibility as a result of using new tools offered by MIS that give answers as well as information. The relative number of people in middle management will eventually decline. An elite and smaller middle group will take over many functions that were formerly top management's responsibility.

The flat structure that will thus evolve will represent two concepts in one. First, the implementation of all decisions will continue to be decentralized. Second, centralized decision making will be emphasized. Relatively few key executives will make fundamental decisions and establish the framework for what are termed "local decisions." However, most local decisions will require the responsible manager either to select from alternatives generated by MIS or to check his solution with MIS. The idea is to have the system optimize overall operations by generating "global" decisions.

Company systems functions will gain new stature. Growth of this type will tend to be geometric. People's enthusiasm to try to automate new applications will generate many new projects, some of which will succeed. Companies trying to catch up with the industry will have the greatest problems. At the present time, upper management's concern with MIS is certainly discernible, but not nearly to the extent that it will be in the more distant future. In the executive suite, MIS analysts will exercise great power.

There will be two specific results of management's need to become more involved in computer systems work. Its role will become much more active, as opposed to its rather passive current state. In this, managers will provide key leadership, which will place emphasis on improving their knowledge of systems and computing technology. Sheer interest will build up at an accelerated rate, providing management with an even greater continuing motivation to maintain its involvement.

Evidence of this is already coming into view. In certain top management ranks, there are presidents and senior executives who can tell a junior systems analyst a thing or two about computers. And there are others who are virtually "snow proof," having gained the knowledge and understanding necessary to enable them to review systems proposals. More and more, computer books are found in executive offices these days. Computer-based systems are a topic that executives will discuss at length, without undue prodding. A lively exchange of ideas and many questions often characterize such discussions. The general degree of receptivity has changed dramatically in the past five or ten years. The future promises even more.

In summary, MIS represent one of the most encouraging possibilities for getting at some of the grass-roots problems of management. Such problems are of long standing and afflict big organizations as well as small ones. Here is what we see in the future.

- Management control systems will permit the organization's activities to be monitored in short time intervals.
- Strong competition in computer-based management systems will evolve, slowly at first, then with fierce intensity as results become more dramatic.
- Few decisions of import will be made without the help of computer-based systems somewhere along the way. The more analytical the decision, the greater will be the reliance on computers.
- Middle operating management ranks will thin out, being replaced by staff specialists.
- Pyramidal organizations will flatten.
- Top management ranks will increase moderately.
- Functional areas—production, marketing, personnel—will dovetail in new and improved ways.
- Emphasis on analytical skills will pull more technical types into the ranks of top management.

* * *

Enormous in their potential for profit, computer-based management systems will continue to be the object of intensive efforts of extraordinary scope and magnitude. The development of such systems will be increased as their potential is realized by the thousands of companies that come in contact with them.

Of critical importance to the success of MIS is management's role in formulating objectives, systems planning, and measuring the performance of these systems. Also of vital importance is its role in applying appropriate controls during the definition and development of MIS. Sound judgment will have to be exercised in order to prevent the real problem from being clouded by the existence of great technological power. Serious attention to establishing system selection criteria is the key, as applications will continue to increase. Management scrutiny in these matters is essential to insure the proper relevance of systems to problem-solving objectives.

MIS should not be looked to for answers that somehow compensate for ineffectual management. MIS will increase management effectiveness only in proportion to the leadership that management brings to it.

MIS Bookshelf Selections

Blumenthal, Sherman C. *Management Information Systems: A Framework for Planning and Development.* Englewood Cliffs, N.J.: Prentice-Hall, Inc., 1969.

Apart from the introductory material, this book will require careful study to absorb the full impact of the late author's message. A book for the systems professional and systems management, it goes into detail on procedures for systems development and contains excellent illustrations and examples to explain various kinds of systems and other points.

Canning, Richard G. (ed.-pub.). *EDP Analyzer.* 134 Escondido Ave., Vista, Calif. 92083

EDP Analyzer is a monthly publication without advertising. Running ten to fifteen pages in length, each issue treats one subject in the computing field. Back issues (to 1963) are available from the publisher. Subjects directly concerned with MIS include data management, fast response systems, methods for business planning and management control, and data-file design.

Enger, Norman L. *Putting MIS to Work: Managing the Management Information System.* New York: AMA, 1969.

This book is unique in its coverage of controls. It deals with audit and security procedures, error detection, reliability and backup, standards of control for software, and it contains a number of management checklists.

Gallagher, James D. *Management Information Systems and the Computer.* New York: AMA, 1961.

Although referring to technological capabilities extant some years ago, this early book has much solid commentary valid for today's administrator. Two case studies are included: American Airlines' Sabre System and Sylvania's centralized information system.

Head, Robert V. *Real-Time Business Systems.* New York: Holt, Rinehart and Winston, Inc., 1964.

Twelve chapters and a glossary explain many of the practical aspects of real-time systems from a vantage point that is obviously firsthand.

Krauss, Leonard I. *Administering and Controlling the Company Data Processing Function.* Englewood Cliffs, N.J.: Prentice-Hall, Inc., 1969.

Provides guidelines, checklists, and detailed information relating to the management of computer-based systems development and operations implementation. Project management is the subject of one of the book's ten chapters and several appendixes.

Lipperman, Lawrence I. *Advanced Business Systems.* New York: AMA, 1968.

Explores MIS applications in many different companies at a level sure to be of interest to top management. With the help of numerous illustrations, the author shows how advanced systems are used for business planning, marketing, and other applications.

Management Information Series: Reprints from Harvard Business Review. Boston: Harvard Business Review Reprint Service, 1967.

Fourteen articles that have appeared in HBR provide very worthwhile reading and a good grounding in some of the not-so-fundamental MIS fundamentals for management.

Martin, James. *Design of Real-Time Computer Systems.* Englewood Cliffs, N.J.: Prentice-Hall, Inc., 1967.

An authoritative reference, this book covers in some detail the important facets of developing real-time systems. Two other books by the same author are *Telecommunications and the Computer* and *Programming Real-Time Computer Systems.*

Meadow, Charles T. *The Analysis of Information Systems: A Programmer's Introduction to Information Retrieval.* New York: John Wiley & Sons, Inc., 1967.

Anyone concerned with the design of data bases will find this book quite readable, notwithstanding its title. Extensively referenced, it contains numerous helpful illustrations.

Myers, Charles A. (ed.). *The Impact of Computers on Management.* Cambridge, Mass.: The M.I.T. Press, 1967.

Eight thoughtful papers and discussion on them are presented in these conference proceedings.

Orr, William D. (ed.). *Conversational Computers.* New York: John Wiley & Sons, Inc., 1968.

Over 20 interesting and useful articles concerning man and his relationship to computers are offered.

Putnam, Arnold O., et al. *Unified Operations Management: A Practical Approach to the Total Systems Concept.* New York: McGraw-Hill Book Company, 1963.

Provides a down-to-earth discussion on MIS for operations management and examines specific areas of system use in some detail. Its coverage of applications, while very good, needs to be supplemented with more current literature on real-time MIS.

Rosove, Perry E. *Developing Computer-Based Information Systems.* New York: John Wiley & Sons, Inc., 1967.

Discusses many of the vitally important management considerations in developing large-scale MIS. The author draws numerous parallels with defense-oriented systems.

Shoderbek, Peter P. (ed.). *Management Systems.* New York: John Wiley & Sons, Inc., 1967.

Organized in 15 sections, each with an introduction, this collection of 51 articles offers much to the management reader concerned with MIS.

Simon, Herbert A. *The Shape of Automation for Men and Management.* New York: Harper & Row, Publishers, 1965.

Refreshing insights into the future of decision making and management with computers are offered in this book.

The Changing Dimensions of Office Management (AMA Management Report 41). New York: AMA, 1960.

An exceptionally fine collection of papers, covering many different aspects of advanced business systems, nearly all of which are written by systems executives. Despite its age, this collection remains a vital reference source.

Yourdon, Edward (ed.). *Real-Time Systems Design.* Cambridge, Mass.: Information & Systems Institute, Inc., 1967.

Though the production quality of this book leaves something to be desired, it nevertheless contains a very fine selection of articles, which are well organized. The editor introduces each section and offers several of his own contributions.

Index